C000283792

The Jungle

Ultra Endurance Running in the Heart of the Amazon

By Mark Hines

Healthy Body Publishing
www.thehealthybodyco.com

Logo by Leonardo Solano:
www.leonardosolano.com
New Media & Communications

The Author

Mark Hines is an Exercise and Human Physiologist, based in London, England. He is currently working on his PhD in Neuromuscular Physiology, and lectures on Human and Applied Physiology. In his spare time he competes in ultra-endurance adventure races around the world.

Acknowledgements

I would like to thank all the people that read the draft manuscripts and contributed to the shaping of this first edition. I am sure that your suggestions and feedback have made this publication far superior to what it would have been without you. Thanks to John B, John Q, Ross, Eddie, Phil and Vicky for all your valuable feedback.

My thanks go to John Hardy, of FASTER Fitness Limited, who is a dear friend and has been an enormous help with my training. Thanks to John any biomechanical creases were ironed out, ensuring that I could manage big distance runs safely. It is through the pioneering work that he does, and via his growing number of students, that we are likely to see a significant change in trends for injury prevention and rehabilitation, over the coming years. Thanks to John, I never received a single running-related injury in the build-up to, or my competition in, the Jungle Marathon.

I would especially like to thank Shirley for working tirelessly at keeping the Jungle Marathon alive, and for always being on hand for help and assistance throughout my preparation and competition. I appreciate that to organise such an event, so far from home and with so many logistical and administrative challenges, that this continues to be a huge undertaking. I am grateful for everything you have done and hope that the JM continues to go from strength to strength.

Further, I would like to thank all of the support and medical staff involved in the Jungle Marathon. Whether providing us with water at the checkpoints, clearing and taping the trails, being on hand to treat medical issues, or being prepared to manage emergencies, we have a safer and more pleasant experience because of you.

Finally, I would like to thank the many friends that I have made during competitions; the adventures would never have been so great without you! I apologise that I could not mention each of you by name in this book, but I assure you I remember you all. Thanks to a certain social networking site, I am glad that we do not simply require chance to be able to meet up again. I believe it is a wonderful thing that we can meet up in various parts of the world, and find ourselves racing together in the most incredible environments. In particular, I would like to single-out John Quinn, for being a tremendous support and a superb friend.

Photography

The race photographer, Gil Serique, took many of the photographs included in this edition, as well as the photograph on the front cover. He can be contacted regarding photography and his work as a guide via www.youramazon.org and www.gilserique.com. My thanks also go to John Quinn and Ian Mayhew, for kindly granting me permission to include some of their own photographs within this book.

For Shirley and John Q

Disclaimer

This book has been written to give an insight into ultra-endurance adventure racing. Whilst I love to compete in these races, there are dangers inherent in all of them, and this book is by no means a recommendation to participate.

Prior to competing in a race such as this, it is essential that each prospective competitor is confident of his or her ability to exercise for extended periods in a jungle environment. Training needs to be of a sufficient and specific standard, and thorough medical checks should be undertaken beforehand. For an alternative and safer pastime, see: www.nicecupofteaandasitdown.com.

"It is in the compelling zest of high adventure and of victory, and in creative action, that man finds his supreme joys."

- Antoine De Saint-Exupery

Paradise Found

This is paradise. This is that which I had never anticipated. To be standing upon a beach of the most perfect white sand, crisp and as powder beneath my feet, with the blue waters of the Rio Tapajos extending like a sea across to the distant shore. A local guide informs me that the river is 10 kilometres wide now, but this is half the width it attains in this region during the wet season. And this, one must remember, is merely a tributary river to the Amazon.

The sky is a cloudless, deep blue, whilst the air is hot but not perceptibly humid. The clamminess of the rainforest lurks beneath the jungle canopy. The virgin jungle commences beyond the huts, at the base of a grassy slope. The communities throughout this region are often inhabited by the descendents of the original Indian population and the early European colonists.

The Amazon is so unexplored that there are still numerous Indian populations, which have never been met by people that would consider themselves 'civilised'. Good thing too. 'The city is not a concrete jungle; it is a human zoo', according to Desmond Morris, and I concur. There is no greater definition of freedom in the modern world than what the families here experience; they are slaves to nothing. It has taken us thousands of years to create for ourselves a world of locks, alarms, banks and paranoia. Here the people sleep freely and contentedly in open huts. It is reassuring that there are still some isolated areas of this planet which we have not yet managed to bugger up.

So, philosophical outbursts aside, here I stand. My new world is encouragingly easy on the eyes, as I listen to the sound of the waves lapping upon the shore and feel the most subtle of breezes against my face, with the grains of sand moving beneath my feet. I could be in the Caribbean, standing upon a tropical island, gazing across to a neighbouring island nearby. Hah! I wonder if such thoughts will occupy the minds of the racers when they arrive at the beach in the next half an hour.

What I had expected, of course, was the view of the jungle from above, as the aeroplane came in to land at Santarem airport. In fairness, however, it was not at first the broccoli forests that I had anticipated. The image of deeply green florets is merely a transitory phenomenon, taking place during the aircraft's descent. From high above, the jungle is as a thick green fibre-pile carpet, laid out across the whole Earth as far as the horizon. Dividing this, the varyingly blue, grey and black waters of the Amazon snake their way along, wider than the English Channel in parts, and over a hundred miles in width at its mouth.

The flight into Santarem was anything but direct. The aircraft acted as a sort of bus service, stopping at each airport in a circuit for passengers to join or leave. Whilst taxiing at Manaus, our penultimate plane-stop before Santarem, the land beyond the taxiway offered me the first glimpse of the Amazon rainforest. The jungle

2

presented a wall of dense foliage, the green tops of which continued off into the distance, seemingly forever, with nothing but a few hills and gentle undulations to break up the land. It would take but a few paces within, I imagined, and I would be immersed into another world. It is a world of fierce nature and ancient tribes: one of the last few relatively unexplored wildernesses on Earth.

Following our arrival at Santarem we were met by Shirley, the organiser of the Jungle Marathon, and shown our way to the bus for the next part of the journey. I had introduced myself to the medical team and chatted at some length about hydration and electrolyte intakes for the competitors. As a physiologist, and particularly as a physiologist with research interests in exercise adaptations to extreme climates, I am fairly well versed in the literature available on hydration techniques for athletes in this environment. The only downside to my increasing knowledge on such specific areas is that I fail to be invited to the sorts of parties that I used to when I was younger. For the best, possibly. Back to the bus, and the atmosphere amongst both the support teams and the competitors seems to be one of suppressed energy and stifled enthusiasm.

So, here I am then. That Peter Pan within me won the day and has me about to embark upon a childhood dream of exploring the Amazon. Perhaps exploration is too inaccurate, for it is not really why I am here, of course, but I dare anyone to argue with that giddy little boy within me that is jumping up and down, giggling like an imbecile at the thought of adventures worthy of *The Goonies*. All the other endurance runners about me are no doubt suffering from that terrible ambivalence of experiencing both palpable anxiety and extreme excitement. It is that latent fuel that drives all of us. Fortunately I am mostly free of their trepidation. This is not my time to race.

* * * * * * * * * * * *

I remember it so vividly that I am still astonished by it. There had been nothing extraordinary about that night's sleep in the Berbere Palace hotel in Ouzarzate, Morocco. We had finished racing the previous day, and throughout the coach journey back to the hotel I had experienced an unfamiliar melancholy. I was feeling subdued by the realisation that I had become somehow institutionalised into the habit of being given somewhere different to sleep each night, and knowing that each day all I must accomplish was the distance to the next camp. Now I had no new site to head to. I was no longer relying solely upon myself to cover whatever distance under my own steam. There would be no run to follow the next morning's sunrise.

What happens now? I had become lost and dismayed by the whole disappointment of finishing. Granted there had been some sense of achievement, but it was overshadowed by the thought that there would be no new day's run. I had become swiftly accustomed to a life of running, eating and resting. Now I was back in the 'real world'; although I felt disgusted by the very idea of the term, I would soon be dealing with credit card bills, ridiculous hours of work and all the other stresses of modern life. Despite my sore feet, tired joints and

4

wasting body, I would have much preferred to have continued on and on; running for the joy of it and running away from those aspects of life I esteem the least: bills, creditors and being overworked and undervalued. Finishing *The Marathon des Sables* had not been as fulfilling an experience as any of the running that preceded it. Finishing was simply the transitory period between the running that I loved and the reality that I might prefer to run from.

Immediately following the race I was experiencing some degree of physical pain, certainly, but running and the company of great friends had been my whole world for over a week. To be sitting on a coach, delicately prising adhesive tape from open sores about my shoulders, hips and lower back, whilst travelling back to the hotel prior to our departure home, was quite a firm slap of unwanted reality. I just wanted to be running again.

Back at the hotel I had showered and removed all physical evidence of the Sahara from about my person; only a light suntan and the wounds of battle to show for all of my efforts. I had slept, calmly, peacefully, and comfortably, in a soft bed on a warm night, with my feet elevated on pillows. The sheets had been kept above the ankles, so as to avoid contact with the broken skin of my feet and the damaged and sore toenails.

In the morning, we had all headed off for breakfast, where one by one we all tried to mount a cunning display of engineering and greed as we piled our *real* food high on our plates. There was only one topic of conversation from the moment that I sat down, other than the obligatory nod of approval and the suggestion that I might have won in the engineering/greed stakes. All athletes, when they have been training for an event for so long, are known to descend into depression, sometimes for months after the actual race has finished.

There is the great build-up, the focussed training and mental preparation, always thinking about the race ahead, all for that one moment when you cross the finish line. Once that line has been crossed a deep abyss opens up; a void that previously was filled with all that mental focus and energy. That vacuum exists from the realisation that we are now without equivalent goal or ambition— perhaps we begin to question our sense of worth and purpose. How would we avoid succumbing to such a depressive state of affairs?

There could be only one solution, and that was what we discussed as we breakfasted. We were sharing our table with a team of runners from the Royal Air Force, and they divulged all there was to tell about the legend of the Jungle Marathon; the real toughest footrace in the world. The real toughest footrace? But surely I had just finished that, I was positive of it. As I was quickly coming to realise, the *Marathon des Sables* was once the toughest, and perhaps the original and best multi-stage, ultra-endurance adventure race, but it was not the toughest anymore. There were now others, and all were pretenders to the throne.

Despite Dean Karnazes' opinion, as voiced in his book *Ultramarathon Man* (which I heartily recommend, incidentally), ultra-endurance adventure racers do not exist in any sort of 'underground'. This is not some secret society of accomplished athletes that meet in dark places, exchange secret handshakes, and conspire about their forthcoming missions. These athletes are some of the friendliest, most open, and professional people that I have ever had the pleasure to meet. Rather than an underground, there is what could perhaps be better described as a 'circuit'. There is a growing number of single- and multi-stage ultra races around the world, and the athletes I was sitting in the company of now had competed in various ones, and were now in the process of regaling the stories of their own experiences and those of others.

Interestingly, they did not need to know all of the races through personal experience, as the tall tales they had heard from others elucidated the nature of the ones they had not competed in. The resounding conclusion, based on the legends which were told, was that the Jungle Marathon was undoubtedly the toughest race that existed at that time, according to those that have either competed in it or heard about it. And that was me sold. We would avoid plummeting into a post-race depression following the MdS by launching ourselves into the training for another race: The Jungle Marathon.

* * * * * * * * * * *

The reason for coming here in 2007, without my tent comrades from the *Marathon des Sables,* was straightforward enough. I had held no apprehensions about the desert race because I had been there before. Every year between the turn of the millennium and 2006 I had visited the Egyptian Sahara. I had completed a number of training sessions there, either by myself or with my Egyptian friends who were riding

7

out on their Arabian horses. I knew the desert. Morocco was different in landscape, but it was nevertheless the same desert. I had never particularly struggled with the heat there, because psychologically I had known that I had already pushed myself so far in training in those exact same conditions, or worse.

There had been two types of competitors that seemed to struggle the most in the *Marathon des Sables*; those that had never worn their rucksack during training, and those that had never been to a desert prior to the race. Although I had oodles of desert experience, I had never exercised in a jungle before. I had spent holidays in the humid climes of Florida in the U.S., Antalya in Turkey and Queensland in Australia, but it was hardly comparable. I had no idea of how my body would respond, how it would acclimatise, or how it would feel to be engaged in a multi-stage, ultra-endurance footrace there. I did not want to turn up for the first time, ready to race, only to discover that aerobically I simply could not cope.

This preliminary visit was about gaining experience, evaluating performance, and clocking up some jungle miles to give me a psychological edge ahead of my return to compete in a year's time. Predominantly my duties would be confined to support crew, although within minutes of being on the bus I was already a firm friend with the medical team too. I would be walking sections of the course the day before the competitors, to ensure that the routes were marked up, and I would be walking parts of the course after the day's race as well, clearing it for stragglers and litter. At other times I might be required to set up the camps at the end of the stages. I had let

Shirley know that I would appreciate any opportunity to get some miles under my belt, but that I appreciated that first and foremost I was here as a volunteer member of her support staff.

From the port in Santarem we had boarded a boat that would take all of the support crews, including some of the Brazilian military, and the competitors to our starting point, some twelve hours or so down the Rio Tapajos. The army lads were with us as an integral part of the support crew. They would be the chaps to pull together in the event of an emergency and help facilitate evacuations. They would also be involved in sweeping the routes for stragglers, communications between checkpoints and the base camp, and protecting people like me from big, scary furry things that might leap from the jungle after us. Their local knowledge and organisational and survival skills were deemed invaluable in a region such as this. The boys had not been given permission to be here on detachment, and so were using up their own holiday to help out.

The rest of the support crew and the competitors busied themselves onboard, with setting up their hammocks and settling into some modicum of comfort. I sorted mine on the upper deck along with the medical team, and then went back to help the others tie theirs up.

The hammocks were tied up wherever there was space, and before long I had proudly (possibly smugly), earned the nickname of Ray Mears, thanks to my purist stance of having actually learnt how to tie the 'correct' hammock knots. Whereas most were content with a couple of half-hitches, I had spent a short time, when I should have been working, perfecting the art of tying a USB cable to the leg of my workstation, using both the Siberian Hitch and a Taut Hitch. The benefit of those knots is that they are quick-release and work well for adjusting tension. The half-hitches are easier, but Mears uses the other two because they do not tighten up when someone lies in the hammock. Having to waste time unnecessarily faffing around, because my knots had become too tight to easily undo, would have been an embuggerance I could well manage without. With all hammocks up and everybody sorting kit or laying back, I headed onto the top deck to do some relaxing myself.

As I lay there in my hammock, listening to the banter of new friends all around me; the boat beginning its journey down the Rio Tapajos in the early evening light and a gentle breeze, I found it hard to imagine being anywhere better. My only concern in the whole world was the knots that I had tied to secure my hammock. I could not help but fear that I may lose whatever tenuous and potentially misplaced reputation I had thus far attained, should my arse descend to the deck with a thud. As the knots held true and the hammock swayed with the pleasant rocking of the boat on the waves, the sun began to set beyond the trees, and I permitted my eyes to grow heavy with the fading light.

Watching the sunset, and then waking at the break of dawn to watch the sunrise above the jungle canopy was a wonderful experience, and a superb welcome to the Amazon. Observing a botu, the legendary pink dolphin of these rivers, was rather pleasant too. This was the Amazon; a place that I had only ever read about or seen on television, and here I was, breathing the clean air and travelling along the Rio Tapajos into the heart of it. Whatever the week ahead had in store for me, I had no doubt that it would be an experience that stayed with me forever.

* * * * * * * * * *

Saturday, 6th October 2007

05:45

I rolled out of my hammock and moved to the front of the boat, so as to change into my kit for the next eight days. My North Face combats offer my legs good protection, and the legs could be zipped off to leave me in shorts, for the occasions when my legs are less at risk of being ripped to shreds by undergrowth. Beneath those I donned some cycling shorts, which I hoped would be sufficient to protect my nether-regions from whatever uninformed critters mistook my privates for a nice place to be. I recall from Lofty Wiseman's survival book that caterpillars and other such beasties rather enjoy the warm and moist environment of the anus, given half a chance, and thus anyone sleeping in the jungle should check themselves for new residents each morning. My upper body was protected with a 'support crew' t-shirt and a long-sleeved shirt over that. I had an army scrim scarf around my neck, as I could use that to stop beasties climbing down the neck of my shirt. It also worked well as a bandana-cum-headnet. My Pro-

Boots should keep my feet safe from the smallest biting nasties, and they are fully waterproof, which is fine so long as they are tied sufficiently tight to the skin to prevent water entering from the top.

I am presently enjoying the sunrise, and shall no doubt begin to investigate the possibility of breakfasting soon. I notice that the recently applied Deet is busy melting the pen with which I am currently writing. The trousers that were impregnated with an insect-repellent are failing in their duty to repel insects, which could become an annoyance should those flying pests have many friends keen to meet me on the mainland. As I sit under the relief of the top deck's small canopy, I am able to enjoy some shade and the sight of a few spiders taking residency not far from my head. At least these are but babies; I am sure that I shall meet some of their larger, more grown-up cousins once ashore. That should make for good therapy.

07:38

There may be more to life than sitting back in a hammock, chatting with the most marvellously pleasant people, and looking out to survey the deep, green and alluring jungle and the wide, calm Tapajos, as our boat progresses upriver. However, as I lay here, basking in the hot morning air, I really am buggered to think of what it might be.

08:25

Jumped off the side of the boat into the Rio Tapajos. Seemed like a sterling idea at the time. The water was marvellous, and sufficiently warm for it to be perfectly comfortable to stay in for some time. It must have been the largest body of fresh water that I have ever swum in. As a consequence, I was able to wash both my clothing and myself, so I returned to the boat feeling immaculately clean and refreshed. Upon my return to the boat I observed a number of dolphins, and regrettably some floating turds. We could not discern if the latter originated from the toilets onboard or one of the swimmers. Glad I did not overstay my welcome in the water with such earthy company.

10:40

Things have been so frantic for me these last few months; I have scarcely managed to do all the reading about the Amazon that I would have liked. I feel somewhat embarrassed to be visiting somewhere that I still know so little about. I did not even manage to learn a smattering of Portuguese. Amidst an average dropout rate of forty-percent, anybody doing this race is either exceptional, or exceptionally daft (or possibly just misinformed). The 'have a go' contingent that appeared at the MdS is very much absent here. This is a good thing.

13:40

Encouraged to become part of the advanced party, a few of us support crew and medical staff climbed into a small motorboat and headed off to the base camp at Itapuama. We spent half an hour speeding across the calm waters of the Tapajos, watching the shoreline and observing the wall of trees beyond it, appearing as a barrier; the gateway to pure, lush, primary and secondary jungle. We reached the beach and made our way up to the huts; the accommodation for ourselves and the competitors until the start of the race. Cashew trees stand guard around the camp; the fruit can be eaten but the nuts at their base cannot unless they have been cooked. Apparently they are so toxic that they can even cause blindness if their steam reaches the eyes during cooking. The trees must be left alone, however, as their fruits belong to the good people of this community.

15:50

Kit and medical checks: I assist in checking first aid kits, or perhaps I simply loiter with intent. One can never be sure.

16:20

'Rain' + 'Forest' = Rainforest. The blue sky has turned to a deep, dark grey, and the heavens have opened up and flushed down. The heavy downpour transforms the beautiful beach into something from *Platoon*. The white sand seems dull and everything less pleasant. The air remains warm though, and beneath the cover of the huts we are well protected.

21:10

A good day. I was privileged to witness one of the most stunning sunsets I have ever seen. The sun seemed bigger than ever in the sky as it set behind the jungle on the far side of the Tapajos. The clouds were transformed from a perfect white to the most orange of all oranges, and then to a raspberry red. For the sake of conformity, the rest of the sky duly changed through its shades of red and orange too.

I have managed to make myself of some use within the camp, although I am not quite able to recall how. I simply felt useful at the time. I think that I may have lent someone a pencil.

I am currently lying in my hammock outside the medical hut, which happens to serve as a local school for the rest of the year. Many of these buildings were purpose built for this event, and the locals may use them the rest of the time for tourism purposes. Besides this small hut, there are five others: three for accommodation, one for briefings and dining, and the other is employed by the army as the communications centre. There are also a couple of rows of 'proper' toilets and showers. The water for the showers comes from the river. Of the three accommodation huts, the military support crew uses one, and the other two are for use by the competitors. The more sparsely populated of the two has an Irish flag outside. Everybody else, save for a few honorary Irish, are crammed into the other hut.

I was on my own, on account of the fact that the medical team wished to sleep on the boat, which suited me fine. It is unspeakably pleasant to find some peace and independence amongst about a hundred and fifty people all sharing the same beach.

Sunday, 7th October 2007

A day of rest

I am exhausted. Well, I am tired at least, and suffering ridiculously from a complete lack of acclimatisation. Whilst the competitors and staff were receiving their jungle training, I had the pleasure of completing the first stage of the race, along with fellow countryman Paul, and two guides. Paul had spent the past couple of months in various areas of jungle in South America, and so I was by far the least fit.

The objective of the day was to check that all was in good order for the first day of racing tomorrow. The trail for the first stage was regarded as possibly the most arduous of the whole event. It took us an unfathomable eight hours to cover approximately sixteen kilometres of horizontal distance. We could have completed it within seven, had we maintained a more admirable pace by not performing the checks along the way, but our speed was by no means sluggish. We had persevered along a route that included many steep and awkward climbs, in addition to short river crossings and areas of boggy, swampy ground.

The trail was close; as soon as we had entered the jungle it felt as though a thick, musty curtain had been drawn behind us. I am fairly used to traipsing over hill and dale, but within the confines of this environment I must work harder for any given distance, and not purely because of the heat and humidity. I also must duck to avoid branches and cobwebs, although I do not miss all of them and regularly find myself brushing my head to remove any newly homeless spiders.

Branches and trees encroach on the path, meaning that one must twist and turn along the narrow route. The centre of the trail has roots criss-crossing it, lying in wait for the opportunity to entangle my feet. Regularly I am snagged as I stride forward and feel the rearwards tug from my ensnared boot, on occasion causing some discomfort to the joints. I am being cut to ribbons too as spikes and spines from various plants scratch at me and lacerate my skin. I find myself out of breath on the climbs and often desiring to sit and rest.

We did, when our guides permitted it, enjoy soaking ourselves in the creek water or lying back on the jungle floor. Naturally we had been recommended against lying on the ground, out of the risk of being promptly eaten by ants and the other denizens of the lower levels of the rainforest. We were not affected, and checked the ground for anything unpleasant before laying back.

Water was an issue. When the competitors race they will have water available to them at the checkpoints, whereas we had only what we could carry. Unlike Paul, I avoided the fresh creek water. Should I be affected by ingesting a water-borne bacterium or parasite then I could become sick, either whilst here or in a few months' time. Either scenario offers no benefit above the nuisance of carefully rationing my water throughout the day. I suppose my problem was that I had not envisaged the day to last so long. Had push come to shove then I would have puri-tabbed creek water, but that had evidently not been necessary.

I was staggered by how tiring this day was. In response to my various cuts, bites, stings and abrasions, I gather that the quote which brought my companions the most amusement was when I stated how I did not mind the jungle, but that the jungle absolutely loved me. Flies had been taking minute chunks from me, vines and razor-sharp grasses had latched onto me to embrace my legs, whilst cobwebs seemed to inundate my head. I must have been five percent dehydrated by the end of the day as well, with co-ordination and focus suffering predictably as a result.

One amusing detail, for me at least, was that I received a cut during the day which remained open until the very instant that I reached the beachside camp. The moist air of the jungle had prevented the clotting process from being effective, and the minor wound required only moments of exposure to the drier air near the Tapajos to clot perfectly. Various wounds aside, I nevertheless have some additional concerns for the second day of exploits beneath the canopy. Water needs to be better managed, at the very least. As for the combined difficulties presented by the jungle environment; it had taken mere hours before I had begun fantasising about lemon sorbet, followed by dreams of a bath of ice cubes with beautiful women pouring icy water over my head. Sadly all I had was mile after mile of bastard jungle, but I loved it, in some quite unfathomable and ridiculous sort of way.

Monday, 8th October 2007

Not the most productive of days. I managed to cover approximately half of the course for stage two of the race. This time I had gone out alone with the guide and bombeiro (military fireman), which made communication fairly difficult, although somehow we managed to cope. I speak no Portuguese and neither the guide nor the bombeiro could speak any English. The terrain was perhaps a little easier than yesterday, but there were still a number of particularly tough climbs.

We took a break where we could lay on top of some felled trees, and dozed for a short while.

Not long after this break we lost the trail. Our guide was not as confident of the route as he had first thought. He tried to work a way through and find it again but to no avail. This had been one of the problems during the previous day, and our poor communication had made it difficult for us to know precisely what the issue was. In the same way we had been unable to contribute any useful suggestions. Today was shaping up similarly. I needed the guide to understand that if we passed along the trail where no markers were present, then we had to go back and put fresh ones up. On the final occasion we stood by the last piece of tape we could find, but of the trails then apparent to us, none rejoined a section further along with any markers.

With none of us knowing the route, we headed along a trail that brought us out of the jungle a few miles up the river from the second base camp, which had been positioned on the beach at the end of the first day's route. We headed back and I confessed all to Shirley. I readied myself for a second trip with another guide, but one of the medical team, Ivan, was sent off instead. It was a bit of a low point for me; I could not help but feel responsible for not completing the day, but what alternative had there been? We did not know where we were going and had no clear option other than to return. Appreciating this did nothing to quell my thoughts that I had let the side down somewhat.

Tuesday, 9th October 2007

No idea of the time. My lifetime guaranteed G-Shock, which had been battered significantly even before arriving here in the jungle, had been finished off by the Amazon. My Pro-Boots, with a sole that had been imperfectly made, will similarly not be leaving this place. Fortunately I seem to be a little more robust, and am finding myself more and more comfortable in this environment.

I had been requested last night to complete the third stage of the race today. However, with support staff mostly staying on the boat at night, I had missed the early morning calling. I had preferred to spend the nights ashore with the competitors, so that they might have a contact should they need anything. In any case, I had wanted to be close to the jungle, as that is why I am here, and there seems to be something too easy about spending the night on a boat.

With no other vocation for the day, I was sent to the end of the day's trail to erect the finish banner for the runners. Since completion of that one rather brief activity, I have been doing bugger-all. I did have a spectacular bath this morning. Rarely is it ever required for me to take an emergency whistle and a machete with me to bathe, but afar from anyone else and in a small creek it seemed the safest thing to do. Heaven forbid I should stumble across a snake and not be able to chop its head off. It would be embarrassing to have to simply stand there and be bitten, possibly for the both of us.

Despite the creek being narrow, it was particularly deep, clear and cool. The bottom was sand, as the water was moving too swiftly for debris to sink all the way down here. I enjoyed my bath immensely, cleaning my clothes and myself, and then returned to the camp. I was pleased to see a bird that I could not identify (I am to ornithology what Bill Oddie is to space travel), the most strikingly beautiful butterfly, and the biggest hornet in the world.

I truly am enjoying myself here. It is a world of wonder and wild nature that pulls at me, creating a feeling that I should return here some day for an extended and sufficient period, so as to truly enjoy a freedom to explore.

Fortunately, the day perked up a bit before it ended. A couple of Brazilian runners came racing over the finish line with their knives out and a look of exasperated terror on their faces. They reported seeing two large black jaguars near the trail. As I had nothing better to do (for I was, at the time, lying in my hammock), I decided to go and investigate. Jaguars are not known to attack adults, unless particularly hungry and in the absence of normal foods. They can be territorial though, and I felt that some of the more petite competitors might appreciate some loud and obnoxious company. Besides, I was hopeful of a good photograph for the National Geographic.

I departed the camp, carrying my water bottle and food, all wrapped in a sling improvised from my shirt. I half-walked, half-ran along the trail. As I met with competitors coming the other way, I would check that they were in good health, and assure them that they were close to the finish line. I asked the English speakers if they had seen anything of concern along the trail. Some claimed to have heard growls, whilst others suggested a strong smell of cat urine. Onwards I went. Having passed Stephania, a young Italian woman, I expected to meet with the Texan, Judah, next.

The trail was, as ever, close, meaning that I could only make out ten metres or so in front of me, beyond which the trail would turn a corner and be hidden out of view. I planned to reach the final checkpoint of the race, and then about-turn and sweep back to the camp, thus ensuring that all competitors were home and safe. A sweep team would be doing this as well, but I expected to be there first, and it was a good opportunity to get some miles under my belt. I was convinced that I was becoming fat and lazy for a day spent doing nothing.

I raced along the trail, aware of how it became obscured from view behind a wide tree to my front. I made it around the tree; I saw a flash of red behind the trees further on. A voice called out, I returned the shout, and then there he was. A bombeiro was pointing his revolver at my face. Damned unfriendly, that was for sure. With such low visibility, and with me moving at speed, by the time we had clear visuals of one another we were already practically touching noses. Upon deciding that I was not in actual fact a jaguar, an anthropomorphic ape, or some jungle spirit, the weapon was kindly lowered. We knew each other from the first day's exploits in the jungle. He had come from the checkpoint himself, and there were no other competitors remaining; they had been evacuated along the river or were joining the sweep team.

We went on, my friend constantly checking the undergrowth and trees for signs of Amazonian tigers. We found a perfect jaguar footprint, just next to the wide tree I had passed before we met up. It was a pristine print, very recent and untouched by footprints from competitors. At this, I encouraged my protector to increase his pace so we could meet up with Stephania, just for my own peace of mind. We still paused intermittently to investigate signs and sounds. On this point, the jungle had become eerily quiet, in stark contrast to the normal hustle and bustle of the animal inhabitants going about their daily business. As my guide informed me: *'the jaguar has no friends in the jungle'*.

The sweep team caught up with us; a dozen or so military chaps along with Kyle from the medical team. We chatted and then the Howler monkeys kicked off. The sun was setting and that made the army fellows unnervingly anxious. With that, we all began to run along the trail back to the camp, in single file and with good pace.

I only fouled up once; I bounded up onto a fallen log and then somehow tripped, which at my speed sent me flying through the air and crashing to the ground. Mid-air I had been overwhelmed by concerns of impaling myself on top of a cut stalk sticking up from the ground. They littered the trail everywhere and presented a significant risk if unseen. I brought myself quickly to my feet and gathered pace again, fortunately doing so without delaying those behind me. Kyle made some snide comment about my wearing my underpants on the outside of my trousers. I was simply dismayed that in putting my arms forward for protection I had split my machete's sheath. Oh well, such things occur in a time of war, and so on.

Following return to camp I was deployed back to the boat for the night, along with the rest of the support crew. I would need to leave to head to the next camp early in the morning, and so my being ready for the off with the others would be most practical. It later transpired that Andrea, one of the American competitors, had come face to face with a growling jaguar in the forest, and had done a good job of keeping her head about her and keeping herself safe from danger. During the night an electric storm lit up the sky, and was later followed by a most ferocious gale. I was on the top deck with Jo and Sarah, our hammocks crossing over each other's and bumping together as the boat rocked with the swell. It was a difficult night for sleep.

Wednesday, 10th October 2007

The rain was still falling as I climbed onto the boat with Sarah and Doug to head over to the next base camp. Narrow river channels on two sides surrounded the camp. I took the opportunity to give my kit and myself another good wash. A young girl stood nearby in the river, washing clothes on wooden benches erected in the water. She left and Sarah came to join me. Later, Sarah left too, and I remained to enjoy a swim.

25

A family of ducks were startled by something beneath the surface and hurried to leave the water. I made my way out as well because, well, you just would, wouldn't you? There are snakes in here and electric eels that could effortlessly despatch a person, and catfish that could easily take off a leg. The caimans are smaller and less likely to attack, and piranha will usually not attack unless someone is already in real trouble. Stingrays are a problem during the water crossings, necessitating us to shuffle our feet into water, rather than to stride or run in.

For men, a particularly real concern is the candiru. This is an incredibly small catfish, and one that typically swims into the gills of larger fish, attracted by the movement of water through the gills. The problem is that it mistakes urine flow from men as this respiratory movement of water from gills. The candiru then swims upstream and lodges itself into the penis; its fins preventing it from being pulled out. I am reliably informed that the traditional cure involves severing of the member with a machete. Women urinating into the water are not similarly affected, apparently, which seems inordinately unsporting. Fair's fair, after all. Importantly, the candiru are not just present in rivers and creeks, but can also be found in swamps and even puddles on the jungle floor. The current details presented on a popular online encyclopaedia are woefully inaccurate on this (not a revelation to this author). There are apparently many documented cases of attacks on humans, including a surgeon's report that the fish had to be removed from the victim's bladder. They have also been allegedly found within the bodies of corpses. Hardly surprising then, that the nasty little sods have a worse reputation than the piranha.

Electric eels, living in ponds, used to be caught by the Indians using horses. The horses would be forced into the ponds, and kept in by the Indians using lances. Many horses would perish as the eels inflicted their paralysing shocks to the vital organs, causing them to drown. Needing to recover themselves, the eels would make their way towards the land, where in their tired state they would be gathered up. An electric eel can be touched by hand and the shock is not likely to be dangerous. In the freedom of the water though, the eel positions itself along the body of its victim, and then directs its electricity into the heart and other vulnerable organs.

The competitors arrive, occasionally in pairs but most often individually. Towards the end of the day I head off to walk the last couple to within sight of the finish line. This has been a particularly long and arduous day for the competitors. Some arrive suffering with severe dehydration. I help them to prepare their recovery drinks, their food, and when I am feeling particularly generous I even tie their hammocks up for them.

One such competitor has an ultra-lightweight hammock, and as I test the knots the single cord that supports the hammock snaps in two. I am in disbelief that it should be so weak, but having become wet the previous night the cord had lost its elasticity. I use a fisherman's knot to tie the two ends together, and suggest that the young chap leaves the cord to dry out for as long as possible. I duly make a mental note not to buy one for my own attempt at the race next year. I have been using a fairly heavy hammock, which I would not use to race with. Many of the competitors require some guidance to reach the river, where they subsequently bathe themselves and cool off.

During the evening, when most of the competitors have retired for the night, I find myself putting Doug's massage table to good use. Steffania is first, suffering badly with leg pain that I source at the top of her ilio-tibial band, which is certainly not an uncommon area for affliction in runners. When I finish, I turn to find that a flock of competitors had arranged themselves in some sort of queue behind me. I oblige them and address their various aches and pains as best I can. It is dark now, but this is not necessarily an inconvenience when giving a massage.

It is whilst standing around chatting with the competitors afterwards that a tarantula runs across the feet of one of them. The poor sod had only been wearing flip-flops, and was in quite a shock after that. The spider presented itself in the middle of the group, as if for our admiration. I requested that the chap that now knew it so intimately move aside, so that I might have space to move the spider back in the direction of the jungle, but the silly boy appeared frozen solid. A couple of other runners, armed with sticks, decide to commence hitting the spider and eventually cripple it entirely. I step in and squash it underfoot, ending its suffering. I cannot help but feel incredibly guilty about the whole episode. We are but visitors here, and it is not our right to hurt, maim or kill the creatures that dwell here. I always feel that we should experience these places with the ambition of setting off home having left not a single sign of our having been here at all.

Thursday, 11th October 2007

Today's race began on the edge of the river, giving the competitors a swim of two hundred metres or so to get into the spirit of the day. With them off and on their way, I head back to the boat to relax for a while, giving me the chance to organise some kit for the next couple of days. Once that was accomplished I was taken to the site of the next camp.

The area was wonderful. No sooner had I secured my hammock, along with Vicky and Doug from the medical team, than we were inundated with small children, all rushing around us and taking great delight in posing for our photographs. I spent much of the morning and early afternoon chatting with Vicky and Doug, after which I repeated my usual routine of earning myself some exercise by heading down the trail and welcoming the competitors that were coming in. Steffania and Judah tended to be bringing up the rear each day. This was hardly surprising; this was Steffania's first ultra race, and Judah had never experienced hills before. I always enjoyed meeting them, mostly because they seemed genuinely happy and relieved to know that seeing me meant they were nearly back, and they would have some company for the journey in.

I moved to take my hammock down in the evening, due to the number of ants that had materialised in that area of the camp (in fact the whole area seemed to be swarming with ants), and received the most impressive wasp sting to my index finger. The wasp was trapped within the mosquito net that draped over my hammock. As soon as it had access to my skin it stung me with such vigour that it actually cut my finger! As well as cutting me the sting itself did smart a tad too. Paul was on-hand to laugh at my misfortune, which I am convinced did nothing to help. Kyle proffered me a cream that seemed to do the trick in no time, once I had removed the broken remnants of the sting with tweezers. The wasp came off worse, predictably.

During the evening I joined the medical team and a couple of soldiers for drinks behind a ruined bus at the side of the campsite. I was concerned that our boisterous and awful singing might have disturbed the sleeping runners, but this was not the case. As we returned to our hammocks the rain started. I took my hammock down and headed, along with many of the competitors and support staff, into a large building adjacent to the camp. Jo and I found space where we could, laid down on the cold, concrete floor and eventually managed to drift off to sleep. We had agreed to cuddle for warmth if we felt we were in danger of becoming too cold. Fortunately we were warmed, in spirit at least, by the appearance of Doug, presenting himself to all fifty or so of us and singing, badly.

Friday, 12th October 2007

I had been carrying dry 'night' kit around with me in my rucksack, which meant that come the morning I had the displeasure of dressing into the wet clothing that I had been wearing during the day. I made use of the camp's fire, provided by the locals to ensure that the competitors had constant access to hot water for their drinks and dehydrated food rations, and stood there for some time to dry out my boots and clothing. Doug, Jo, Sarah and I were taken by 4x4 into the jungle to the overnight checkpoint for the day's stage.

Today saw the start of the long stage; over ninety kilometres in length, and an overnight checkpoint would be enforced for competitors reaching it after a particular cut-off time. This was due, we were informed, to the presence of a large number of jaguars in the area, as we did not wish to have competitors fumbling through the dark in such company.

We reached the checkpoint and the heavens opened, yet again. We had a rudimentary shelter in place at the site, so that kept us dry as we awaited competitors. A couple of runners reported a deep gully a few kilometres before this checkpoint, which had become treacherous and required ropes. Accepting that it would take some hours to have it arranged for ropes to reach us, I donned my poncho and headed off into the rain to investigate. I was in rather a cheery mood, as it happened, and quite enjoyed being out on the trail in the rain. It made a pleasurable difference to the oppressive heat, as the temperature had certainly dropped a few degrees, and the added moisture enhanced the smells from the plants and other foliage.

I met with a couple of competitors along the way, including my firm friends James and John, both of whom confirmed that they had experienced difficulties with the gully. When I reached it, I found Andrea sitting down in the muddy trail at the base. When I enquired as to why she was sitting there, at the time filled with worry that she might have been injured, she informed me that each time she tried to stand up and move she simply fell over in the mud. Bugger. It was a steep slope, and the path was practically a stream over soft mud. It was too slippery for me to reach her directly, so I scanned the space around the path. At least the rain had eased off. The remaining clouds protected the jungle from the sun, allowing the temperature to remain far cooler than we had become used to.

The trees were a few metres away from the path on both sides, with thick foliage making up the space between those trees and the trail. With my machete at the ready, I cut a liana from a tree and used it for balance as I swung down and began cutting a new path. When I reached the end of the liana, I paused to cut down a thin tree and then to half-break a branch to give me more leverage and room to move. So much for leaving only footprints. I sheathed the machete and took Andrea's hand, then turned and began to make my way back up the slope; making use of the trees, branches and lianas as I had done on the way down. No sooner had she arrived at the top than more competitors reached the creek at the base of the gully.

I helped to pull up Bert and Steffania, by which time the new path was adequate for Phil to make his own way up behind Steffania and I. We were close to the top and I prepared to make a new route where the path joined the original trail, as it had become too slippery to risk using. I brought my machete down through a large plant and the air filled with golden, shimmering, fluttering lights. I was taken aback as my mind attempted to fathom this stunningly beautiful yet novel phenomenon. Then realisation landed with a thud. Bees!!! I rushed Steffania and Phil off away from them; the bees were still circling upwards and had not begun to investigate the cause of their recent eviction, and cut a new trail to the other side of the existing path. By the time I reached the creek another couple of competitors had reached the far side of the gully and were beginning to make their way down to the creek. When Andy and Peter reached the base of the climb, I pointed out the new trail and watched as they made their way up unaided.

Judah was the only competitor to reach the checkpoint late enough to be forced to stay over. Some competitors had talked about staying over out of choice, just to experience spending the night in the deep jungle, but thought better of it when they had fully come to appreciate the distance still to be accomplished for the stage. When night came I enjoyed aiming my Maglite into the jungle, and seeing hundreds of pairs of eyes shining back at me. One can surely never feel alone in such a place! The rain ceased and we settled into our hammocks to sleep. Others from the support crew had left, and had been replaced by about a dozen soldiers; their noise assuring us that any animals wishing to know us better would have to be quite, quite mad (or deaf, possibly).

Saturday, 13th October 2007

I awoke at ten to five in the morning, but remained in my hammock until half an hour later. Judah needed to get going, and with no sound of activity from his section of the camp I had to get up to spur him on. He was ready to leave at six, and what followed was an incredibly long fifty-five kilometres. Judah had really never managed to train on any hills whatsoever, and at a walking pace his progress was slow. This was coupled with him becoming tired from his efforts, and frequently just lying down across the trail as he pleased, in order to rest and take on some food and fluids. It was quite surprising to the soldiers that joined us, and myself, just how much rest he felt he needed and how regularly. But still, he was here and persevering, and there are not many people in the world that could manage this.

Even though the pace should have been easy for me, it was the hours spent on my feet that took their toll, and I soon became aware of sore joints and aches and pains as the mileage built up. We were not in the jungle for long before we emerged out into open settlements near the Tapajos. We paused briefly to observe dancers practising, the women wearing the most gorgeous dresses, and everyone enjoying themselves. We met Kyle at the next checkpoint, which is where Jo left us to head back to the boat, and I continued on with Judah and the two soldiers.

I had intended to keep Judah company, partly to give me experience of a good length of trail, and partly to ensure that he was not discouraged from finishing. Trail became track, which became road. At the next checkpoint Ivan, from the medical team, arranged some good food for the soldiers and I, and then continued along with us to the finish. The route from that checkpoint led back into jungle, then road again down to the Tapajos, then road took us to the beach itself, and then back up onto roads, across a stretch of river, and then back along more roads. I had to keep my boots on for the river crossing, and as water entered in over the top my socks became saturated. Over the final ten kilometres or so blisters and sores developed that made progress painful, if not a little slower. Finally the route took us back to the beach, which we kept to until we reached the lights of camp. It was a quarter past ten at night when we reached the finish line. Judah was too late to have made the cut-off time for the stage, but Shirley would be allowing him to finish regardless. As she put it, she would not have someone come this far in good health and then prevent them from completing the last thirty kilometres to the final finish line.

I spent the night on the boat, and the wind and waves had me swinging uncomfortably high in my hammock. I was too tired to get out and raise it above the level of a bench that it kept knocking into. This would be the last night of sleeping in a hammock on this trip; tomorrow night I would be sleeping in a hotel bed, which I curiously did not relish. I had been enjoying this short excursion into the Amazon, and felt reluctant to be resigned to leave it so quickly.

Sunday, 14th October 2007

In the morning the competitors set off for a thirty-kilometre run along the beach to the finish line, in the small town of Alter do Chao. The adventure would soon be over for them, and for me too. I sorted my kit for the hotel and the flight back, and then made my way to the finish, by boat, to welcome the competitors across the line. I did have a couple of blisters to show for all my efforts, which I certainly deserved. As had become tradition, I went off to meet the last couple of competitors and walk them in. Food was supplied for us in a local restaurant. I ate my way through plates filled with rice, beans, beef mince and chicken, washed down with whatever drinks were put in front of me. Fed and watered, we all made our way back to the hotel, where I enjoyed a shower before heading out for more food and more drinks.

I relished the thanks and praise that came from my efforts during the race. For Andrea, she had become a part of her own rescue in an adventure movie; Bert thanked me for saving his life, although I have no idea why, and James thanked me for the fond memory of the lunatic in the mac, appearing from nowhere in the middle of the jungle and the driving rain. The bombeiro had a translator pass on his gratitude for my coming to rescue him from the jaguar, and Per from

Denmark informed me that I looked like a nerd. All in all it had been a thoroughly successful trip then.

I had experienced how my body acclimatised after five or so days following on from my arrival, and how much more comfortable that allowed me to be when exercising. I had gained confidence in my own abilities to cover ground in the Amazon, which I would be relying upon when I returned in a year's time. Importantly, I now had a good understanding of various sections of trail, the terrain, the hills and the terrors of the razor grasses and tripwire roots. Not least, of course, I had made some great friends and seen a part of the world that I might not have been inclined to visit had I not become involved in adventure racing. What remains is for me to return to England and prepare my training programme for my own attempt next year.

Empathy and Evolution

I see them there as I stroll along the South Bank of the Thames, as they are struggling away; these red-faced new runners. Huffing and puffing as they go. If I were mean, then I would think first of a defibrillator. My naïve base reaction is to feel sorry for them. Pain, anguish and discomfort are written all over them. But the sympathy passes as quickly as their heartbeats, and is replaced with a warm sense of pride.

I feel that I should run after them and congratulate them on their sterling effort, but I withhold for fear of reprisals. Heaven forbid that I might attract accusations of being condescending or patronising. Forget about the respect and admiration I have for Haille Gabrasellasie, Lance Armstrong, and my fellow ultra-endurance adventure runners. These men and women sweating here are probably my real heroes. The successful endurance athletes (however one might measure success) have crossed over the brow of the hill. They have turned a corner in their training. Nothing hurts in racing like starting to run for the first time.

I can see it in their running pattern. It is inefficient, laboured, flailing. They are wasting so much energy just to move each foot a few inches in front of the other. When it connects with the earth it is heavy, weighted, stressful. Sometimes it makes my joints ache just to watch. I spent years watching runners on the streets and on treadmills. I learnt how from seeing one foot hit the floor I could understand how their entire biomechanics operated. In Malcolm Gladwell's *Blink* it would have been referred to as instinctive intuition. It comes from seeing something so often that any deviation from the norm can be picked up at once; understood in the mind long before the thoughts could be properly contemplated and articulated. I would drop a knee slightly, twist at the hip, all to mimic their action, from which I could understand where their body became most stressed. It earned me a fair number of personal training clients, back in the day when I was raising funds to pay off my student debts. I could approach a runner on a treadmill and pinpoint a particular area and ask them if they experienced pain there. Most of the time I was right, although not always. Sometimes people do not do sufficient miles to really cause themselves damage, and at other times it has been there for so long that they are no longer aware of it.

I trained my staff to do likewise. It is simple enough: to observe so many people that you can recognise the difference between normal and abnormal joint movement. One can then see which side contacts the ground with the most force, and look for the joint that seems to be bearing the brunt. Sometimes it is the ankle, but more commonly it tends to be the knee, hip, lower back or shoulders. From there, knots (trigger points) can form in other muscles along the kinetic chain, all of which can usually be recognised and often found by feeling or massaging the area.

Now I have given up on such antics, as there are far better people than I working on rehabilitative sports medicine. But I can still feel it. I can see the way that a laboured foot hits the pavement and shocks the shin and the knee, maybe the lower back, and in a way I feel it too, and again I feel sorry for them. But if they carry on then their technique might improve, and they may learn to lengthen their stride and the repetition improve their mechanics. Maybe. Perhaps they will learn to run more upright. Why do they cower forwards? Are they self-conscious and embarrassed and fearful that people will see their faces? Faces that they do not want to be seen? Do they think that this is how runners are supposed to move and so they are mimicking something unnatural?

Maybe it is just from so many years of trying to fight the flab with endless stomach crunches, that now they cannot put force through a foot without the back curling forward as if still crunching away. That is easy to spot. The neck usually juts forwards in rhythm. Will people ever learn what the abdominal muscles actually do? The information has been out there for years, but then who cares? Crunches and sit-ups hurt, so they must be good for you. Besides, all those hunks in the fitness magazines chiselled their fine abs from crunches and sit-ups, didn't they? Maybe if these runners are experiencing pain, then they will have the sense to have the source checked by a professional, before their running ambitions become woefully curtailed.

I see it borne in those runners' faces too. All that pain and anguish. Their cheeks are puffed and their whole head appears

40

flushed and inflamed. They are burning up on the inside. Their heart is beating so fast it must feel as if it is going to explode. Their lungs are constricted within the chest cavity, as if they would need to expand beyond the ribs to take in sufficient air. All that work. Those tired hearts and lungs, working so hard to deliver oxygen and fuel to the working muscles, and remove the waste products and the carbon dioxide. The legs have become so heavy that they must feel like mighty oak trees rooted to the ground. The shoulders are a tiresome burden and the spine curves forwards as the body lopes on. And those hearts and lungs, working so hard yet they still cannot work hard enough.

All that energy being used up, and the body is so inefficient at cooling itself. Those poor souls. Ever since their first few paces they have quickly been heating up. Now it must seem as if a furnace burns away inside, riotously, treacherously, lulling the runner into the belief that it can only become harder, that their body simply does not have the capacity for more. All those biomechanical imbalances make their running inefficient, in turn causing them to use more energy to cover a given distance than they would without such issues. But regardless of such details, their body will become fitter if they keep pushing themselves; if they continue pressing on.

How do they do it, these heroes of mine? How do they get out here, on the streets and in the parks? When they were preparing to venture out on this run, what motivation was it that drove them to be here? They knew that they were not as fit as others. They knew that they might be overtaken by other runners, and even by some walkers.

They knew that people would be looking at them, mocking them (for some people mock all those that are different). These runners might be the most self-conscious and easily embarrassed people there are. But they made it. They knew how much it would hurt. They knew how much it hurt last time, and how it took only seconds of the run before the pain started, and how it became progressively worse throughout their journey. But they did it anyway.

At some point, when they were pulling on their training shoes, they must have known how it would be so much more agreeable to simply relax in their nice warm home, on a comfy sofa in front of some thrilling televisual treat whilst scoffing some delicious hot food, together with a beer or a glass of wine and followed by a nice cup of tea or coffee and something sweet. But they chose to forego that, and all of their comforts. These bloody heroes sallied forth through the front door, which may just as well have been the very gates of Hades, and they slapped Cerberus in the face, embraced the fires of Hell and went out for a bloody horrible run. Heroes? They are the very salt of the Earth, and I salute them.

The fact is that I do not care who someone is as a runner, or how much they have achieved. All that tells me is what we can learn from each other, or at least where we can begin talking. Why run outside at all; why not join a health club? Well, I suppose that if someone feels self-conscious then it might be easier to know that if they are running outside then people only see them for a fleeting few moments. In a health club they might be trapped in the stares of other members and the staff for the duration of their training session.

Besides, nobody needs to pay a hundred pounds a month for the privilege of going for a run, along with fifty pounds a session to have a personal trainer telling them to put one foot in front of the other, and then to speed up a bit. Tish and pish; I am being far too unfair. There are some excellent health clubs out there, and some personal trainers that are worth their weight in twenty-two carat gold, but there is far more to running than simply a training programme. In fact, I might just be so bold as to say that the training programme is one of the simplest factors there is:

- If you want to run further, then run further in your training sessions.
- If you want to run faster, then prioritise running faster in training.
- Ensure that the volume of training, the recovery time, and sleep and diet are all sufficient to promote progression and avoid plateaus and regressions.

The rest is all the fine-tuning. The core of all of this is experience. A good running programme will be based upon what appears to work the best for the majority of people, of similar levels of fitness. But once that generalised training is underway, all of the fine-tuning comes from the experience of the runner. A good instructor might recognise the signs and hazard a guess and the best means of progression, but at some point, in the future if not now, every runner should be able to throw off the shackles of regimes for the masses and refine their programmes to suit themselves. It all just comes down to those few simple rules. These poor sods battering themselves half to death on the pavements are taking their first few miles into a new world not just of physical fitness, but into a greater understanding of how their bodies work too.

Well, I grant you that we can complicate a training programme a tad more than that. How, for instance, do we go about best-estimating an appropriate duration or distance of training session, and what pace or range of paces should be utilised? How many sessions might be optimal each week, and how ought the diet be manipulated so that it best suits preparation and recovery from the sessions? When should the programme be tapering up and tapering down? How might a heart rate monitor, GPS, or watch-based thermometer be best integrated? What is the pattern for a week's training, and how does that fit into the overall macrocycle covering the months leading up to a competition or testable milestone?

There are myriad different variables that can be considered in light of the various training goals. So, in other words I concede defeat; you are absolutely right, we can make a training programme as simple or as convoluted as we choose. Perhaps it is our nature to want to make things as complicated as possible, or perhaps we just like to be able to talk about the intricate details, because then we might feel superior to those following the most basic approach.

As Friedrich Nietzsche puts it in *Human, All Too Human*: "In social dialogue, three-quarters of all questions and answers are framed in order to hurt the participants..." Ever since evolutionists discovered the reality of our place in nature, a disappointing majority of people (including some of the said evolutionists), have strived to show that even though we might be a part of nature, we are nevertheless on the top of the pile. We are so, because we are more complicated. Bacteria are simple and they are rubbish, but we, *we humans*, we can create the arts and literature, we can enjoy poetry and music, we can read and write, creating wonderful things and separating ourselves completely from the world around us. We cannot possibly describe such things without getting complicated in our explanations. Of course a training programme has to have a hundred different layers of complexity to be any good. To simply entertain the notion of going out for a run is preposterous; it would never work.

I, however, am not interested in creating confusion or dismay for any self-satisfying benefit. As a lecturer I take great delight in *assuming* a limited knowledge amongst my students, and that means that I can begin with the basics and work through all of the complicated details, hopefully, without anybody noticing how I threw them in. That is how I strive to be when I write my lectures, and it is certainly how I approach my own training (and my own life, for that matter, and I simply cannot think of a better way of doing it). Disagree, by all means.

Anyway, I have digressed because I fear oversights and insufficiencies galore. I had meant to be discussing my running heroes, and their great and glorious struggles as they fight and battle to get over all those hurdles between where they are now, and that moment when they realise that their greatest pains have been permanently trodden into the paths behind them. Do I envy them their glory? I doubt it. I have it easy now, and anybody that knows me well knows that I always dream of the easy life.

I remember my running history comparatively well, considering that the mind always tends to blank out the memories of pain. It would be unfair to say that I was never a runner, but nevertheless entirely accurate to declare that I was a useless one. Well yes, I used to be one of the brave few to compete at school in the 800 and 1500 metres, but that was only really because there were so few people that were prepared to have a bash, that there was a fair limit to the number of people that could feasibly finish ahead of me. I had no competitive edge whatsoever at school. I was just a tall, lanky, ugly, pathetic pillock that got beaten up by idiots even more pathetic than myself, and this was partly the reason that I had no self-confidence, no self-belief, and no idea that I could ever be any good at anything where I was competing against others. The sad thing is that I was not actually that bad, but it took twenty-odd years for me to realise that.

I began learning to swim before I could walk, and by the time I was at secondary school I was pretty fast in water. Yet when it came to competition I never really had the aggression to try to do well, and the only time that I do remember swimming in competition, I handicapped myself by doing breaststroke when the others were doing front crawl. The annoying thing is that I might have either won or come in a close second, but none of my friends were paying attention, and my usual low self-perceptions made me assume that I must have done too poorly for it to be worth asking whoever was taking note.

Going back to the running, we used to have a wonderful cross-country course around the fields of Lord Leventhorpe's School in Sawbridgeworth, Hertfordshire. The route led from the pavilion past the tennis courts, skirting the periphery of the main sports fields, then through a short section of woodland, and along a path up a slight hill to a farm, and then returning to the pavilion via the other side of the playing fields. I used to be in the front half of the runners when we did that, but my frustratingly disappointment-fuelled youth required that I omit that from my memory until now.

On occasion I even elected to go out for that run during my lunch break. Now, I clearly recall returning to the pavilion, hot and sweaty, and one of the older boys asking me how fast I completed it. I read out the time on my watch and was greeted with nods of approval. It must have been something like seventeen-and-a-half minutes for a two-mile route, which thanks to the hill and our collective lack of training might have been considered impressive. But such thoughts were expelled from my memory.

What I do remember, oh so well, was the one occasion that I represented the school at cross-country. I came in close to last. I had completed no training whatsoever, and it was a long and unfamiliar course. There were also sections along roadsides which immediately led me to such boredom that I slowed to a walk, totally unmotivated and depressed that yet again I was about to demonstrate to the world at large that I was no good at sport.

As for those 800 and 1500 metre runs. I did not come last; I know that. But it really did not matter. I did not notice the people behind me, only the people that beat me, and yet I was always resolved to defeat. I had no competitive edge, and yet I hated being beaten. If there were ten of us running, and I came in fifth, then as far as I was concerned there were six of us that came in last place, and four others that beat us. That was the sort of mentality that makes me wish that I could visit myself in my past and shake some sense into me. Telling my twelve-year-old self that my entire world would change for the better in the years to come would have done us both a world of good. I probably would have given him a hug too. Soppy git.

There were other races, and such like, such as cross-country running and sports days when I was in the Air Training Corps, but these were one-offs and followed a similar theme. I did okay in the cross-country, because everybody had a stab at it and nobody seemed to have done much training. I was awful at the sports day because I tried my luck at the 800- and/or 1500- metres (memory does not serve on this one), and came in either last or close to last. On that occasion, my fellow runners had trained, and I felt my usual disappointment, compounded with the guilt of letting the side down, but with the solace that 'I'm not really any good at sport anyway'. Looking back it was so depressing that I have no idea how I ever made it through puberty.

I left Leventhorpe at the age of fifteen. In September of that year, I began my A-level studies at the Hertfordshire and Essex High School in Bishops Stortford, just up the road from my previous school. The need to change came partly from my being exasperated from my many years of torment at the hands of my aggressors at Leventhorpe, and partly because I was not offered the opportunity to make a hash of my desired A-Levels there because the subjects suffered timetable clashes. Anyway, Herts and Essex was only a mixed sixth-form school; it was an all-girls school up to the fifth year, meaning that being a boy put me in the minority. At least it meant that there were fewer people to give me a hard time, and the guys all stuck together at first, for there was safety in numbers, and we all muddled through our first rather anxious year as one.

I began strength training at *The Challenge Gym*, a cosy and intimate club that seemed set up with bodybuilding in mind, yet tried desperately to appeal to that great majority of the health-conscious populace of Bishops Stortford, who were simply interested in toning-up and slimming-down. I was under the guidance of manager and bodybuilder Wayne, and through him actually discovered something that I was not bad at. Because I had no-one to compete with but myself, I had no real issues with how much weight I needed to lift. With an ultra-skinny frame, at over six-foot in height and nine and a half stones in weight, I could only become heavier (or snap, obviously). Hence, I was bound for success.

Thanks to some excellent direction (for which I shall always be grateful and indebted), and what seemed like a prescription to eat as much of anything as I possibly could, my bodyweight soared to about thirteen and half stone within only two years. My bodyfat levels were always below ten percent, and on occasion down to six, which meant that my skin looked see-through and my veins chose to reside on the outside of my body.

I was lifting staggeringly heavy weights as well. Within no time I was taken under the wing of Barry, a local powerlifter, and we were soon performing some of the heaviest lifts in the gym (although I was still nowhere near his standard). I had never used any drugs, and it seemed that I had a good sense of awareness of my body, which tied-in nicely with my new-found love of food and a less stressful way of living. Most important of all, my natural testosterone levels seemed unusually high, which for someone that was such a damp squib for so many years before, came as a surprise and a shock to all of us, I can assure you.

I made an abundance of new friends at the gym, mostly senior to myself, and felt that I had become a part of something greater than myself, but in a way by which I was accepted and nurtured until I could take others under my own wing. I worked there part-time as well, around my studies, and it was one of the best jobs that I ever had. I naturally screwed it up, but then I screwed up almost every job I ever had because I have been monumentally awful at working for other people.

I had tried and tested a few martial arts from a very young age, although my lack of spirit meant that I could never actually call upon any of it during my youth, when the occasion might have called for it. I dabbled in Judo, Wado Ryu, Aikido, Maui Thai Kickboxing, Traditional Kickboxing and Philippino Kickboxing. When Krav Maga, an Israeli hand-to-hand combat system arrived in the UK,

Wayne was one of the first instructors and I learned by his side. When he started to teach his own classes, I was able to fill-in as the experienced helper and demonstration guinea pig.

When I was a child, idiots loved to pick on me because I was seen to be an easy target. By the time I was eighteen, idiots wanted to beat me up because they thought it would mean something if they said they had beaten up the biggest gangly student in the pub. It never worked though. I was so calm and laid-back that any attempts to start a fight were simply ignored. Besides, I patronised pubs simply brimming with gangly students, and no doubt any serious attempts at violence would have led to at least half of the patrons, and most of the staff joining in. If only that twelve-year-old had known that one day he would have some good friends and well-warranted self-confidence.

One of my best friends at school was Russell; a popular lad that everybody liked. Russell had asthma; so naturally at the time I thought that I should have it too, and was so satisfied when my G.P. diagnosed me that I truly believed this brought me closer to my friend. But, whereas Russ would have an asthma attack and end up in hospital, I would actually require my father to tell me that I was not breathing properly. I was always so sure I could never make a fuss about anything, which meant that I subdued the signs and never recognised them. My asthma was exercise and allergen-induced, and subsided gradually with time, although the sensitivity to certain allergens remained.

Over the years that followed I maintained some level of martial arts training at home or occasionally in a gym, whilst my

51

attentions to strength training became sporadic and of little long-term consequence. I was moving around because of my studies and later on due to my work, and a perpetual lack of funds meant that I was working on so many projects outside of my work, and/or my work was so demanding of my time, that my opportunities to have regular productive training sessions became fewer and fewer.

Then, in March of 2005, whilst living in Cambridge, I elected to compete in the *Marathon des Sables*. As an exercise physiologist, surely I could train myself to run one hundred and fifty miles in a weeklong race? And if I could not, then surely nobody should be able to! I was in the perfect position to research everything within my field of academia, so as to learn what was required for such an undertaking. It was only going to be a one-off. Just this one flirtation into the world of endurance running, and then I would come back and focus once more on all things strength- and battle-orientated.

I had never been enamoured with the idea of running the London Marathon. The problem was not the distance, although at the time I would not have been able to complete it. I was raised in Sawbridgeworth, a rural escape sandwiched between the larger towns of Harlow to the south, and Bishops Stortford to the north. I could walk five minutes from my door and be immersed in countryside; in fields with rivers and the sound of civilisation out of earshot. I was never a fan of the cities. The idea of running around a built-up area had never appealed to me. Besides, thanks to my sickly childhood I was also allergic to pollutants, and that included whatever horribleness lurked in the area above our great capital, which descended upon me and forced a flu-like, histemic response.

Now that the years have been kinder and I have gained some tolerance, I am only affected if I am out of the city for an extended period and then return. I had, up until that point, spent some time each year since 1999 in Egypt with friends. Mahmoud had a stud farm by the desert and I used to spend some time in the Sahara during the hottest of days. Knowing that I could walk around the desert gave me the confidence to think that I could walk for a hundred and fifty miles across the Sahara. If I could train myself to run, then I could run the sections that I wanted to, and walk whatever remained. It seemed to me to be a splendid idea.

Now we may go back to those new runners. I remember that first run of mine so well, way back then in the Spring of 2005. I had donned some training gear, including far too many top layers because it was cold outside, and I did not have the foresight to realise that I would quickly warm up. I had no running trainers, just some stiff-soled Reebok Classics, which had always been perfect for my strength-training sessions. I added some weight to a rucksack in the form of clothing and a five-kilogram dumbbell, put on my heart-rate monitor, and headed out of the flat and onto the street.

My heart rate was a hundred and forty-five beats per minute just having come down the stairs. This was anxiety again. It was me, twelve years old, expecting that I would be useless. My peace came from knowing that I was not competing with anyone other than myself, and that this session would hurt all the more to ensure that later sessions would hurt me a little less. And then I set off...

Every time I see someone struggling I must experience the perception that it is me again. The first few hundred metres had been acceptable, but already I was feeling warm within my sweatshirt. My heart rate increased and as I headed away from town my body temperature continued to rise. Eventually I was forced to a walk and resolved not to quit until I had done what I had set out to do. Hot, flushed and sweating, I got myself back into a rhythm, slowed down and steadied my pace, and completed the circuit.

I had underestimated the distance, worn too much clothing, carried a pack that was far too heavy and cumbersome, and arrived back home feeling wretched and pathetic. Did it hurt? Each step my gathering feelings hammered at my head, begging questions of what I thought I was doing. Somehow that run had proved more positive than I had anticipated. It had hurt: the distance, the lack of fitness, the heat from the clothing, and the weight on my back. But that was a good thing. I managed to get through it. Next time I would be fitter, because the effects of my struggles dictated that it would be so. The weight on my back would become easier to manage, because the pain and soreness in my shoulders and back would make my muscles stronger for next time. *"Out of life's school of war: What does not destroy me, makes me stronger."* (Nietzsche).

And so it went on. My training during that first year was sporadic, at best, right up until I took a job in London where I was asked to lead a running club. A short four-mile circuit was the perfect distance for me to work on my speed and become comfortable, thereby developing a strong base of running fitness. As my jobs changed, thus reiterating my inability to keep almost any professional position, I had to invent new ways to work running into my life.

A few months prior to my attempt at the *Marathon des Sables*, I transferred to a health club roughly a half-marathon away from where I was living. I finished my shifts at any time from two in the afternoon to two in the morning. Then I got changed into my running gear, a process that was no longer the amateurish faffing around to throw on whatever was to hand, but a fully-fledged ritual during which I would be mentally preparing myself for each stage of the journey to come.

I would stroll off across Hammersmith Bridge, take the option east and then go through the final stage of run-preparation just on the path by the riverside. The surplus layers would come off, the laces on my Salomon's would be pulled tight, and I would go through the brief phases of my mobility work. All the time I meditated on the run ahead of me. I would pull the rucksack straps tight, ensure that everything was tucked-in and secure, and then check the time on my G-Shock as the first heel strike marked the commencement of the training session.

Always the first ten minutes were the hardest. Those poor guys finding it so tough to make it through their sub-hour sessions… I worked hard for the first ten minutes, after which everything settled down and I reached a state of relative comfort. There can be little wonder how I have come to believe that those developing runners are working far harder than I.

My dues have been paid now, and after over four years of forcing myself to run further, faster and harder, I can now relax and enjoy myself. If I want to run fast, then I increase my pace and my mind ticks over the figures. When I reach Putney Bridge how long have I been running? If I continue at this pace at what time can I expect to reach Wandsworth Park, Battersea Park, or the Anchor Pub? I was constantly calculating and assessing, then modifying my pace by small amounts as required, and keeping focussed on my timings and how I was coping with it all physically.

Most of the time, however, any ambitions of timings are not considered. I know my fastest and slowest times, and as long as I complete the run somewhere in between, then I am satisfied. On those days, I simply lull myself into a quiet meditation as I go, permitting my mind to daydream and I drift off into my own private thoughts, loosely aware of my timings and the landmarks, and still taking pleasure in greeting my fellow runners as they come and go.

And still, as those final few months progressed and time ebbed away before the *Marathon des Sables*, those first ten minutes were always the hardest. I recovered sufficiently to be able to manage half-marathons on consecutive nights for six days a week. I was aware that if I took more than one day of rest between sessions then I would feel more sluggish in finding my rhythm. As those last months passed me by, the ten minutes of hardship became eight, and then six, and then four.

Maybe if I was not well-recovered, or had been working longer hours than usual, or if I had been deprived of sufficient sleep or adequate nutrition, then it would be back to ten minutes before I recovered from my early-exercise oxygen debt. For that is all that it is. Our heart rates increase, followed by breathing rate and depth, but there is a delay. We begin running at what we consider to be our normal running pace, yet our body is delivering oxygen and nutrients to the body in accordance with what we were doing immediately before. Thus, there is some carry-over of that, when resting or walking volumes of blood and oxygen are feeding muscles engaged in exercise. Over the course of a few minutes, the required physiological compensations begin to take place.

As we become fitter everything about us changes and adapts to the stress. The body develops in response to the stimulus of training. Our cardiovascular system becomes better at taking oxygen from the lungs to our muscles. Thanks to changes in our red blood cells and haemoglobin, our blood carries more oxygen, and can remove more carbon dioxide. Our hearts become stronger and can even grow in size (left ventricular hypertrophy). We have an increase in capillarisation, that is, an increase in the number of fine blood vessels that surround the muscles, thus giving a greater surface area for oxygen and carbon dioxide to be exchanged between the muscles and the blood.

The muscles themselves have a greater oxygen carrying capacity, due to an increase in their myoglobin content (the muscles' equivalent to the blood's haemoglobin), and the fibres themselves adapt to become better at aerobic work. Once the oxygen is inside the muscle cells (a process made more efficient by the increase in associated enzymes), then there are more mitochondria, a vital organelle for aerobic metabolism. Again, that final process is improved due to increases in the related enzymes, the chemical catalysts that allow the various reactions within our body to occur at the rate we need them to.

So, the reason that I have it comparatively easy is because my body has made those adaptations, and whilst I continue to stimulate further improvements, my body is already far better adapted than it was when I went out for that very first training run. Our new runners are still in the early phases of those physiological adaptations, and as a result their lungs, hearts and muscles are all struggling because they are not as efficient as they will be in the years to come. As a consequence they are feeling hotter, less able to manage that heat, and their minds are having to battle with the body's cues to end the pain and stop the effort. All that I had to focus on was getting through those first ten minutes, because once beyond that threshold then my whole world became a much more agreeable, pleasant place to be. And those first ten minutes only really constituted being a little warmer and less comfortable than might be ideal. Those new runners have it so much harder, and I truly hope that they all persevere and reap their rewards.

One of the things that surprised me the most, when I began my formal training for the Jungle Marathon, was just how much further my physiology had come. On most days, even early on, I had no noticeable effects of any oxygen debt whatsoever. I began running at a comfortable speed, which, when I timed myself, actually demonstrated that it was faster than my pre-MdS speed. Yet, the need to focus on getting through those initial ten minutes was gone. Running had just ceased to hurt anymore. Yes, I could decide to race; I could set myself challenges and aim to beat personal bests. Similarly, I could just choose to run flat-out until I reached exhaustion, but the point is that my body would reach exhaustion in an efficient manner. The point of exhaustion itself would still hurt, and I could still become incredibly hot by working harder than I usually would, but my general training had become pain-free.

As an ultra-endurance runner, I never wanted to finish running at the end of a day and feel exhausted, because in competition I needed to be able to run again the following day. If I worked too hard on day one, then a snowball effect might ensue that could see me too fatigued or injured to complete the race. I needed to finish my training sessions at an intensity that left some fuel in the tank, whilst having maintained a speed that I felt was acceptable. To be able to do that now, for me, makes me feel that I have really turned a page. All of the physiological processes that were reflective of my pre-running days have either adapted or been superseded by what has been required to make me an endurance runner.

For the first time in my life, I am actually satisfied that I have achieved something, even though I see this as a journey in which I still have a long way to go. This is why I feel a connection with every other runner and endurance athlete in the world, whether they can manage 500 metres, five minutes, or 500 miles. To have accomplished even this feeling of pride in oneself, and the personal achievement, is something that I hope all runners have experienced or will experience. This is the level at which we might all be equal, because this satisfaction is the result of paying our dues over the miles passed; it exists free from other ambition, goal, or competitiveness.

Perhaps it is the latter that dictates why I must forego the luxury of complacency, and why it is that I have found myself needing to train harder than ever for that next big thing. I want to know what it is to be competitive, not particularly against others, but against the fellow I was a year ago, or a month ago, or last week.

Back to Bedlam

I was nervous, and ridiculously so. I had been nervous all day. The time to get back into running proper had come. In my mind I had been playing and replaying the tape of the evening's run over and over in my head. It was just a few short miles from work close to the London Eye to the tube station at Canada Water. But it was not the distance that concerned me. Not at all. I had not only mentally rehearsed the run itself. I had rehearsed everything; even getting dressed for the run. It was the feeling of running that was putting a lump in my throat, quickening my heart, and loosening my bowels.

I had been running on and off ever since finishing the *Marathon des Sables*. Mostly the runs had been brief efforts, lasting less than an hour, and they were often to keep a friend company. As a consequence they were not the quickest of runs. But tonight would be different. I would not be running with clients or with friends. I would be by myself again; focussed on that next big thing. I could sense the air rushing passed my face, my long stride carrying me along the south bank of the Thames, as if the sea breeze had reached in to carry me home. I could feel that searing heat again.

I was fitter now than I was back then, back when I started. But the first directed session would hurt, even if just at first. I would make it so. My heels would hit the paved ground, but I would not be

61

pounding it or stressing my joints. Each heel would touch down only to allow my back leg to sweep forward, my knee and ankle to bend, and for my body to continue rushing along. All would be gentle and nothing excessive. I could sense the momentum. I knew how it would feel from the moment I passed through the building's revolving doors. I would be outside, free to the elements, and running again. Even the thought of running resonated within me. All was anxious, the air palpable and my heart quickening. I had to be out there again, running for myself, readying myself for the jungle.

The distance was not to be far, but it would be sufficient. I would know how my new running gear felt and performed. I would know how much work I had to do to get to where I needed to be. I needed to leave this oppressively dull and mindless place of work where I was temping, and shift my lazy carcass at a respectable speed again, resurrecting life into it once more. Would people look at me? Some would. It certainly is not a highlight of a run, to be stared at as if deranged. It occurs to me that they are looking at me as if I am somehow alien, or foreign. Or perhaps they suppose I am about to explode. But I am used to the looks. In a pathetically sad way I have become accustomed to that. I know that my legs are thin. Whenever I sleep in a forest I do so in fear that Ray Mears might happen upon my legs and try to light a fire with them.

I heard enough shouts when I was training for the MdS. Mostly it was encouraging, even if mockingly so. Girls mainly. Sometimes drunk, presenting themselves as that latest addition to our national identity. There would be some sort of shout or scream and then perhaps an applause and a 'Keep going!' I could manage that okay. I would often be holding up a hand in acknowledgement or volleying some response. It helped the time to pass quicker and amused me for a while. But I can still feel some of those stares. The way people chose to stare almost always at either my legs or at my crotch. What on earth can be entertaining them so? There is certainly nothing of interest that comes to my mind, I assure you. When dressed in my running tights I have been accused of having bionic legs, because they look far too thin to actually contain normal muscles sufficient to carry my bodyweight. It was only sometime later that I came to appreciate what the more well-versed psychologists already know: looking down is simply being submissive or respectful, either deliberately avoiding eye contact or a natural response. Not realising that at the time always had me glancing down in bafflement.

My shift came to a close and I headed to the toilets to get changed, going through the motions that I had mentally rehearsed again and again during the day. I undressed and pulled on my black Salomon running tights and a pair of running socks. Then I pulled on my black running shorts, also Salomon, and my Berghaus navy blue running t-shirt. I would be wearing my trail running shoes for all training, my Salomon XA Pro 3D Ultra GTXs in place of my Asics Cumulus trainers, as I would be wearing the Salomon's in the jungle. I hoped to loosen them up sufficiently to have them feeling like slippers by the time I flew out to Santarem.

I had a rucksack with me, containing clothes and some other bits to add weight. As I would be carrying a rucksack during the race,

I intended to use one for all of my training, to ensure that my whole body was used to running with the weight on my back. There seemed little point in improving cardiovascular fitness if my muscles all collapsed at the start line when I strapped on the rucksack.

As I walked back to the office to place my work clothes into a drawer, my heart was pounding. My face and skin felt flushed as my anxieties and excitement for the run grew. I told myself it was ridiculous; a run of five kilometres or so was not going to be difficult. But this was not about making the distance; it was about doing it well, and using my performance as an indication of fitness levels and how much I needed to improve before the race.

I took the lift down and exited the building. Once outside I pulled the shoulder straps tighter on the rucksack, ensuring it would be kept close to my back and not bounce too much. I should have walked for a few minutes to warm-up; I had been sitting down behind a desk all day. I contained myself to walk for a few metres only, gathering speed all the time. I bounded up a few steps that brought me in view of the London Eye and the park in front of it. I broke into a jog to take me onto the green. My pace increased; by the time I reached the Jubilee Bridge I was already at my 5-K running speed, as I ran along the south bank eastwards towards Canada Water.

By the time I reached Waterloo Bridge, a few hundred metres further along, I was already feeling hot and in full realisation that I had started off too fast. I took the edge off my pace only a fraction and allowed my breathing to calm down. People wandering along the front of the Oxo building forced me to slow to move past them, and similarly so as I passed under Blackfriars Bridge. Beyond that, it was clear enough to increase my speed and make up on the lost time and enforced rest. I passed the Founder's Arms pub, the Millennium Bridge, and the Tate Modern. Southwark Bridge, Clink Street and London Bridge followed, with the slightest of squeezes past pedestrians until free space arrived again just next to HMS Belfast. The GLA building, Tower Bridge, and then a quick and clear run the rest of the way to Surrey Quays; the end of the run before turning off and walking to Canada Water underground station.

It had been a good run. I had felt hotter than I would have liked at first, and my breathing was more laboured, but I recovered well within those first few minutes and maintained a good average pace throughout. I would repeat this run a few more times and then increase the distances: 10-Ks and half marathons at first, and then runs of between twelve and twenty miles. For almost all, I would be carrying the rucksack, and wearing my trail running shoes in preference to my road shoes.

I had been entertaining the idea of wearing the running tights in the jungle, so as to protect my skin from lacerations from the undergrowth, but already I knew that they would be too warm. I would have to stick to shorts and accept a few cuts and grazes here and there. So, plenty was learned and my running training for the Jungle Marathon had officially commenced. Excellent.

* * * * * * * * * *

Ever since a conversation with Steve Diederick, the managing director of Best of Morocco (the company that manages British entry into the *Marathon des Sables*), I have recognised two, often distinct, aspects of my training. Steve had told me that fitness was only ten percent of what was required to complete the MdS, whilst the rest was mental. Although, over time, I have come to disagree on the balance, I still agree that the mental aspects of adventure racing should never be underestimated.

I think that the original advice applied to at least half the field of competitors. If we are struggling, then we tend to be relying on our mental will and determination far more than our physical abilities. Even during the most arduous times, when parts of the body are howling in pain and begging cessation of the agony, then we still have the physical ability to put one foot in front of the other and carry on. There might be exceptions, such as during extreme dehydration or a heart attack or following a fracture, in which it is physically impossible to continue (or else continuing would severely risk health). But those are clearly the unlikely exceptions, and training itself should have helped to guard against such horrid eventualities. At the most common of dark hours, those times when pain and suffering fill our world with anguish and hatred, then it is certainly our mental constitution more than physical that carries us through to our own personal victories.

But what if we are fit enough to never even be close to succumbing to the dark times? What if we can run each day as good as pain-free? We run well, we eat well, we sleep and recover well, and we manage our feet well. During these times the mental aspect of training is almost redundant. One hundred and fifty miles, or thereabouts, might require little, if any, reliance on special motivations. On such occasions, and in such individuals, then I have to confess that it is all *fitness, fitness, fitness.* But how can we know such things in advance? Having known all of the competitors in the 2007 Jungle Marathon, I have come to appreciate that there are broadly up to three ambitions that competitors in such an event might have for themselves. Some have all three ambitions, whilst others might have only one of them. They are as follows:

1. To win
2. To finish the race in a position or time that they would regard as acceptable
3. To finish

There is a fourth, although the American tower of strength Terry, was the only one to make me aware of such an ambition:

4. To take part

Yes, I know that everybody that turns up wants to take part, but that is rarely the ambition in itself. For most of us it is taken as read. We want to win, or to finish well, or to finish the distance, and in order to do so we also enjoy the pleasure and privilege of taking part. But Terry had some joint problems that meant he soon found he could no longer stay in the race. This had become apparent fairly early on the first day. Instead of throwing in the towel, Terry kept heading out to complete a section of the course each day, just for the challenge offered to him by taking part in the manner in which he could.

Now perhaps Terry did turn up to finish, and in his eyes to finish well, but he had struggled during the *Marathon des Sables*, and had not managed to complete the JM in 2007. That is what I remember; he never finished a full stage, and from what I understood he simply walked a section from one checkpoint to another, and that was what he did each day. Perhaps he occasionally managed two checkpoints, or even more, but the point is that he was never going to realistically finish the whole race, not when he found how difficult it was for him to move at pace through the jungle. If he had been in any doubts about that before the race, then by the end of the first day he could have had none.

But Terry was a lion. He was quietly spoken, and he moved slowly and deliberately, and he existed in his own world out there. Really, he *made* his own world out there. He moved at his own pace, he rested when he needed to, and at the end of each day he would be smiling and happy with what he had achieved. Fitter men had quit when they realised that they could no longer finish well; Terry kept putting one foot in front of the other until he was content with what he had accomplished. Some could not fathom how the likes of the super-strong, super-fit and determined, such as the Canadian Daryl, could possibly quit, when it was perfectly clear that he could still make it to the finish. But for Terry and Daryl alike, the goal was not to finish, and just as Terry would never have accepted quitting altogether, so Daryl could never accept finishing if it meant that he could not finish where he wanted to. Daryl's race was over when he realised he would not achieve his goal, and so to actually plod on to the finish line would have been pointless for him. He knew that he could finish, so why bother? He had nobody to prove anything to.

Terry knew that he could not finish, but he would not be content unless he put the work into each day that he demanded of himself. Some people failed to understand either of them. I would never be so arrogant as to assume I could understand anything substantial about anyone, during such a short space of time, but rather to appreciate only the most superficial of details. Nevertheless, I have nothing but the deepest respect and admiration for the both of them.

My first goal, like Daryl's, is to finish well, but I also have a second goal, which is that if I cannot finish as I would like, then I might be content to finish as I would *not* like. Naturally I would want to be fit enough to manage the full race with no pain and no suffering, with no temptation whatsoever to rest with the demons of defeat. Maybe things will go wrong for me though. Maybe I will suffer injury, or my feet will blister or open sores will appear. Maybe something will happen that dictates no possibility of finishing in a position that I am satisfied with (it is a race, after all, although with my projected fitness I can have no realistic ambition of winning). Should such a barrier occur, then I cannot predict what it might be, or how much it might lead me to suffer.

To finish the race, all that I need to do is to put one foot in front of the other, and ensure that this happens at a pace sufficient to see me across the finish line before the allocated cut-off time for the day is reached. That is when, amidst what might have become a whole world of pain and agony, I must be able to just keep on moving. That is why, if to finish is to remain a goal, we must have incorporated sufficient mental training into our programme.

How on Earth can this mental aspect of training be specific? I am resolved to consider that it must be mostly impossible. I cannot cut away the flesh of my feet to ensure sufficient agony as I walk along. I can neither encourage stress fractures nor induce severe dehydration. To do any such thing would be to compromise the rest of my 'mental' training, my fitness training, and even worse to potentially risk my overall health. I could potentially inject myself with the various poisons or suffer the various bites and stings that I will likely be subjected to. But why would I? I am confident that the hordes of snakes, spiders, scorpions, bees, wasps, and ants will all have their shots at me when the time comes. There is no point now in spoiling their fun and stealing their glory, far be it from me to ruin their precious bastard moment.

No, I shall permit myself to do what I have always done when I demand a personal test of character and constitution. I shall repair to the hills and mountains of our great land and pit myself against the challenges therein. Running, for me at least, is about short-term pain. Even if I struggle for two hours, then I am at worst only suffering for two hours. In reality, of course, most of my running is fine and quite enjoyable. I might get hot or tired, but that hardly counts as suffering. Perhaps I will get to the point where I am ready to quit, but that usually comes at the point where I intended to quit anyway, and the reason for any additional strain on my reserves was because I had increased my efforts accordingly. Big walks, however, can test me physically for full days on end. The weather might be miserable, I might find myself to be cold, wet and hungry, I might become tired and thoroughly fed-up; my feet might become sore and tender, and my joints weakened and in need of rest and recovery. Yet these are the times when I must force such distractions to the very deepest, darkest locked and barred closet of my mind.

I must still navigate accurately with my map, I must be able to cook and to feed myself as required, I must be able to source water to stave off dehydration, and I must be able to locate adequate campsites for each night. I must be able to keep my wits about me when there is no-one that I can call upon to do the thinking for me. I must maintain the ability to keep on putting one foot in front of the other, and marching on until I am good and ready to stop. The cause of the pain or suffering is relatively unimportant, so long as it does not compromise my overall health and ability to continue other aspects of the training.

It all comes down to challenging the will and desire to stop and throw in the proverbial towel. It is to find oneself up shit-creek without a paddle, and still consider that it is there to nourish the greenest fields growing under blue skies in the miles downstream. It is to use one's size fourteen boots as rudimentary paddles until a more effective oar can be fashioned from deadwood. It is to snigger in the face of defeat, and to tweak the nose of self-doubt. It is to keep going when others would long ago have given up, and to know that you are the better human being for doing so.

It took Richard Askwith (writer of *Feet in the Clouds*) a long time before he could accomplish his goal of completing the 'Bob Graham Round'. From memory (mostly inaccurate and never to be relied upon), Richard had come to a point where he thought he might never be able to complete the long run around the Lake District. Family and work responsibilities were such that he felt he was doing all of the training that he could possibly manage. In the end, he came to realise that it was not his training, but his determination and resolve that was lacking, and when he fully accepted that, then he got out there and bloody well finished that run.

One day, I might rather like to get up to the Lake District to have a crack at getting all those forty-two peaks covered in the allocated twenty-four hours, but I am sure that it is far beyond my abilities now. Focus and obsession lay at the heart of many of these ventures; we can train as specifically and sufficiently as we care to, but should never lose our sense of the passion that is driving us. We must never become complacent that our fitness alone might be sufficient to get us through. When we have failed then it might be too late to discover what we should have done better. There are too many races, too many responsibilities, and such little time to rely only on learning from our mistakes. If I fail to complete the Jungle Marathon, then I have no idea if I will ever be able to have another go. As is printed on the back of Terry's t-shirt: '*The road is long, life is short...hurry.*'

And so it was that I contrived an idea to head to the Lakes...

Disaster at the Lakes

Thursday, 10th January 2008

I would venture that few people become excited at Wigan North Western Station. I must have been one of the few. It was only at this point (geographically speaking) that the stresses and strains of the past few weeks subsided sufficiently to allow me to truly grasp the particulars of my current situation.

Here I found myself, on a swanky Virgin Pendolino train heading to Penrith, from where I would commence my five-day stroll around the Lakes. It was upon hearing a news report the previous week, which warned climbers in the area of the risk of avalanches at Helvellyn, that I made the decision to come up and take a look. I was quite shocked that there was that much snow reported. I had dreamed of seeing British mountains covered in snow for some time. I have also had this particular expedition, or something close to it, in my mind since I was a teenager. The goal was quite simply to climb the three highest peaks in England: Skafell Pike, Helvellyn and Skiddaw, during a single trip of a few days (I only realised whilst at the Lakes that this order has now changed, and Skafell is independently classified as the second-highest peak, behind Skafell Pike, with Helvellyn and Skiddaw dropping a place accordingly).

73

The Jungle Marathon

I have not bagged a British mountain since Ben Nevis the day after my twenty-ninth birthday, the previous August, and the Munroes were anything but beautifully adorned with fresh snow. As a matter of fact, the Munroes were barely visible because of the effects of our typical British summer; they all wore grey skirts of dense, damp, miserable cloud.

Somewhere between Wigan and Penrith I found myself considering the fact that my original route had been planned for summer time and during daylight hours. Tomorrow I would have to summit Helvellyn in only a few hours before making camp, *en-route* to Skafell Pike. Still worse is that Helvellyn, as I have been reliably informed, is a full day's walk. Having looked at the map, I could see that I would be approaching Helvellyn from the East; a fairly steep climb with a few cliff faces along the way. If it really did turn out to be snow-covered, then I had no crampons and ice-axes with which to make a confident assault. I would have to review once in a better position to judge. The plan was thus liable to change at short notice.

Then I considered the time issue, seeing as I had originally planned for less than half a day to complete Helvellyn and make camp several miles away. It was then that a wry smile went across my face. I was not planning on a simple walk. I was planning to move *at pace*. Safely, yes, and with kit so heavy that my feet sank into the concrete as soon as I tried it on; but I definitely would not be aiming for a leisurely stroll around the park. Not this trip. No chance.

Following the train's late arrival, I headed out of the station, took a right turn onto the main road, and started heading out of

Disaster at the Lakes

Penrith. The rucksack did not feel too heavy and the weather was pleasant; a spectacularly clear and calm starlit night sky.

When I reached the main road there were no longer streetlights, so I was strolling along the hard shoulder in the dark, and jumping onto the grass verge on the very few occasions that a vehicle came along. I had passed a turn-off ten yards earlier, and anticipated no more excitement for while to come. It was at this exact time that my back-up Stormlite key-ring torch became my primary torch. The reason being that the torch I had meant to bring was safe and sound with all my outdoor kit that had been considered superfluous and duly left behind. Bugger. I left the road and took the next one towards Ullswater. The road was single-lane and surrounded by fields and the occasional bit of woodland or stretch of river. At times the breeze would go from gentle to slightly cheeky, and then back to gentle or even non-existent.

After a total of six miles of walking I reached Ullswater and turned onto a minor road to skirt around it. I treated myself to a quick break and then headed out of Pooley Bridge and towards a campsite. My actual camp for the night was intended to be by some woodland on a hill further around the water. I was going to get there via a caravan and camping site, and hopefully pick up some drinking water along the way.

My relief at finding a drinking water tap at the campsite was met with equal and opposite disappointment when I put my Platypus water bladder under the faucet and no water emerged. Come to think of it, there were no tents or caravans either. Brilliant. I headed up and out of the 'campsite', negotiating a barbed-wire fence as I did so, and made my way uphill and around the woodland until I found a flat enough section on which to erect my tent. One spot of rain, two spots...*oh buggerit*...it had friends. The heavens began to open as I made a start on pitching the tent in the dark. I set up inside the tent and clocked the time once I was inside the sleeping bag: 03:03. Not bad.

Friday, 11th January 2008

08:00

The rain tapped down on the tent's canvas, but it was coming and going. I gave it the benefit of another hour to check and see if a tropical paradise fancied appearing and, when it did not, I rose anyway. I sorted my kit and headed uphill, leaving the field of sheep by the gate at the top. I turned right and stopped dead, awestruck by the snow-capped mountains, far off in the distance; they looked magnificent.

I headed off towards the mountains. Navigation was the way it should be; I knew the route and the path was clearly marked, so I only used the map to confirm position and to get an idea of distances remaining. When I reached the far end of the water, lower areas, including the footpath, were flooded, so I had to extend the route a touch. I reached Glenridding at around 13:30, but by this stage the clouds were rolling in off the mountains and there was no safe means of completing Helvellyn and making progress towards Skafell this evening. I headed up the first part of the track to Helvellyn anyway, and found the best campsite in the world: picturesque, flat as a snooker table, and with a couple of well-placed trees and a good view of the lake. I pitched the tent and then headed back to Glenridding to collect some water and additional food. I had Puri-tabbed approximately half a litre of water earlier in the day and it had tasted nasty, so I treated myself to some of the good stuff. I returned to the tent and cooked some dinner, and was in my sleeping bag ready to sleep shortly after dusk at 17:00.

Saturday, 12th January 2008

I awoke to the gentle patter of rain upon the canvas, and gradually started going through the process of getting up. I cooked some pasta on the Trangia and had a hot chocolate and a Pepperami whilst I was waiting, then finished up and packed everything away. The legs of my trousers had been steaming owing to wet fabric meeting warm legs.

I headed up the first few metres to the top of the hill on which I had been camped, so as to get a good look at Helvellyn. I then went back down, around a pond, and was soon on a path with other climbers heading up from another direction. Most people were far better kitted-out than me, with better jackets and simple day-sacks. I rested a few times on the way up for a bit of food and something to drink, but on the whole my progress was faster than that of most others (a good sign considering the weight of kit I was carrying), and I had a chat with a few climbers as we paused to rest at the same place.

A few lads took their hats off to me when they saw the kit and heard my plans for the next few days. It did not seem fair really; I had not made it to the top yet. As a matter of fact, I took my hat off to them for being such young scamps, and it was splendid to see energetic, attractive, youthful males so far from a pub and making good progress in taking themselves still further away. There were no derogatory comments or conversations about women-folk, and each one of the chaps seemed to be a sterling example of what we need in tomorrow's generation: a bit of get up and go, an awareness of a world outside of pubs and games consoles, and friendships based on common goals and mutual ambition, rather than just alcoholism and sex (presumably, although one can never be sure).

I reached the snow base after an hour or so of traipsing, and the general trend was for dropping kit, fuelling up, and then kitting up for the colder weather. I was engulfed by cloud within minutes, and the air temperature was below freezing.

A small lake (Red Tarn) was in front of me, with two crescents rising up and around it to the summit. Striding Edge was the ridge to my left, and was very much the order of the day. The crescent ridge to the right of Red Tarn was Squirrel Edge, and the summit lay in the middle of the two (but was currently obscured by cloud). Most people were attacking the summit via Striding Edge, as this was the more difficult of the two, and would then descend via Squirrel Edge.

I progressed a little further and soon found that everyone was once again on their backsides. A woman asked if I was going to climb in just boots, or if I had crampons too. I confessed that I was planning to take a look, and if it were not suitable then I would head back. Simple as that. She had been up before, and was amongst a party of four. We then watched as several others passed us and went on up without crampons, and decided to crack on and give it a closer look.

Striding Edge is just that; steep slopes descending on either side of a narrow path, which is marked out by rocks, and the fact that there is no other route that does not require climbing gear. It is not the sort of thing you necessarily associate with danger. Granted, one false move and you could slip over the edge and fall to your death, but then one false move when crossing the road and you could also be dead. Step off a tall building and you would probably be dead. In fact, it is quite safe, just so long as one can stick to the path.

It only becomes dangerous if there are high winds and/or some other treacherous weather, or if one is not in suitable kit. With that I took a moment to feel rather bad for a father and his son that had been found dead here a year or so ago. Their exact position had been made clear by a small memorial stone where they had cuddled up together as they died slowly of hypothermia.

A little while later and we were approaching a chimney: a short climb down between some rocks before a steep snow- and ice-covered clamber to the summit. One man passed us heading back from the top, declaring that we would not make it without crampons and ice axes. Another chap told us that the worst was behind us and we would be fine. I commented to the group of four lads behind me that I would go with the opinion and experience of the latter, purely because he had the better beard. This was a comment that met with resounding and heartfelt agreement and approval (I had also seen the aforementioned bearded gentleman traipsing forward and back, to and fro, round and round, for some time now; up to the summit, back, around some rocks, and so on. He was either testing out his crampons or he just did not want to leave the mountain quite yet).

I began to climb the ice field and progress was good, as it invariably would be, until one becomes stuck. I did not have a good, deep foothold and I slipped and slid down the slope, halting myself with my umbrella-cum-ice axe. I ended up on my side, leaning against my kit. I tried to dig my foot in and push myself up, but at this angle I could not kick-in and I slipped again, saved once more by a brollie-arrest. Bugger. I looked down. Chances were that I would slide right off the side to my death. I tried again with my foot but no success. I looked around to see if any climbers were coming up this way; but with their crampons they could go a more direct route. There was a foot indent in the ice, about four inches across and about an inch deep. It was a metre or so away horizontally, and half a metre above the height of my shoulder. That was my only chance.

I raised the brollie and dug it in a few inches higher and clambered a few inches up on my side. The brollie could dig in as far as any ice axe on this surface, which was fortunate because it was all I had. Climbing a few more inches took a few seconds and I felt as if I had burned a thousand calories *'Right then, yer big girls blouse!'* It was the first time I had really felt tired this whole weekend. I tried again, a little higher, but the foothold was still level with my chest and over a metre away. I looked down, to death. I looked up, hoping to see someone. I looked across the slope; out into nothing, as the cloud came in and thickened, and I felt the chill in the air. I would not last here until the spring thaw.

'What to do if you find yourself stuck with no hope of rescue. Consider how lucky you are that life has been good to you so far. Alternatively, if life hasn't been good to you so far, which given your current circumstances seems more likely, consider how lucky you are that it won't be troubling you much longer.'

- Douglas Adams

I looked up. Death or glory it would be. I tried again; a little higher, but again nowhere near and I needed to catch my breath. I looked up and the girl from an earlier group had come back and was standing at the top. She offered to come down and take the rucksack but I refused; it weighed a tonne and she would not be in a better position than me once she had it. At the same time it was the only reason I could not right myself. I knew she could see my position and options better than I could so I asked her to stay where she was for a minute, and I told her I could see a foothold. Right, I told myself, no

81

more pissing about. This was it, death or glory. I pushed hard again, two or three times and stretched my leg out and it reached the foothold. I transferred my weight across and turned towards the slope, swinging my rucksack around behind me.

With that I dug my feet in and started moving up; fast. The girl, seeing that I was fine, disappeared off, and I made my way onto the summit. A collection of others was there, sitting around and fuelling up. I was getting the odd look, mainly disbelief that I made it with all this kit. And that was the whole point; I had brought it because I wanted to take the southwest path off and head over to Skafell, but looking at it, it was quite impossible without crampons, so I would have to carry it with me all the way back down Squirrel Edge to Red Tarn. I could have dumped the lot there in the first place, and then picked it up and started off again from there afterwards. Oh well. I am here now and I have made it through the worst of it.

As an Everest climber who I know was once told, upon radioing base of his success at reaching the summit: 'Well done, but you're only half way'. True enough, but I had been reliably informed the descent down Squirrel Edge would be far easier than what was now behind me. I dumped my kit, and took photos of the lads with their camera, and one of them took one of me with mine. I then went to offer some chocolate to the group that had walked crampon-free, and to thank them for coming back to check on my whereabouts. The girl said she was used to seeing two people behind her, and when it was only one she had to check it out. The other girl agreed and said they could not lose me; they knew I had the hot chocolate in my bag.

Disaster at the Lakes

They set off towards Squirrel Edge and I tidied away my kit and headed off as well. Whilst walking across the snow and ice the cloud moved in and I could no longer see anyone. I realised that I was walking on deep snow, and there were rocks to my left. Was I meandering onto the cornice that lay to the right of the summit? Could this whole lot fall away at some point? I wandered back onto the rocks and found a short ice field down the side. The other group were just ahead of me and called back to say that it flattened out later on. Good news, but I would refrain from setting off the fireworks for the time being. I scrambled down the ice and was happy for the additional security of the rocks. Extra purchase was very much welcome.

Progress was slow and steady. I was choosing routes close to the more jagged rocks, ensuring that I could keep hold if I was to lose my footing. Where that was not an option I would push the umbrella in and place my foot above it. On occasion I had allowed myself to slide a short distance down to a clearly impressed footprint lower down. I worked my way to the path that led off the ridge, and began the descent proper (always checking Red Tarn to see it growing closer).

The shout went up from the end of Striding Edge closest to the summit. We turned and the chap in front of me pointed to the slope beneath the summit. The man must have fallen from the summit itself; his arms and legs flailing out away from his body as he connected with the rocks and began to roll down the slope. There was no movement from his body that was not initiated by momentum and the rocks. Either he was already unconscious or very good at being limp. My hand was reaching into my pocket for my mobile, but the girl in front of me already had hers and was confirming she should call 999. "*112!*" I corrected, and answered her next question with "It isn't routed through your service provider like 999; 112 will take whatever it can get". This is an important point in such a situation, as 112 is theoretically less likely to lose signal, and more likely to obtain a signal in the first instance.

She called out her options as the chap ahead of her and I called out "Mountain Rescue" in unison. We confirmed the casualty's location and what had happened, and after that she asked for a grid reference. I had the map in my hand and passed it to a woman walking up requesting it. If she could read it quicker than me, then my map was hers. She was probably more familiar with the area anyway and it was the right thing to do. The call was lost before she could read it though. I took the map and made my way down past the others. I had to get to him; I had a good medical kit that I could use; plus a shelter, and a sleeping bag; everything.

In my real life (at the time) as an operations/health and safety manager, my staff and I had more lifeguard and first aid training than anyone else I knew. Whether or not I could use any of it I would not know until I got there, but the basics of first aid would be a start at the very least, until help arrived: Prevent the condition from worsening and preserve life. Adrenaline kicked in and I flew down the path to Red Tarn. I was still minding my way, and accepting a less than direct route to the casualty, as now was not the time to turn one casualty into two.

A burst of pain shot up from my ankle as I went over a rock; I must have put it through its paces a bit somewhere along the climb, but the pain seemed to get me fired up even more; *a poorly ankle?* Hah! As if that would slow me down. I reached the far end of Red Tarn and asked various people to confirm where he had landed. None of them had even seen him fall! He had fallen right in front of them! I continued around the lake.

Time itself had slowed down and I did not seem capable of moving fast enough. I wanted to dump my kit, but it had everything in it that he might need. Adrenaline was taking me to him now, but I knew twenty minutes had passed since his fall and the helicopter would probably get there first. But I had to try. I might be useful, in some way, somehow.

At times my feet would fall through the snow and I would lose my leg into it up to my thigh. *Still with kit, but pressing on.* There was a group there now. I had seen a few climbers near the casualty where he stopped falling and more had come down since then. They were using a more direct approach and so were presumably in crampons. Who were they? Could it be mountain rescue already? Did they need anything I was carrying? If not mountain rescue, was anybody there medically trained? If not, then the lessons of my instructor, Ben, would be put to the test. There was no fear or apprehension. I just wanted to reach the casualty and help in any way that I could.

The Jungle Marathon

As I approached the casualty I could see him covered with a sleeping bag, except for the head, and a group of men with insignia on their jackets were there, working a radio. Mountain rescue were here; they must have already been on the mountain. *"Commence C.P.R!"* I made my way around the men at a respectful distance; I could not get in the way. I spoke with the rescue leader and he confirmed that they had been descending not far from me, but had better kit and had reached him first. A doctor was amongst them and they were frantically working between the radio, and a mobile phone belonging to one of the small group of climbers that were already on this part of the mountain. They were trying to confirm the time for the helicopter evacuation, and additional members of mountain rescue were reaching the scene all the time.

I kept with the four people that had been climbing on this section of slope, and dropped my kit down. The casualty was breathing deeply, and a steady, bradycardic pulse (~forty-five b.p.m.) had returned, but with his blood lining the route of his descent, he needed a transfusion. The casualty stopped breathing again and cardio-pulmonary resuscitation (C.P.R.) was resumed.

I had cleared my kit for the helicopter approach, and headed back to the doctor. He had a good team with him, and all that I could see was professionalism. C.P.R. is apparently deeply tiring after only a few minutes, so I let the doctor know he could ask me if he needed someone else to step in and take over, but he had plenty of help already. I would not have asked an 'unknown' to join in either if it was not necessary.

Disaster at the Lakes

Instead, I took their kit and stashed everything loose away. The helicopter would be here within minutes. We were instructed to lay on top of our rucksacks and warned that the down-pressure of the helicopter's blades would be fearsome. My kit was fifty yards away and secured behind a large rock, and so I got into position on the half-a-dozen rucksacks belonging to mountain rescue.

In it came; a yellow RAF rescue Sea King. A couple of flares were used to direct it in, and the paramedic was winched down with his kit. He rushed over and attached the defibrillator. As the Sea King approached it was forcing ice into my face and the pressure was clawing at my skin. I was fixed looking at the blades, which was easy enough because they were at eye level and within ten metres of me. I wanted to look so I could see if I should try to get out of the way – *no chance* – and the ice was stinging me so hard I had to bury my head into the slope to protect my eyes.

Some talk ensued between the doctor and the paramedic, as the helicopter moved off. Work ceased. Time of death was called. A defibrillator works by correcting an out-of-rhythm (fibrillating) heart. It cannot do anything if there is no rhythm at all. In that case, the casualty is dead.

I helped mountain rescue with their kit, and the leader instructed us to sit tight as the stretcher and bag were lowered when the helicopter came in for a second time. We did so. A climber then came over to inform mountain rescue that he and his team had just brought the casualty's wife down from near the summit. The two had been separated at the top and he had gone to look over the edge; over the cornice. A police officer was amongst the group of climbers that were first to the casualty, so I gathered that he was to speak with her. How horrid. How wretched. Here she was halfway up a mountain and about to have it confirmed that her husband had just been lost to her. How could she be comforted? 'It was quick?' 'He did not suffer for long?' If I am correct about mountain rescue finding a pulse then 'he fought hard?' 'Fell into good hands?' Ultimately, there was no time for goodbyes, and he was gone in an instant. What a walk for her off this place. What a sickeningly ghastly walk.

I collected my kit and headed back around the lake, stopping to take on some food and drink and sort my kit out. I tried to look at the map but my mind was running in circles. I could not safely reach Skafell from here and I had lost all taste for such a climb to follow this one. I wanted to distance myself from the incident and gather my thoughts before continuing on. A night in a proper room and some proper food was in order. I would head back to Glenridding, which was my only other option from this side of Helvellyn.

As I left I saw some other people heading off to the left of my original route, so I started heading off that way. It was too cold and I still could not focus on the map, but I was already considering a route around the mountain towards Skafell. As I descended down the path it became apparent that night would fall long before I could find a safe route around. Skafell was now off the cards, and it was for the best. I could take a look at Skiddaw still, and come back to Skafell another time.

A view from the
plane of the
Amazon River

The author
enjoying life on
the boat

The huts at
Itapuama

Above left: Following the Bombeiro through the jungle
Above right: Not wanting to get my boots wet on a river crossing

Below: The cheeky spider that ran over Al's foot

Above: Helvellyn in the Lake District: The approach along the start of Striding Edge, the remainder and summit hidden in cloud

Below: The summit, still partially obscured by cloud, overlooking Red Tarn

Above: Kinder weather greeted us in Snowdonia

Below left: Views just beneath the summit of Mt. Snowdon
Below right: John, shortly before we reached the summit

Disaster at the Lakes

Having refused a couple of lifts (offered due to the sight of the rucksack I was carrying), I reached Glenridding after nightfall (shortly after 16:00) and found myself a room at the Best Western. I called in my route changes to my emergency contact, John, and settled down for one massive pizza and a couple of particularly pleasant ales. I did feel markedly depressed about the day, but not in the sense that I was distraught and my mind preoccupied with dark visions. I was appreciably miserable and struck with the gravity of what had happened. My thoughts kept returning to the woman and the husband she lost over the edge of Helvellyn.

The mountain rescue leader had checked that we were all right and warm enough before we left the mountain, and it made sense since this sort of incident could traumatise people. I just focussed on what I could learn from this and what I would be doing in the immediate future. Whether or not I might suffer psychologically I had no way of knowing, although I doubted it, but it was nevertheless a new and horridly saddening experience. I could only plan to take it easy on myself now and play it by ear.

Sunday, 13th January 2008

I checked out of the hotel just after 11:00 and a fair English breakfast. The hotel staff had informed me that a bus could take me to Penrith, from where I could get another bus to Keswick, from where I could prepare for my charge up Skiddaw tomorrow. No buses today; the staff had been so helpful but had not mentioned that. Having informed me that there were no direct buses to Keswick, I think that they just wanted to say 'yes' to everything else. Oh well. I left my kit and went for a wander. My options were to take a taxi, or to postpone everything for another day. It was pouring down. I found a B&B for half the price of the hotel, with a bed twice as big, and so shifted my kit over to the Beech House.

I went back to the only outdoors shop in the village to check out the prices of crampons and ice axes. Skiddaw is only about twenty metres shorter than Helvellyn, and according to the map it is a steeper and rockier ascent. Without crampons it probably would not be worth considering.

They did not fit. None of them would fit. My boots were just too big. What now? Buy new boots to try to get some tight enough for crampons? But my first priority was walking, so I needed comfortable walking boots, not climbing boots. So no winter climbs above the snow level? Urgh! I was not going to take another risk like Helvellyn. Lesson learned. Do-able it might be, but safe it was not. I would have to hope for a better selection of crampons at Keswick, or else I would have to choose another less interesting challenge for the day.

Skafell could be for my friend John and I to do together, but if I cannot get crampons then I will only be able to climb smaller mountains/hills or only climb out of winter conditions. At least I still had my health; I would always find ways of pushing myself, and I hoped that I could still get stuck into some good climbs.

For now, the plan is still to head over to Keswick tomorrow; set up camp around the base of Skiddaw, and then to investigate outdoor shops. If there is no joy, then I will take Skiddaw as far as I can, and then postpone a climb to the very top, if necessary, until another visit when the snow has cleared. I would spend the rest of today wandering around in the rain and absorbing the events of the weekend so far. Ullswater, whether in sunshine or rain, is breathtakingly beautiful, and I am glad I came here.

Monday, 14th January 2008

Torrential rain was still beating down outside. According to the forecast we would have rain in the morning but showers in the afternoon. I gathered that was suggestive of rain all day.

I sorted my kit and checked out of the Beech House. I was the only person on the bus from Glenridding to Penrith; I was very much here out of season. From Penrith I caught another bus to Keswick. I got off the bus and strolled through the high street. The density of outdoor shops was astonishing.

I worked my way through the town and headed north, onto the road towards Carlisle. I took a footpath right towards Millbeck and wished I had stayed on the main road until the primary route to the village later on. I found myself spending more time picking my way around water-logged ground and pulling my feet out of the mud. From Millbeck I made my way onto one of the main footpaths up towards Skiddaw. After a few minutes I met a couple of walkers coming down from the mountain, but they had not reached the top as it was cloud-covered and they had not wanted to negotiate the rocky path after nightfall. We chatted for a while and then we headed off in our respective directions. At the top of some woodland, at the base of the main route up the mountain, two streams converged.

Using some sort of intuition, I took a left turn up to the brow of a small hill adjacent to the stream. I found some relatively flat ground and decided to set up home for the night. I could see that I would have to use the rucksack to help stop myself rolling down the hill, but it was that or camping in the middle of the stream. The rain was still coming down too. The forecast suggested that it would clear up by the morning, so that would be it; my one chance of success before having to catch a bus back to Penrith and my train into London that evening. I was in my sleeping bag by 17:30. I sent out a sit-rep (situation report) and location to John, and then cooked up a couple of dinners on the Trangia.

Tuesday, 15th January 2008

The gentle pitter-patter of rain came to an end and I ensured that all of my kit was tidied away in my rucksack, save for the tent itself and a small day-sack (containing some food, water and emergency kit, stuffed into my tent bag and supported over my shoulder with a security strap). I greeted the world by relieving myself (I am a man, and the world is my toilet) and then proceeded up the track.

The path was easy to follow for the first few hundred metres, but then became lost amongst the streams and scree. I paused once for about five minutes, in order to take on some chocolate and water, and then continued on, into the clouds. The valley had disappeared from beneath me as cloud cover moved in and consumed it. Above me, around me, everywhere; nothing up, down or around but white clouds. It was not cold though, and it was not raining, so I was satisfied enough with that.

I headed up until I reached a path running left to right from Carl Side onto the summit of Skiddaw. It was on a small plateau, and straight ahead would be descent. By comparison to the narrow path I have been on up until now, this new path was wide enough to land an Airbus on. I took the option right and the route became markedly steeper. I paused to catch my breath every now and then, often using the opportunity to consult the map. Only a few hundred metres of elevation remained, and then I would be on the summit ridge. Perhaps a thousand or so paces.

There were some snow patches along the way, but there was no sign of an ice field or any great snow covering whatsoever. I met a path off to the right, which I had been expecting to come across. I continued along to the left, amidst piles of scree that had been built up into cairns. Just a couple of hundred metres more and I came across the trig point and a small Silver Jubilee commemorative stone. The whole area was empty, devoid of any other life but me. This was far easier than Helvellyn. I took a few photographs and had some food, but with nothing else to delay me further I commenced my descent.

I headed down with some speed this time. The ascent had been at a fair walking pace, but I included some good running on the descent, during which I had caught sight of a ridge emerging out of the bleak white abyss in front of me. The cloud lifted to my right and I clearly saw down into the valley to that side and to a ridge in the distance ahead. The view was breathtaking; almost scary to see how steep the mountainside was, as I had been able to see none of this on the way up; nothing but white cloud.

I took a few more photographs and then continued my half-walk, half-run down to the plateau by Carl Side (diving back into the clouds). Once there I picked up the pace; this time a combination of running and scree-surfing, sliding downhill on the flat stones that marked the way. I considered that this was far too enjoyable to qualify as 'mental training'. When the path evened out I broke back into a more civilised pace and eventually reached the small hill where my tent was waiting for me. I checked the time: 11:40. I had some food and enjoyed seeing the clearer skies, and then packed everything away, tent and all, and walked down through Millbeck to the bus stop.

A walk around Penrith was put off due to the station's reluctance to accept left luggage because of the 'continuing terrorist threat'. As a consequence I had no option but to accept the terrorist threat by whichever faction of whichever cell it is that objects so strongly to the rural northwest, and set myself up in a pub to await the train back to London.

Reflecting upon this trip was quite awkward for me. I had truly enjoyed and relished the challenges of walking with the heavy kit; persevering through bad weather when I could, and sitting it out when I could not. I created contingency after contingency to manage myself safely and effectively in the light of events and weather conditions as required. But this long weekend will always be marred by the memory of what I had witnessed when I was coming down from Helvellyn. I left the Lake District with a heavy heart and a new sense of the fragility of human life, along with the dangers inherent in climbing during the winter months.

Shenanigans in Snowdonia

Well, shenanigans is a word not used often enough in my considered opinion, yet I recall few occasions spent with John when any other word could possibly be more appropriate. I had met John in Ouarzazate just prior to our attempt at the *Marathon des Sables*. We struck up conversation on our first evening at the Berbere Palace hotel, and decided that what we both fancied doing, once we had finished enjoying our supper, was to explore the delights of this north-African town. Well, John had been intent on exploring, whereas I had been intent on seeking out a patisserie to purchase a box of traditional desserts. We were both sufficiently pleased with our outing.

John and I had shared a bivouac during the race, along with Carl, Richard, Mark and Selwyn. John had the onerous and entirely unpleasant and unrewarding task of tending to my medical needs in the regions I was unable to tend to myself. Favours were returned accordingly but I am sure I had the lion's share of attentions. We also had the distinct pleasure of sharing our love of Monty Python, a pleasure that resulted in frequent renditions of various sketches, songs and phrases. On the last day, for example, I had been on my last legs and John was generous enough to keep me company across most of the sand dunes until we both reached the finish line. We had crossed the final sand dune singing, as I recall and much to the amusement of some cunningly placed photographers, *Always look on the bright side of life*.

Back home in England, most of us from *Tente 99* cemented our friendships by maintaining contact. I could wile away hours on the telephone with Carl, reminiscing about those good old days in the desert, and similarly with Richard, although regrettably never for as long or so frequently. Carlos, however, was a firm friend with Richard, and conversing with one permitted an intimate insight into the news of the other. Similarly, John stayed in close contact with Selwyn, so I received news of Selwyn's return to normality whenever I spoke with John. Selwyn, it seemed, had become a little depressed since completion of the race, and I could imagine why. He and I had chatted one evening about how the *Marathon des Sables* had been his one big focus for so long, and being more senior than the rest of us, his relationships and responsibilities with his family were all the better grounded. Hence, for him to have reached this one great goal, he had found himself without direction, or so it seemed, and was taking the return to his old life a touch harder than the rest of us.

Carl had exams coming up, Richard was off to Afghanistan, John was off to Russia and then to Dubai, and I had been focussed on the jungle. Selwyn, who I have always held in the highest esteem, seemed to have made the MdS the zenith of his ambitions, and now could only see a depressing route back to normality. It is probably the same for all athletes. It was our fear of such depressions that had many of us planning our next event before we had even left Morocco. For goodness sake, John and I had been singing *The lion sleeps tonight* and the theme tune to *George of the jungle* whilst queuing up to check-in at Ouarzazate airport.

Mark, our last boy scout and a dispenser of more vital kit than Field and Trek, had disappeared off the radar, somewhat. We knew that he had gone back to Italy, but communications were difficult and little passed around the group as to where he was and how he was doing. For the rest of us though, it was a splendid demonstration of the bonds that can be forged in the fires of battle, even if that battle happened to be no more than the achievement of an arduous and very personal goal. We were united as comrades with our personal ambitions, and have remained as friends ever since.

Unfortunately, perhaps, we were retelling stories many times over from every possible angle, which really should have been laid to rest the first time through. I could only imagine that should we all ever meet up at a dinner party or such like, that other people would find us very tedious and trying company very quickly indeed. But then, I still do not get invited to those sorts of parties.

And so it was that I was not only delighted to find that John would be joining me in the jungle, but further that he was returning to the U.K. from Dubai and would be interested in spending a couple of days in Snowdonia with me, hiking and so on whilst heaving heavy rucksacks and enjoying gay banter of splendid days gone by. I am usually a loner when it comes to these sorts of exploits, but that has most often been because I decide to do such things at the last minute. Alternatively, everyone I ask who I think would love to have the opportunity to join me tells me to sod off, often making outrageous claims such as they would rather chew their own legs off. Well, I mean, there was never any need to be spiteful.

Of course, there is always the possibility that I prefer to be on my own anyway. I enjoy the quiet contemplation, the peace, the being far away from everyone and pretending that all the countryside and nature that surrounds me is there just for me and for me alone. I enjoy not having anyone else to rely upon, thereby having to depend upon myself entirely. I enjoy, in some perverse way no doubt, the apprehension and anxiety that comes from having no-one there to ask for a second opinion. I like having no-one to help me if I am in trouble; to save me from a deathly drop into some gully far below, or to run and get help when I am savaged by genetically modified sheep (films never to watch before a weekend alone in the hills: *Black Sheep*, *Dog Soldiers*, and *American Werewolf in London*). Well, as a matter of fact, I do tend to watch all such films before spending long periods in the wilderness. In some bizarre way I enjoy allowing my mind to wander, becoming occupied with associated dreams and fantasies. It helps me to draw from the landscape and weave stories from it; the more stimulating the better.

So, now I have been presented with the opportunity of spending a weekend not only punishing myself, but to drag a very dear new friend into Purgatory with me. How splendid indeed. Naturally I was tentative and somewhat apprehensive about the whole idea. What if John turns out to be a complete arse and I regret every moment of it, simply wishing him away so I can be back by myself? I mean, I rather enjoy having just myself to talk with; such times constitute those rare occasions when I receive sensible answers. On the whole though, I concluded that no everlasting harm could come of it, and it would do me good to see whether or not I had become a social reject in the art of hiking with *other* people.

Saturday, 16th February 2008

Having travelled up to Chester the previous afternoon, I was now sitting comfortably in John's Corsa, *en route* to Snowdonia for the first training weekend that I have ever undertaken with someone else. The scant disregard for vowels in the place names clearly identified that we were approaching Wales.

The plan was to take full kit up to the summit of Snowdon, and then do some other tough walks and climbs in the area, for the two days before John had to get back to work. John had been sat at that breakfast table in Ouarzazate when we had made the decision to enter this year's Jungle Marathon.

We parked up at Pen-y-Pass, and sorted our kit, making arrangements with the car park attendants for a two-day stay (we did not want mountain rescue out looking for us when the ticket expired). We put on our rucksacks, took the northernmost path out of the car park and began the steady climb.

This was beautiful. This was utterly magnificent. With the possible exception of a previous training weekend in the New Forest, this was the best weather that I had ever experienced when training.

There was not a cloud in the sky and it was shaping up to be rather warm. We made our way past a few other walkers and I pointed out a rocky outcrop to John as a potential resting place. It was agreed. With full kit we seemed to stun the people around us as we broke into a fair-paced run.

We were surrounded by the grassy banks of the mountainside, with the blue calm waters of the shimmering lakes down to our left. How could we just stay to a comfortable pace and enjoy ourselves? This was *training*! We dodged the loose rocks along the way and avoided the frozen puddles and black ice that coated the path, and began to climb up the track. When it became too steep for a respectable run, we eased to a strong walk, and moved across to our resting area.

We stripped off our outer layers, drank some water, and took a few photos of the surroundings. Such antics were sufficient for plenty of the people that we had passed to get ahead of us again on the path. We kitted up and this time John took the lead, running of course. It did not even need to be said. We could, so we did. We received more bemused looks as we ran, strode and leapt up and along the track; 'It's because we're very *special* boys', I was telling myself ('special' being one of the most ridiculous and meaningless words in our language). It was a moment afterwards that one of those special boys, John, announced a massive cramp was inconveniencing his left calf. He sat down on a rock and between us we managed to work the calf loose and then continued on our way. I put it down to the stress of running up steps with the kit, and just hoped that he could keep it at bay for the remainder of the ascent.

We took a brief pause as the path became its steepest just beneath the ridge, and then we headed up. Some strong walking and the occasional burst of running saw us to the top in a couple of very comfortable hours. We enjoyed some food on the grass beneath the summit, overlooking Snowdonia westwards. Her lakes, peaks, rolling hills and mountains all looked spectacular and were breathtaking to behold as they shrugged off their shroud of morning mist in the warming sun. We then headed back down, swiftly of course. There is a second route from the main path back to the car park, which follows along next to the lakes. We were expecting a steep descent and then a flat route for most of the remaining distance, so then we could fit in some more running. The only issue was that we could not see the path down. We could see it by the lake, but we could not see how to reach it. "Let's freestyle it" was John's oh so splendid suggestion. "Sterling idea" should definitely not have been my reply.

We headed down onto some rocks and began working our way down the slope. The path most certainly did not come this way, but we were committed and it was safe enough (just). We worked our way down a hundred metres or so of scree, and after a short pause for water we headed off at a run back towards the car. Once again the cramps were back, this time affecting John's thighs. This could not just be the physical stress on the muscles. "Perhaps it's salt?" I suggested. We had been taking on water, as well as some food, but maybe there was a sodium deficiency that was affecting how his muscles were working.

We walked the rest of the way back to the car park and headed into the café. I had been struck by clarity on the way and had decided that a nice cup of tea and a bacon roll would fix everything. The £3.50 for a couple of rashers of bacon in a sandwich was steeper than the ascent of Snowdon. We decided that we would eat into their profits by being a little overzealous with the salt, and John concurred that it did indeed taste fine, a good indication that he was short of the stuff. I was too, for that matter, and we both prepared our salt stocks for later on and had plenty to drink.

We refilled our water bottles and headed off across the road away from Snowdon. A path from there took us up towards our second climb of the day. Two days in Snowdonia? We were not likely to just quit after the first climb. However, daylight hours were still short and we had quite a way to go. The plan was to take the path north to Glyder Fawr, at 999 metres, before working around a small lake (Llyn Cwn) due northwest, and then descending down through the Devil's Kitchen. We would then pitch the tent somewhere between the next lake (Llyn Idwal) and the next mountain (Pen yr Ole Wen).

I had assured John that the route would be fine because it was mostly flat, although I was mainly referring to the main path from Pen yr Ole Wen to Carnedd Dafydd and Carnedd Llewelyn, ranging from 978 metres, to 1044 metres and 1064 metres, respectively. As it should be a return journey, that would be an awful lot of flat ridge

103

walking. It was certainly flat by comparison to what we would have to do first, but I was working on averages. We would have several steep ascents and descents before we reached Pen yr Ole Wen, and we would not arrive at the base of that sheer climb today. After three-quarters of an hour though, John did indeed concede that it was 'mostly flat'. "If you lean back far enough," he volunteered, "it's almost like walking downhill!" I missed my own company so very, desperately much.

The first height on the map was 646 metres, and the climb from there to the other side of Glyder Fawr was not too bad at all, save for some work around a few rocky areas. John led the way down to the first lake, 'freestyling' of course, as we could not see any path to assist us otherwise. It took a few minutes to establish that we could most certainly not 'freestyle' down through the Devil's Kitchen, although it would have been an awesome abseil, and we spent the next few minutes trying to find the correct route down.

One thing that I distinctly recall was John mentioning dinner, and that he was really looking forward to his chicken curry. He was gone. I have never seen a human being, laden with full kit, move at such a pace down such an icy path. He was a man possessed, as it were, with visions of curry. I have never seen it so acute, and I called out to him to give me a moment to catch up and all that I received in response was a: "Teatime, Fatty!" Outrageous! Still, at least the salt and better administration seemed to have taken care of the muscle cramps.

I made my way back into the lead after John took a route that I had no intentions of taking, and off we went. We were going at a strong pace, and we were racing the sunset. Dusk was very much upon us. John led the way across a nightmarish stream crossing. The stream descended into a narrow pass between the flat where we were, and a rock face on the other side. The distance was nothing, but the flat wall, narrow footholds, and icy stones were cause for concern. John made use of a foothold less than an inch wide to swing his other foot into a solid hold, before moving away and waiting for me. We had just accomplished it when I heard people.

John was tearing off again, and by this time our torches had come out, but at least we had reached the second lake and could set up camp on the other side. There were definitely voices. I scanned up to my right and made out a couple of figures on the side of the rocks, halfway up the face. There was a diagonal crack the length of the face that they were positioned on, but it was covered in snow and ice and they apparently had no climbing kit or torches.

I carried on moving and shouted out to John. He was gone now though. I could see his body moving along the path, but in his mind he had already opened up the sealed pack and poured in the hot water for tonight's gastronomic feast. I looked up again; what were they doing? This was a stupid time to start climbing, and they were not calling out for us to help them. I was getting flashbacks to the previous training session in the Lake District, and fearing something dreadful.

We made it to the other end of the lake and pitched the tent. It was dark now and cold. Ice was already forming on the inside of the canvas. We sorted out our kit and got our stoves on the go for dinner. During the day I had been living off South African Biltong, Droewors, and some chocolate. Now at least I could make up my chicken curry as well. Utterly splendid.

Mountain rescue came over to us within the hour to inform us that a few people were stuck up in the Kitchen and there would be quite a bit of activity during the night as they worked to get them down. It would seem that the Devil's Kitchen is one of the few places in Snowdonia that people can receive half decent mobile coverage. The lucky bastards!

Sunday, 17th February 2008

The problem with burying oneself in a thick mummy-style sleeping bag is that one can never tell when morning has broken. You just sort of stay tucked up and hope that it has not. I peered out and enquired as to whether or not John was dead yet. He was in his MdS sleeping bag and it had been well below freezing during the night. He made a quick inspection and asserted that he was, indeed, not dead. It was 07:30, and he had managed less than an hour's sleep since 3 am, primarily due to the cold. I tried to be sympathetic, as I lay there nice and cosy in my Snugpak Antarctica 2C sleeping bag. The model has been tested down to -35°C, and is not particularly comfortable above

–5°C, and I love it. I have four usable sleeping bags nowadays, and despite having owned this one since I was fifteen, it has been well looked after and has kept me alive in some horrendous conditions in the past.

John assured me that in about half an hour the sun would penetrate into the valley and the temperature inside the tent would soar. I naturally had no reason not to believe him and agreed that we should rest until nearer the time. Such a time obviously showed no sign of being realised, so I dressed and we both had breakfast on the go whilst packing away our kit. Water was a problem, or two problems to be more precise. The first was that there was not enough to get us much further than breakfast. The second was that most of what we had was frozen. At least we had kept our boots inside the main section of the tent, and not left them with the water bottles in the porch. It must have been incredibly cold last night.

We sorted out our kit, amid walkers and climbers passing between the lake and us, and we were all exchanging pleasantries. I was busy eating more food, whilst John was busy examining the differences between two bottles of his urine; one collected during the night and another during the morning. Satisfied with finding the secret of eternal life in his samples, he released the fluids into the wild and set about packing away the tent. We then strapped on our rucksacks and headed off down to the road, hoping for a shop where we could stock up.

We were in luck, and promptly relieved the kiosk of their entire bottled water supply, and a few flapjacks, before heading off across the road to the first of the day's climbs. We could have managed without the expense of bottled water and just used Puri-tabs on stream or river water, but it tastes horrible and that in itself reduces consumption and promotes dehydration. Even for a day, if one becomes even a little bit sick then progress is slowed and efficiency falls. If you want to do well, then you make sure that you have what you need to stay in good health.

We just beat a trio of other walkers to the base of Pen yr Ole Wen, our 978 metre first climb. We took the path up to what looked like a solid wall of rock, and started scratching our heads. The path must have carried on further up, but there was nothing to really indicate that the path was actually there. I checked with the trio, and they confessed that they were simply following us. Oh dear; we must have been looking confident again.

Well, John was up onto the rock and I was ready behind him. I selected a left foothold, placed my hands high up on the rock, and stretched my right foot up and around. With everything in place I pushed up through both legs as I reached my hands up higher, and promptly heard a tear from the gusset region. Oh dear, oh dear. It definitely was not organic, so it must indeed have been clothing. It sounded exactly like Velcro, although I could not think where any was that could have been affected. I climbed up onto the top of the rock and inspected my trousers. Genius. There was a gaping split from the base of the zip to the seam further round. That should have put the trio off.

In fact, after about half an hour of climbing, the trio had clearly given up and sought adventure elsewhere. To me the path was perfect; a great combination of easy stonework and occasional scrambling. It had just been those first hundred metres or so of near-vertical ascent that had tested us a bit. John and I stopped to take on fluids and refuel, and then carried on up. The path diverged and we made the decision to climb further using the smaller scree and bracken to the right, as opposed to the larger scree and rock face to the left. It fast became a nightmare. The gradient was steep, the rocks were loose, and the bracken was tearing at my hands as I used it as a lifeline. It took another forty-five minutes to scramble our way up the most dangerous surface that we had encountered so far. I enjoy a climb, but this was bordering on treacherous, and one slip would have really inconvenienced the other person. Once above all that, the rest of the route to the summit was littered with huge rocks, which were far safer and easier to negotiate.

We sat down on the summit and took on some more water and food. The view out across the Welsh highlands was breathtaking. The views from here were even better than from the summit of Snowdon, and I would recommend walking around this area to anyone. It was absolutely stunning, and considering the weather that I usually have to put up with, it was a real treat and a pleasure. We could see the ridge leading around to Carnedd Dafydd and Llewelyn further round. It was only a little rocky and the gradient was wonderfully gentle. We set off, almost running, and made it to Dafydd in a matter of minutes.

We had the briefest of rests and then made off for the highest climb of the day: Llewelyn at 1064 metres. The ridge became more interesting, and as this was our second day of beautiful blue skies and barely the hint of a breeze, we were in no danger of being blown down the side. An easy but swift pace took us down to the base of Llewelyn. Despite a difference in elevation of only twenty metres between the two peaks, the subtle descent along the ridge meant that the climb to the top would be over a hundred metres, and it was steep.

One of the good things about the two of us doing this together was that we could manage speed. When one person was taking it easy, the other would tend to take the lead and press ahead, pushing the pace. It was good because it made us effective. We were completing distances in less time than we would have managed individually. I had led the way up this climb, but John and I very much reached the summit together. I sat down and gorged myself on biltong, whilst we worked out a route back to the car.

We essentially had two options. Getting off the mountain any way but along the route we ascended on was a no-brainer. That initial climb was not something that we would want to repeat, and certainly not in reverse with our bulky rucksacks. We could 'freestyle' a route down to the A5, and from there it would depend upon the time. If we had enough daylight left, then we could just cross the road and head up to the top of the ridge on the other side, between Glyder Fach and Y Foel Goch. Then we could head down the other side and meet up with the A4086, to take us back towards Pen-y-Pass and the car.

110

We headed off and worked our way back towards Dafydd. Before reaching it we bore left and made our way off the mountainside, descending via Lake Ffynnon Lloer, and then aiming for the farm and the road beyond it. The first part of the descent was through deceptively boggy ground. Everywhere we stepped materialised into a stream beneath us, something we could not have seen from higher up. We made a few good guesses as to the direction in which the water ran, and found our way to firmer ground. Soon we were beneath the level of the lake and on far more co-operative terrain, as we headed on towards the road.

We passed a couple of ladies on the way. We had seen them climbing up behind us on our initial climb that day, but they had since disappeared, only to be seen again now, not far from that first peak. The one that had been leading was now bringing up the rear, and her friend was in the process of committing the cardinal sin of all walking partners. She was clearly moving faster than the other one, and so had sat down to wait, whereupon she then stood up and moved off before her friend had properly caught up with her.

As a walker it must be the most demoralising thing in the world, when you are tired and struggling, to have a friend with you who is marching off ahead, and when they rest you think that you will get a rest too once you reach them, but alas they barely even look at you and just get up and carry on. It really is awful teamwork, and very inefficient. When something gives one a knock like that, then confidence, self-perception and motivation all take a nosedive. The individual often reverts to behaving like a child; starting to deliberately drag heels whilst staring at the ground.

By the time we passed them John was in the lead and had broken into a run as soon as the ground evened out enough. It was great. We were hot, we were carrying kit, and we had just completed three fairly respectable climbs today, and we still had enough energy left over to run for the road. We headed across the A5, and as soon as we were at the start of the next footpath, John was rummaging inside his trousers with the Vaseline. Nice.

It was after 17:00, and the sun would be setting just after 18:00. We would be pushing it but we were committed. The ground was boggy, wet, and icy and the path seemed more a state of mind than anything that could be identified on the ground. We were climbing in the shade now as well, and we had to beat the sunset. As long as we reached the top of the ridge in light, then we could make our descent by torchlight, but we did not want to be climbing up in the dark. That would be too dangerous and too much of an embuggerance to make for a pleasant finale to our little weekend. The ridge looked like a nightmare too. There would be a couple of climbs before the start of the main section up to the top, but it looked mean. It looked a long way off as well, and when we found the path proper it was time to stop and rehydrate anyway.

I shared out the last of the chocolate bars and we checked the time: 17:30. We really had to move. Soon we were up and progressing at pace, again, and careful not to make any mistakes. The path was lost as we prepared for the main climb. A combination of scree scrambling and clambering up the grass took us to a rock outcrop below the ridge. The sun was setting behind us, and I agreed with John to take a quick breather as I helped myself to the camera from the top of his rucksack and took a few shots. John assured me that he was nearly wrecked, and that he would be entirely by the time we made it to the top, but I did not believe a word of it. We were about five minutes away now, and our timing was spot on. We could take another rest when we were there.

Up we went, hoping above all else that we had not been climbing for a false summit, and collapsed exhausted on the ground at the top. It was dusk now, but with a clear sky, and a gibbous Moon, we at least had that and the stars to help us find our way. The path was not clear, and as we left too hastily to get off the ridge, we missed the route by a few hundred metres. Freestyling had been very much our theme for the weekend, but it was not preferable to using a path in nothing but moonlight.

Our torches were fine for identifying ice and picking our way across rocks, but we did not want them on continuously for fear of running down the batteries. John was off again and this time I did call him back. I really just could not believe this man. He had been absolutely tremendous, and I had loved spending this weekend with him, but as soon as he thought about his stomach he was gone! I just needed him closer this time as the bracken was a nightmare, and if the person in front slipped, it did not make sense for the person behind to run the risk of slipping on the same ground. We slowed down a bit to

113

help each other out, acknowledging that it was as dark as it would get, so we had nothing to rush for.

We spotted a wall over to our left, about half a kilometre away, and made a start around the hillside for it. We climbed over and descended, and the road that we wanted lay dead ahead. After negotiating another couple of fences we were there. It had taken an hour and a half to get off the ridge and make it to the road, which seemed like a long time spent falling through holes concealed beneath bracken, but we were there now. We patted each other on the back for a job well done. In two days we had managed to climb a number of high peaks in the Welsh Highlands, including three of the highest mountains in Wales.

Once we were on the road we could move much faster than we could on the softer earth, and we charged our way up to the car park at Pen-y-Pass. I felt a little nauseous when I was back in the car. I had been trying to use biltong because I get through carbohydrate-rich foods very quickly, and tend to be very hungry afterwards. Meat, by comparison, gives me a slower release of energy and is something that my body deals with much better. In addition, when exercising for a whole day the body is relying heavily on fat stores, hence the benefit of fatty meat.

The reason for feeling a little sick, I decided, was because of the high amounts of protein. Protein requires a fair amount of water for digestion, and people in hotter climates tend to eat less protein than people in colder climates. It is quite reasonable to suppose that I should not eat meat during this sort of activity because it compromises my hydration status. The only way around this would be to carry more water, but then the added weight would cause more of a burden as well. Either way is a compromise. The alternative would be to have more carbohydrates during the day, and then protein and fat in the evening.

Still, it is useful to learn something from these weekends, and from this one I have learned that John has an awesome pace and is a great chap to do this sort of thing with. Snowdonia, on a good day, is one of the most beautiful places in Britain. I know that I can cover a fair amount of ground, even with full kit, if the need arises. Further, during activity I should limit protein consumption unless I can compensate for the increased water requirements. All in all, a good experience and something to log into the memory bank under '*good times*'.

Those Beautiful Runs

It was during my mid-twenties that I came to hear of the *Marathon des Sables*, and, in need of a new focus and drive, I registered for the event and began training with gusto. In all honesty, the training never really seemed to compare to the weight-training and kickboxing that I had enjoyed previously. The exercise in the gym had been short and sharp, involving intense pain and focus, over the duration of a set unlikely to go on beyond a minute. Such excitement felt lost on running.

During my build-up to the MdS, I discovered a shift in how I perceived myself and how I managed my exercise. Was I really enjoying myself running? I would do everything that I could to take pleasure in my sessions, and would find myself running along the Thames, contemplating its tidal reach stretching back behind me all the way to Teddington. I saw the Thames as a link to the estuary, beyond which was the North Sea and the Channel. From there, the world awaited, and I associated the river with escape and the vastness of the world as a whole. I had to, because I loathed London, as a training ground at least, with a passion.

It is not that London is not charming in its own way, but I am here because I have to be for my work, not because I feel belonging. I see myself as a bird in a cage, forever reminiscing over the East

116

Anglian countryside where I grew up, and the even more beautiful places where I see myself living when means allow. But here I must remain, for now, and the river is my link to a wider world. It is the river that could take me away to other lands, to adventures and to freedoms beyond my work and home.

In terms of my mindset for training, I find the power of the seas humbling to the meagre aspirations I have for whatever endeavour awaits me. I use the river as an inspiration, as though my very existence is somewhere between the awe-inspiring and incredible power of nature, and the depressing futility of humankind's ambitions. At least I consider this true in terms of the average Londoner; spending most of what ought to be their leisure time actually working in some mind-numbing job of no real importance to the world, or else drinking or watching uninspiring, dull and tedious twaddle on the television.

I dream and pursue an existence possibly higher than my station, and for that I make no apologies. There is a conflict that occurs between the realms of satisfaction and ambition. I am at least not content to simply dedicate my life to paying back debt and being a slave to economies. Such things can never be a priority for me; merely a step on the path. Beyond this city lie places of wild nature that no civilisation could endure. I like that, and it gives me hope in a world I frequently find unspeakably challenging to tolerate. Such contorting notions, paradoxically uniting anguish and release, allow my thoughts to wander as I daydream, as myriad different perspectives fill my mind. Each thought has to be reconciled, because were I to conclude that I truly hated London and economic life then I would descend into depression, so I can use my runs as reflective times to contemplate philosophies of the world.

In truth, if something helps me to maintain a positive attitude, then I will probably take it, however ludicrous it might appear upon reflection. I am certainly not one for dwelling on the fluffy attitudes in life, and I carry no superstitions. But, on a technical level, the tidal Thames can represent a part of our coastline, all the way up to the lock. It is not too much for my mind to consider that it is the sea breeze that I feel against my face. Nor is it too great a stretch for me to feel that this water connects with the North Sea and the Atlantic, thus representing passage to other lands and the whole world beyond. It is an effective reminder of the scale of the world and that, when I look for it, there is far more here than the built-up city in which I live.

I had noticed that when I ran at an easy pace, my mind could daydream for most of the journey from Hammersmith to London Bridge. When I ran fast, however, then I could not dream at all. I would be checking my timings at particular landmarks and gauging performance accordingly. The intervening periods would be spent contemplating breathing rate and depth, checking stride length, and seeking out anomalies; movements or muscles that felt peculiar or as if they were being overworked. In that sense, such runs could be likened to a deep meditation or trance. Whether or not I actually *enjoyed* it became something of an issue for me. If I was not, then surely this was all futile, regardless of the bigger picture and my ultimate goal?

I remembered the days of my youth and early twenties, when I lived to train in the gym, and to absorb myself fully in the intensity of the moment. And then there I would be, plodding along past the Tate Modern, convinced that I was not deriving enjoyment from this running at all, but more simply tolerating it.

Then, a few weeks before the MdS, when I was still increasing training mileages, I received a slight injury. I had attempted a longer run than usual, and as my lack of confidence and experience forced a different pace, the shift of stresses around my body caused an overuse injury in my calf. I had to hobble for a while, and it took weeks to heal satisfactorily to permit a good distance run, and it had certainly not healed entirely by the time I left for the desert. During the period that I was unable to run I discovered something. I missed running. It was alien to me because I was still relatively new to it, and until now I had only really dwelt upon my strength-training days. I most definitely missed running. At the time I simply could not understand precisely what it was. I vividly recall watching runners pacing along outside the Tate Modern themselves, and as I walked on by I was overcome by both depression and envy. Somehow, despite the monotony and the duration of the activity, I had fallen in love with it. How despicably and unforgivably clichéd that I should only realise how I felt about it when it was kept from me.

After that, I came to view my runs differently. Even during the *Marathon des Sables* itself I still loved running. I accept that time erodes the negative perceptions of the unpleasant past, but I recall nothing but enjoyment throughout the event. I remember the

119

camaraderie, the forged friendships (many of which still remain), and the thrill of running up and down sand dunes, over peaks and across open plains. It brought a sense of excitement beyond that which I could obtain simply from walking.

I became absorbed within the landscape, such as to become a part of it, one man moving across the landscape to reach his bed for the night. There was no battle against the earth. There was nothing physical to conquer. I was persisting in an endeavour to work as hard as I thought sufficient, whilst travelling across some of the most wondrous and challenging land on the planet. As Robert MacFarlane so eloquently suggests in *Mountains of the Mind*: we attempt great things in our pursuits to experience the sublime.

* * * * * * * * * * * *

My diary notes for today should have been positive; they should have hailed of greater accomplishments on the path to fitness for the Jungle Marathon. But, clearly, they did not. I was still battling with anxieties as I prepared for a run.

I build up a new distance in my mind as if it will be a great progression and another superbly fulfilling experience. But most importantly, I view the run as a challenge, a race against myself: a chance to prove myself, to myself, once again. I was excited about the prospect but the reality was that it caused stress; a side-effect of which was that I became nervous and my digestive system began falling apart. It might be a mild inconvenience if an important interview or public engagement is looming close, but if one needs to keep in good order for a long run then the consequences can be disastrous. Dehydration is the first problem; discomfort is the second. Acknowledging both, in turn, gives motivation an awful knock. It seemed, in the early stages at least, that nerves were getting the better of me. Everything would settle over time. Initially, however, it just seemed that I was placing a lot of stress onto myself to do well. I suppose that my expectations were simply too high.

I had left work looking forward to my first half-marathon of the training. My last half-marathon had been back in April, fully two months ago, but I had not trained for that and I am certainly fitter for this one. I turned off the Strand and headed down the steps at the end of the road, across the embankment gardens and turned right to run along the side of the Thames. I ran with a good pace, and my rucksack was not particularly heavy. I moved past a few runners and took the left turn to run across Westminster Bridge, running in the cycle lane as there were no bicycles close to overtaking me, and the pavement was filled with tourists. I moved up a couple of gears to cross the road and then headed along the South Bank westwards.

I had run along this stretch of pavement many times, but in the opposite direction, when running back from Hammersmith during my preparations for the MdS. I reached Vauxhall Bridge, and ran across it then back eastwards along the North Bank. At the palace of Westminster I crossed the road, then made my way to St. James' Park, then onto Green Park, Hyde Park, Kensington Gardens, and then back to Westminster, the long way round. From Westminster I ran eastwards, again along the North Bank, crossed over the Millennium Bridge, and ran along the South Bank to Canada Water, where I finished.

Some aspects of the run went particularly well. I experienced a stitch twice, and both times I thought 'Great; this is *training*!' The more pain that was thrown at me the more I would have to deal with, and the more tolerant I would become before my next run. I ran the hardest way possible; not cutting any corners, running along the sandy tracks around Hyde Park, and I ran up any additional inclines or ramps that I came across; anything to make it harder. I did it for the same reason that I appreciated the stitch. The harder I made it for myself, the more tolerant I would become next time. *'Pain is just weakness leaving the body'* (source unknown). The more pain that I experienced, the less weakness I would have next time around. It was all *training*.

But some things did not go so well. It took me two and a half hours. Why?! I had started out at a good pace, and I had pushed myself no matter what. The inclines were pathetic, hence the inclusion of steps, ramps and anything else I could use to increase the workload, but nevertheless this should have been an easy run. Could it really be that such feeble inclines were causing me problems? It was warm, and I was struggling to breathe because of the pollution, but that should not have actually affected me so perceptibly.

I thought back to my MdS training, when most of my running took place over the winter months, often in the middle of the night or early hours of the morning, and all along very flat ground indeed. The only 'hill' then was up to Battersea Dogs' Home. What had happened? I had been forced to a walk on a couple of occasions. I had not felt that bad, but my running pace was off. I would run too fast and too hard for a few miles, and then I could not manage a reduced pace. I would burn myself out and then walk to recover, and then repeat.

It was only when I crossed the Millennium Bridge that I discovered a pace that I never thought I had. It was a surprisingly easy pace. This was a pace that I could easily maintain without getting tired at all (but for the fact that I already was tired). I kept that going for the remaining few miles to Canada Water, but I must have walked at least three miles during what should have been a continuous run, and I was disappointed with my efforts. Later that evening I checked the route on Google Earth, and it came out as fourteen-and-a-half miles, which was further than I thought, but nowhere near far enough to justify the time. On the whole, this was not good. Today was Tuesday; on Friday I *would* do better, because I would give myself no choice.

The run in the jungle is likely to be the most arduous challenge that I ever attempt. I am sure that it is twice as hard as the MdS, and at present I am not adequately fit to complete that. I have time, but I consider myself dirt; I feel pathetic, useless and awful, like some sort of failure. All this because I finished later than I expected to.

In retrospect, I remember that the first time I came back from Hammersmith. I had walked the entire distance, with the express intention at the outset of committing to memory all of the little areas where I had to turn away from the Thames. This was to save back-tracking when the 'Thames Path' abruptly ended care of a new housing development, or whatever else. But I did not want to walk the new route today, and I did not need to. Why had it taken so long? I think that I walked because I had become despondent due to the run taking longer than I had predicted, and feeling harder than I had anticipated. I had no water to drink, and only some chocolate in my rucksack. Next time I would do the right thing, the Boy Scouts' thing, and I would be prepared.

I can analyse all the details of what went wrong and what I can learn from it, but it is basics first. I was dehydrated, and dehydration affects performance. My food had been wrong, and my anticipation and excitement had caused stomach problems. Next time I would have sufficient water before and during the run, and I would manage my food better.

I have managed the distance, which means all subsequent runs will be building on the pace, which is just simple training and so I will not be as anxious. I know the route now and I would control myself to avert the pre-run anxieties. Next time, I would do much, much better.

* * * * * * * * * * * *

I loved so many of my training sessions, and relished each moment spent running. I would enjoy drifting past other runners as I progressed along the riverside. I always felt a pang of guilt as I did so, hoping that I would not be harming their motivation as they saw me easily run past. To overtake others was never my goal; I only intended to maintain my own speed. However, when actually running I would see others ahead, and calculate how long it might take for me to pass them. Somehow, to pass someone else seemed like progress, but I fought to switch off such ridiculous and misplaced feelings.

If someone overtook me, then I would find myself a little knocked for it. The voices began resonating within my head: *Take them back. No! You are going for distance, whereas they have probably just started. They are fresh; they are not running as far as you; they are not carrying as much weight on their back. Just stick to your own pace; you can be faster than them another time. You are going for distance, not for speed. **But they are in the lead!***

Why the voices, and should I silence them, control them, or derive something positive from them? When someone moves past me I might speed up a fraction, often not by conscious design. Sometimes I deliberately slow myself down though, just to emphasise to myself that I must run at my own speed. But then whenever someone runs past me I naturally believe that they are faster in general, and that means that they are better than me, and if they are the superior runner, then I am inferior. And then the notion of inadequacy surreptitiously sneaks into my mind, and my now bruised male ego becomes outrageously peeved and annoyed. But I have to let it go; there is no benefit in overtaking them only to be suffering a little way further on. Right now I am training; my race is in the future, and even then I am my only genuine competition. Everybody else will be there with a similar goal; to get to the end and to do themselves proud.

Perhaps it is because I am rarely overtaken that it still chides me each time, although I do not share this to brag, I promise you. If I were in a race then it would be different, but we are all just working ladies and gentlemen out here that have finished our day's work, and are having a run for whatever goal it might be that is driving us. We are all equal, but sometimes I really, *really* want to be more equal than everybody else! Blame whatever failing you like, and if you cannot think of any then make some up. Perhaps the more people that overtake me the better. Perhaps it is my lack of experience that means that I give myself such a tough time so unnecessarily. Perhaps this is one of my greatest weaknesses? Maybe it can all easily be boiled down to my needing more humility. *Just focus on the task in hand, and the race in the future.* Over time I learnt to switch off; to enter my own zone where whatever goes on around me is taken as superfluous. It took me a while to get there; pride and egoism (and probably egotism, too) can be enemies to much in life, including running.

But this is easy now. I can manage myself well. I become warm but not overly hot. I can control myself at a temperature that suits me well. If I were to speed up then I know I would become hotter, and then I would soon feel exhausted. This is just right. The Royal Parks that feature heavily in my training have their 'gradients', but it is hardly a fitting word. Inclines and declines are not terms that can seriously be entertained, nor can the word 'undulating'. It might not be as flat as a snooker table, but it is most certainly not in the realms of hill training.

Having thwarted the mental demons that tempt me and poise themselves to corrupt my preparation, the training ground represents my greatest physical dilemma. I know that distance covered and aerobic training will help somewhat, and not only with the real hills but also with acclimatisation as well, but they are poor surrogates. All I can do is focus on the now and what I have available to me. To accept this is good; it is an acknowledgement of how to better my training. To complain, or to accept this as a worthy excuse, would be self-destructive, or might somehow detract from my motivation. I suppose that what it comes down to is that I accept what I have presented myself with, and do the best that I can. In the future, I will know what I can do better; and I am happy with that too.

* * * * * * * * * *

In Hugh Symonds' book *Running High*, the author refers to those easy runs along stretches of road or pavement. As he runs he feels that he is gliding above the surface, his legs moving seemingly without effort, as his body is propelled forwards. Such runs, such beautiful runs, were what came to be the goals of my own training sessions.

That feeling of drifting over the ground at speed, with breathing and heart rate controlled, my mind wandering off into daydreams. My feet touch the ground but the impact is unnoticed. No stress worries my joints, and no aches or pains trouble my tissues. I feel no heat, no discomfort, and no concerns. I float over the ground as if I am being carried. The air may be warm or cold; there may be stillness or there may be wind and rain, but all the while I perceive myself as a constant. Simply existing in space; running swiftly yet without effort, my body content for me to progress in this manner for mile after mile, hour after hour. The world appears tranquil as it passes me by; and always the runner is moving through it.

There is poetry in those runs; there is form and function and a deep satisfaction. A personal victory arises from completion of such an outing. And the other runs? The runs where I find myself experiencing a little more discomfort? Then I am simply paying my dues; each time my body feels as though it is working hard I know that my fitness will improve, so as to ensure a similar run following recovery will be beautiful. Whether I am able to enjoy such beauty upon that next time, or if I choose to persevere and push myself that little bit harder; such considerations I will only know during the run itself.

I enjoy the beauty of the easy runs: those floating, gliding runs. I also relish the beauty of the challenging runs; the runs where for a time I anticipate defeat and a requirement to cease from exercise. When I meet with such disappointing prospects, and I find the means to push through whilst correcting the problem, those sessions become particularly precious to me. During the course of my training for the jungle marathon, I enjoyed the satisfaction of all such runs, whether simply beautiful or beautifully challenging. There seems little wonder that I should so much enjoy the thrill of training for a big race.

The goal of my training had been to be able to run good distances, of between eleven and eighteen miles, four to six days a week. I rarely ran less than fourteen-and-a-half miles. Some runs were beautiful, and some merely had moments of beauty. All had greatness to them, whether due to adversity or ease, and always there was something that could be measured as a triumph.

A Coast-to-Coast Washout

The pros of taking a 'rain-check' were not sufficient to quieten the reality of my having to back out. My feet were macerated. The pus stuck my skin to my socks and later even my feet to the floor of the shower. Stopping when I did was absolutely the right thing to do. If my goal had been to finish the course then I would have done it. However, my goal was to complete some training for the Jungle Marathon, and if such training threatened to compromise my fitness for the real event, then it would have been beyond counterproductive. It would have been sadistic and self-ruinous and that was not what brought me here.

What I took away from it, however, was far more than I expected. I discovered that I cannot use a bivi bag as a realistic shelter in inclement weather. I cannot combine trail running shoes and heavy kit, but neither can I combine walking boots with heavy kit and still run effectively. The best course of action would surely be a repeat in which I would walk but carry a tent, or else run and stay in B&Bs. Water is a difficult to find on this route, with few villages to pass through and sparse natural sources.

The idea of doing a coast-to-coast crossing of England was the foregone conclusion of having read Matt Beardshall's book about his run. The journey is typically walked in twelve to fourteen days, based upon the various books by Alfred Wainwright, and takes in the Lake District, Pennine Way and Peak District. The walk traditionally begins at St. Bees, just south of Whitehaven by the Irish Sea, and concludes at Robin Hood's Bay, just south of Whitby, by the North Sea. The distance varies according to the route, but is generally considered to be between 160 and 190 miles.

I had thought that I could use the coast-to-coast as an opportunity to get some last-minute hill-training in before I headed off to the Amazon. The current Jungle Marathon course is almost all hills, with perhaps fifteen percent of running along flat beaches, mainly on the final day. Having been living in London I was positively envious of anybody that lived near the hills or mountains. In the absence of local hills for regular evening runs, the next best thing would be to take weekends away in hilly countryside so that I could still fulfil that aspect of my training. In my case it was finances that prevented me from travelling away so regularly, as well as the burden of work commitments, including weekend teaching and course writing. If the finances had been available, then I could have managed some of the work commitments from a B&B, but for me the situation was too dire to even manage a coach fare to anywhere useful.

I began my lecturing position at the beginning of September. With three weeks before I had to teach a short biology course, I was given the opportunity to swap days around and have a clear six-day break. Six days? I *had* to take a look at the coast-to-coast. It was too soon and I was not in a position with my training to seriously entertain the prospect of a continuous run, but I had to do something. This

131

would be far from ideal, but considerably better than doing nothing. I could half-walk, half-run the uphills, then run the downhills and flats, and recover as required.

I attacked the outdoor shops with gusto, buying myself, amongst other items, a Rab Storm Bivi, thus eliminating the necessity for a tent. Matt and his friends had stayed in B&Bs, but I did not have the funds and would not have been able to estimate my distances well enough in any case. I bought food and new water Puri-tabs and neutralisers. In the two days before I set off I bought my coach ticket to Whitby and train ticket from Carlisle to London. I felt apprehensive buying the return ticket but it would be four-times cheaper to do it this way than to buy a standard ticket upon my arrival at the station. I looked at routes and printed off waypoints, which I then programmed into my Memory Map and uploaded onto my GPS. I had never used a GPS before, but considered that it was about time to start learning how.

I never planned to use the GPS as my primary means of navigating, purely because things can go wrong with them. GPS can lose satellite connections, become inaccurate, or lose power. A map is far more reliable (provided that it is not so old that houses and roads have been constructed or demolished since it was printed, something that has caught me out in the past), with a compass it is better still, and GPS remains as an option for double-checking or back-up. I would attempt to honour that philosophy, and not rely on the GPS out of laziness and convenience.

The rucksack was heavy. It was too heavy. It weighed in excess of twenty kilograms, which meant that I would not be able to run at anything like a reasonable pace. The load was due to the combined weight of the rucksack itself, the sleeping bag, the food, my stove and the fuel, as well as water. I also had medical and survival kit in there. I could not compromise on these things and expect to stay safe. Instead, my compromise would be on speed over the ground. Again, as this was to be a training expedition, rather than a goal in itself, I would happily walk the first two days as I adapted to moving over hilly terrain, during which time the food weight would be reduced.

I left work at midday and took the seven and a half-hour coach journey from London Victoria to Whitby, arriving just before nine pm. In the first days of Autumn, night had fallen but the sea breeze coming into the harbour was warm and clean. I offloaded my rucksack from the coach and began to make everything ready, packing away what I did not need, ensuring that waterproofs were at the top, and switching on my GPS to set the first new waypoint. I sent a text message to my I.C.E. (In Case of Emergency) contact, to confirm that I was in position and preparing to set off. I then heaved the rucksack onto my back and headed off around the fishing port to pick up my route south.

When I reached it, the small road that I needed to take was fearsomely steep. Despite all sense I went from a strong walking pace into a jog, struggling to get one foot above the other on the pavement, against the weight of the rucksack. My heart was pounding and I began to overheat. The heat came on suddenly and relentlessly, overwhelming me and begging me to stop. I made it barely two-thirds of the way up and was reduced back to the strong walk. I enjoyed it, in a way.

I was unfit for hills. That was why I was here, and this first opportunity to test myself taught me nothing new. The glee must have been from the knowledge that I had come here to set this straight, and that valuable lessons would be learned that would help me in the Amazon, from a mental perspective even if not sufficiently from a physical one.

I reached the top of the road, with Whitby Abbey over to my left, and I headed right, along a pavement down a dark, gently undulating road. I could not resist it; there was no traffic so I stepped out into the road and picked up the pace. The road and pavement surfaces were both lost to the darkness, but whilst my eyes adjusted I was confident that the road would present fewer trip hazards. I began to run along, down and up. Any notion of not running uphill was fading fast. I kept telling myself to reel my neck in, to reduce the stride length and to take it easy. I was not fit for hills. If I did even an hour of hill running then I might make my muscles too sore for me to be able to manage another day, and I had aspirations of running to the other side of the country.

I left the road for a bridleway, my Mini Maglite lighting the way. Then the rains came. I threw on my waterproof and secured the silver rucksack cover over the front of my Berghaus and expedition roll mat. I maintained a walking pace all along the bridleway, out of fear of tripping in the dark as much as concern of stressing my muscles too much. The descent into Robin Hood's Bay was steep, but in the dark my attentions were drawn to the countless B&Bs, the wondrous depth of character and individuality of the houses, and the small shops and pubs that lined the way to the beach.

That descent *was* steep. At points I let myself go and gathered pace, from walking to jogging to charging down, mindful of the locals heading home from the pub. Those fell-runners; that awe-inspiring breed of athletes, they gather incredible speeds when descending from the peaks. To force the muscles to control a steep descent at a moderate or steady pace is to inflict significant levels of stress on the muscles and connective tissues. To let go, whilst maintaining sufficient control, builds tremendous speed and momentum, but seems to put fell-runners at less risk of injury than completing their descents at a slower pace.

Perhaps the swing of balance towards speed is also affected by the need for speed itself, and I can barely imagine the sight of fifty fell-runners charging down from a high peak at full-tilt. It must be quite fun to observe; certainly exciting. But their logic is no-doubt preferable to that of playing it ultra-safe, and ironically increasing the risk of soft-tissue injury by doing so. In fact, having read Ashcroft's book and contemplated the logic of why they run as they do, I am convinced of it.

I reached the bay, having half-walked, half-hurtled down from the top, and made my way down the slip road and onto the beach. The tide was far out from where I stood, and in the inky black of a cloudy night I could only hear the sea, as it was so far from view. The beach was stony and slippery, and I dared not wander off for minutes to find the water's edge. I turned back, picked up a small pebble as I did so and placed it in my pocket (it is a tradition when attempting this journey, after all). I set my kit down outside a shop, had some food and sorted my kit, put the Mini Maglite into my pocket and extracted my headtorch from the rucksack, and then I headed off. I headed *up*. My only recollection of the walk up that steepest of roads was that I kept beneath my lactate threshold. My legs had been kept clear from the acid burning. I knew that had I attempted to run with this kit, I would not have managed more than maybe three steps.

My map and compass were protected from the elements by their waterproof case, and I navigated my way out of the bay and onto the coastal path, on a course northwards this time, back towards Whitby. I had now commenced the official route. The path was slippery and wet; far too risky for me to run. I reflected on my 'rules'. I was here to train and to experience some hills. Completing the coast-to-coast was not the goal in itself. The reason for this was simple. I had a race in a month's time. I could recover from soft-tissue injuries, but anything more serious could rule me out.

This was a training opportunity; to improve my ability for getting up and down hills, which would be of huge value for the Amazon. If I were to receive a nominal amount of soft-tissue damage, then I would still be able to get back into running within a week, and I would still meet my anticipated levels of fitness by the time I flew out to Santarem. If I received more severe soft-tissue injury, then I might not be able to train for any more than a week before I flew out, in which case the mental aspects of hill-training, together with any carry-over of physical improvements, would have been negated. If I tripped, then similarly the resulting damage could be too great for me to recover from in time.

I could have run along this track, but I would probably have slipped, tripped and fallen more than I would have deemed acceptable. It was better to play it safe and hold back on the running, rather than becoming injured and unable to run or derive benefits from the hills. I walked on, slipping nonetheless on the shiny pebbles, but appreciative that the consequences would have been potentially more dire at a running pace.

I turned right, through a caravan park, again uphill, and out along a winding road. The road headed northwards, then southwards, and with the minimal of westwards. It was frustrating, but I knew that this was the way of the route, and I intended to stay loyal to it rather than to make my own way across. On the more secure surface of the roads I found myself charging downhill, along, then up for short sections. Then I walked and recovered. I wanted to make some headway before I slept. I came off the road and onto a footpath, which eventually led out onto the start of the Yorkshire Moors.

The earth was muddy, saturated and boggy. The heather was drenched with moisture and soaked my trousers as I plodded on southwards. In the dark I lost the footpath, or at least I thought I had. The path had become just a stream, then all seemed lost in the tall grass. I tested and probed possible routes through, but I could not discern a definite path. I took a bearing from the compass and headed on.

My Salomon trail running shoes released water through their gore-tex. I told myself that if I had been in boots then my feet would still have been dry and I would have been comfortable, but that I would have lost the potential of specificity of training, as I would be wearing the Salomon's in the Jungle. Furthermore, the trail running shoes would allow me to run effectively when I reached the hills.

I flung the rucksack and map case over a fence, and then flung myself over after them. I had reached a road and would use this to get back to where I should be on the route. There was no fun to be had in dragging my feet through the bogs, and no progress to be made from such a tiresome enterprise. The area was flat and high; the strong sea winds howling over the moors and threatening to prevent me from finding somewhere to sleep. I found where the footpath was punctuated by the road and checked my watch: 02:20. I made the decision to camp for the remainder of the night in a small area of woodland by the roadside. I had been tempted to continue on, but I resolved that further and happier progress would be made during the hours of daylight.

I rolled out my mat and pushed my sleeping bag within the storm bivi, before removing my Salomon's and climbing into the bag. The shoes went under the rucksack cover; the whole thing next to my head to help protect me from the wind. As the cold crept in I zipped up my sleeping bag and felt the warmth and comfort at once. I had imagined the bivi bag to be claustrophobic, as if I were entombed in my own coffin. It was certainly suffocating. The marketing spiel assured me that it was manufactured from the most breathable fabrics yet designed, but fearful of carbon dioxide poisoning I opened the end of the bag, and immediately felt more at ease. Warm, snug and tired, I drifted off to sleep.

* * * * * * * * * * * *

I awoke just after 07:00, climbed out from my sleeping bag and layered up with my Sprayway midlayer fleece, Rab fibre pile jacket, and the cheapest Thinsulate woollen hat that next to no money could buy. I packed everything away and headed off once more, still heading south.

I jumped over a stile to land in a swamp. The path disappeared under deep water, which continued a little further on to form a fairly reasonably sized pond. I wasted minutes working out a way around. I had to take a detour through higher ground before I once again met with the correct route and proceeded along a small farm road. I was still soaked for all my efforts, just the same. A path through shoulder- and even head-height ferns ensured that I was drenched from head to foot, but with the pace of walking and the weight of my kit I was at least warm.

I made it into woodland, where I broke-up my walk with short runs, but again the track was too wet and too dangerous for me to feel confident enough to maintain a fast pace. Besides, as I kept trying to remind myself, the first two days needed to be the easiest so that I would feel more confident with the kit. I had done this before. Even with the most minimal of decrements in kit weight from eating the food, after a couple of days of carrying the rucksack it always feels perceptively lighter than it actually is. The body can be kind like that, whether it is due to actual strength improvements (via improved neuromuscular pathway activation, to be specific), or just a dulling of the pain.

Today saw some good short climbs, but it was mostly flat, with plenty of roads and tracks to follow. I met an American couple, maybe in their fifties, who were coming the other way. For them, this was their final stage, having walked for almost a fortnight, and they were elated to be within a half-marathon of completion. We chatted and I congratulated them on their achievement, before I headed on. It was like that a lot. I would meet many people coming towards me, and they were all on the coast-to-coast; all having been walking for about a fortnight, and they were all saying the same thing. They all loved it. The scenery had been absolutely beautiful, and it had been an incredible experience for them.

I suppose that I had been envious in a way. I had not really been able to enjoy this. I had too far to go and I could not run as I had wanted to. These travellers were staying in B&Bs, and they were all on a course to be finished between midday and 14:00. For me that was when I was starting the second stage of the day. So far today it had been sunny and pleasant, with the only negative being the nature of the ground that I had to trudge through when crossing the fields and the moors.

By the early evening my feet had grown tired, although the rest of my body was surprisingly fine. I could sense that water, which had been inundating my shoes and socks, had caused abrasion problems with my skin, and I was in no doubt that I had several blisters on the way. Good. Sort of. Just enough stress would allow the skin to become tougher. Again there were rules. I would have to concede if my feet were damaged to the point that they would not heal to allow me train within a week.

The other danger was that damage to my feet, whether to the skin or the muscles, could cause compensations in my gait, as my body attempted to protect damaged areas. Over a long distance, this could ultimately lead to stress fractures, and then I would be in danger of not recovering for months. I also decided that I would concede if I were at risk of losing a toenail. Although losing a toenail is not an issue in itself, it can sometimes take weeks for the underlying tissue to die off and for the nail to be pulled free. Again, that could interfere with my training. There would probably be other possibilities, such as having the nail removed by a podiatrist, but I was unsure of costs and time and so on.

As I walked along the track and up what I hoped was the final incline of the day, a helicopter pilot spotted me moving along, and circled round to give me a fly past and check I was in good order. He was on his radio, probably communicating back about some fellow emerging from the moors a few minutes before sunset, but grinning like an idiot so was probably all right. In fact I was racing the sun. I wanted to begin my descent before the sun dropped behind the hills on the horizon in front of me.

As the long trail headed down, I could see where my finishing point for the day would be, just at the base of this hill. I managed a few more minutes but had to stop for fuel and water. I heard a pitter-patter of what could only be a runner. I knew there was no-one behind me on the trail. I looked down in the direction that I would be going, but the track disappeared over the edge of the hill and out of sight. I looked and listened, but nothing. The sound disappeared.

I sat and ate and then the sound came back. I looked off to my right to see a man in a fluorescent jacket and three-quarter-length running tights heading up towards me. A fell-runner. I felt honoured. I sat there and watched as he approached and then disappeared off towards the brow of the hill, and we exchanged the briefest of pleasantries as he passed. What a nutter! It was cold and he had no extra kit with him at all, and he was just heading up the steepest hill that I have seen so far, and off into the cold, damp night. I secretly appointed him my hero for the night and then gathered up my kit and continued down.

A couple of minutes passed and the pitter-patter came back and I stepped off the track and onto the grass to the side. We again exchanged our pleasantries and continued on our respective journeys. He was flying though. His technique was spot-on for a fell-runner too. Not just the downhill, but also the uphill was just as it needed to be as well. People often debate running technique but it is mostly ridiculous. Look at how a school child runs. They have not had the injuries and countless biomechanical compensations brought about by one-sidedness in carrying and contrived physical activities. People create nuances and quirks out of nervous-system issues, and then it seems that people discuss the potential benefits of their obscure adaptations.

We have been improving on our movement patterns through millions of years of natural selection. That is, nature has selected the individuals that can move the most efficiently and effectively. Now people will actually discuss whether or not they can tweak millions of years of evolution by simple thought processes. A similar approach has caused sufficient problems with our diets, which should initiate alarm bells ringing at the possibility of doing similar with our biomechanics.

I see far more variation in technique during a single run of a few miles around London, than I do when I watch elite ultra-distance runners. Elite runners are all very similar, but amateurs tend to be grossly more varied. Often that is likely to be the result of injuries, however slight. The body compensates to protect itself, so other muscles take the strain to remove pressure from an injured area. Then the new area experiences increased stresses, and so further compensations arise. What results might be pain-free, but it is clearly inefficient and ineffective, permitting reduced speeds and reduced distances.

This fell runner was no different in his technique than a world-class marathon runner, except that he picked his feet up a little more, which generated more of a vertical component. In this case he was sacrificing a few inches of stride-length in order to reduce the risk of slipping. Thus he was compromising his technique, favouring a reduced efficiency in order to maintain longevity in fell-running. That seemed fair enough to me.

Please, I beg you, do not even bait me to get started on distance runners avoiding heel strike and running on the balls of their feet instead. Whoever thought of that had no understanding of how soft tissues dampen joint stresses. It is certainly one way to promote knee, hip and lower back problems. Obviously it is fine if you do not intend to use those joints into old age, but I certainly do, and I give them enough of a battering as it is without compounding the problem with novel and ridiculous self-inflicted adaptations.

I concede that it might be fine for sprinters, who do not require as many heel strikes in their entire careers as many of us get through in a single training session, but that is for them and not for us. You doubt me? I have a foot plate/force platform in my laboratory that simply itches to be put to good use in supporting such matters. Anyway, I digress…

Having concluded my internal ramblings on the subject of fell runners' biomechanics (well, and that of endurance athletes and sprinters), I reached the base of the hill, and found on my map that I had indeed reached Clay Bank Top, the end of the day's journey. Since my arrival at Whitby the previous evening, I had covered approximately fifty miles with heavy kit, and had managed to experience a modicum of hill training, although nowhere near enough

144

running training. With no other options, I laid out the bivi bag by a fence, and made a shelter from my basha and the fence posts, using my rucksack and a bush to secure the other two corners. I treated myself by removing both my shoes and socks, and resolved to attend to my feet in the morning, once they had dried out and the air had had the chance to facilitate healing

* * * * * * * * * * *

During the night my body heat had created a considerable amount of condensation within the bivi bag and beneath the basha. By morning my legs and torso were soaked from sweat, although my feet had at least managed to dry. My feet had been fairly shrivelled when I had removed them from my shoes and socks for the night. Blisters had begun to form where the saturated socks had caused rubbing.

I packed everything away and headed across the road and up a narrow path. The hill was steep and appreciably high, but the lower sections of the path were made up of rocky steps, which was a superb help. The morning air was damp and the sky overcast, as it had been throughout the previous day. More rain was coming. From the top of I was presented with a succession of similar hills to ascend and descend along the route. The stone steps were smooth and slippery in their wet state, forcing me to maintain a controlled pace, but I progressed as quickly as I could.

I passed a few other walkers along the way, many wearing ponchos as protection from the persistent drizzle. I left the steep hills and exchanged them for a longer, gentler climb through woodland, which later emerged onto open, shallow moorland. The ground was so wet. Long grasses soaked the lower areas of my trousers, and the boggy mud constantly inundated my shoes with water. This slowed progress and my feet became tender as the skin softened and rubbed against my wet socks. Even when I left the countryside for sections of road, I could always observe how water leaked out from the trainers.

My feet would be in a terrible state if the ground and weather conditions remained like this. There was now a very real risk that I would have to throw in the towel to ensure that my feet recovered sufficiently for continued, effective training for the jungle race.

Having negotiated my way around a field of particularly fearsome and intimidating cows, and a bull that put me in mind of a similar challenge confronted by Matt Beardshall's team, I found myself wading rather than walking. Farmland with paths around the periphery had become so wet that they were several inches deep in water. The rain was still drizzling down, relentless enough to ensure that conditions would only become worse.

The rain did not bother me, nor the poor ground conditions. What I did object to was how the conditions combined with my inability to protect myself from them, and how that was the root cause of my discomfort. Had I been wearing my fully waterproof Magnum boots, then I would have been quite comfortable and confident of my ability to complete the journey. But I had chosen not to wear them out of a need for training specificity, and the weather reports had not indicated that conditions would be this bad.

I waded out of the farmland and onto roads, towards my campsite for the third night. According to my GPS I had covered approximately ninety miles in these last forty-eight hours, over challenging terrain and tough ground conditions. I had a hundred miles still to go, but knew that with the conditions likely to worsen, and my feet in desperate need of some tender loving care, that it would be in my best long-term interests to call it a day. I was fairly dejected as I came to accept this, but knew it to be the correct decision. I could stagger on, but it would mean losing skin from my feet and bruising toenails. In addition to this perfectly sensible rationale, because I was not equipped to deal with such persistently testing weather conditions I was not really enjoying myself. Live now, commence healing tonight, and enjoy some good training opportunity before the Jungle Marathon. The coast-to-coast will have to remain for another occasion.

I checked into a B&B and showered; an incredibly sore and character-building affair, after which I tended to my bodily rucksack sores and the awful state of my feet. This was something that would have been incredibly difficult to manage outside in the wet and cold, where I needed everything to be dried so that sores could be effectively dressed.

The next morning I headed off, almost limping from the sores on my feet, and made my way to the local bus station. As I did so I passed a field that the trail would have taken me across. It was almost a metre deep in water, with the gate almost out of sight beneath the newly formed lake! On lower ground people had sand-bagged the doors to their homes, with rivers threatening to burst their banks at any moment. What a week to attempt such an endeavour!

I vowed to return, hopefully mid-summer and with long days and amidst glorious sunshine, with a view to enjoying every moment of it. When I do so, I shall dress in my adventure-racing kit, and carry my ultra-lightweight rucksack and equipment. I will stay in B&Bs so as to ensure that I can focus on making set distances each day and be able to tend to myself effectively in the evenings. I had made the correct decision, unquestionably, but to quit, even for the sake of a victory later on in the race I was actually training for, still smarted and smacked of failure. I could have pressed on; I knew that. I chose not to for the sake of the greater goal. I think that I write this more to convince myself than you.

I keep assessing it over and over in my mind. I can blame my kit or the weather, or even my feet, but I know that my performance was a reflection of decisions made; attempting the feat during the only week available to me, wearing the clothing most practical for training specificity for the jungle, and carrying kit that was too heavy to enable me to run, but that did not contain a tent which would have helped me to better look after myself (although I cannot imagine how I would have pitched it, with such horrendous ground conditions on that third night). I questioned myself repeatedly on the journey home, and I still do. Vindication will come following my successful completion of the coast-to-coast at another time.

Final Preparations

Hill training should be a priority in a running programme for the Jungle Marathon. Almost all of the JM is over hilly or undulating terrain. That is, almost one hundred and thirty miles of inclines and declines. Basic aerobic fitness is the foundation, and hill training is the key to making the programme specific to task.

In this respect, my training has been inadequate. London is as flat as a snooker table and not nearly as green. There is no real specificity of training other than distance and kit trained in. Ideally, had time and finances permitted, then I would have made use of weekends to fit in some days in hilly countryside. The reality, disappointingly, was that neither time nor finances permitted such excursions. So from the outset I accepted that my training could not be to the standard that I would have liked, but when is it ever? There are a lucky few that can bring all of the right ingredients together, whether by design or otherwise.

I became better at managing the inclines that featured along my normal running routes, but mostly that was confined to the bridges and Royal Parks; woefully insufficient. The main focus for heading up to Whitby in September had been to get into hilly areas as I worked my way across the country (by beginning the journey from Whitby, I would have been encountering progressively steeper landscapes on my way to Whitehaven). That, of course, was largely a failure due to my inability to beat the weather. I had managed a good distance of ninety miles in two days, but it had been across the flattest parts of the full course. Fortunately, however, the inclines and declines that I did encounter were nonetheless far more demanding than those I had become accustomed to in London.

Ideally, hill training ought to be incorporated as early in the training programme as possible, so as to permit a good degree of useful muscle adaptation. For me, it would be more about the mental benefits of knowing that I could at least make it to the top of punishing climbs (for example, I had easily worked my way up the steepest sections of the mountains in the Lake District and Snowdonia, but these were far too long ago now to have much physiological carry-over to my present conditioning).

The week prior to the race I had to journey to my hometown of Sawbridgeworth in Hertfordshire, to receive my medical checks and jabs. As these took place over two days, it gave me the opportunity to tie-in some light hill-training in the nearby countryside. As this was the final week before the race, I had intended to decrease training volume, so as to allow my connective tissue, muscle tissue, and heart muscle to recover from the high-volume work that went before.

Tapering down would also allow me to recover my energy stores better between sessions, so that over the course of the week I could focus on maximising my glycogen (carbohydrate) stores. At this stage, I would not object to carrying a little more fat either, partly because I would lose it before the end of the following week, and partly because I was at this point the lightest that I had been since I was seventeen (74 kilograms, down from a respectable weight of 84 kilograms, and a favourable weight of 88-90 kilograms).

There are various ways of performing hill training, and a lot of what to do is determined by the nature of the hills available and fitness level. Most of my training had involved getting from A to B, and it was only in the last week before the race, when distance was no longer the goal and hilly terrain was available to me, that I could actually focus on a more traditional approach. I even had the pleasure of my father's company, as he had been working an early shift at a nearby hospital and wanted to join me (a decision I hope he does not regret!).

We met up and he helped as I sorted my rucksack, Platypus and hydration mix, and then we were off. Pishiobury Park is a pleasant area of greenery, and even though it sits by a main road, the trees along the border of the first field block out the noise. The fields are used by cattle, dog-walkers, and very little else. We would confine ourselves to the main field, about a mile in circumference, and as we ran round the periphery I was busy trying to discern where we could base ourselves for the main training. This was hardly Skiddaw.

The intention was to find an area with the right combination of steepness and length; I wanted to avoid areas that were either too short, or else not sufficiently steep. The best that I could find was on the east side of the field, about halfway along. The incline was a hundred metres long at most, and although the steepness varied, it started off relatively steep and became gradually worse, until a clump of nettles close to the top marked the area where the ground flattened and would suffice as our turning point.

We had managed a lap and a half of the field as a warm-up of the typical ten minutes in duration. The plan was simple: run up at a steady pace, and run down faster. Whilst I may have learned how to run downhill care of Askwith's book, it was during the *Marathon des Sables* that I had learned to run uphill. It was during the part that I had been looking forward to especially. At just after 14:00 on the first day of the long stage, Mohamed Ahansal and the other elite runners passed me by, following the three-hour head-start us non-elite runners had been given. I had just descended from a short hill and was on a flat some way before checkpoint four. Just ahead of me were some high sand-dunes. I tried to feel his running pattern, stride lengths and pace in my mind as I watched. I tuned in and waited to see what would happen when he reached the first sand-dune. I watched.

He reached the base of the sand dune and easily made it up and over, but that was no surprise. What I noticed, even from a distance, was that his pace and energy did not change. His legs seemed to move at the same rate as when he was on the flat. For me, I would dig in a little bit on the hills; I would then lean forwards and push up more through my legs, and my whole running pattern would change slightly as a result. Not Mohamed. His legs moved in a similar manner and at the same speed, and his energy simply became divided into upward as well as forward elements, but the total energy that he was putting in did not appear to be any different (it might have felt different, due to different areas of muscles being incorporated to different extents, but the revolutions and energy going into those revolutions was constant). The only aspect of his running that changed was stride length, as his feet were brought up higher and he gave himself less far to travel horizontally.

That stayed in my mind, even though I did not know how to apply it then. Since I began training for the Jungle Marathon though, whenever I came across inclines I would endeavour to do the same; I would keep my legs moving through the same number of revolutions per minute as when I was on the flats, and I would attempt to not put any more effort into the climb (suppressing my usual urge to bound up). My stride length decreased, and there was a greater vertical element, although even that was nowhere near what it had been when I had climbed hills in the past. It seemed to work; it felt more efficient than just digging in and trying to get it over with.

Out here in the fields, the tactic was simple interval training. I was not used to steep inclines, so I began by running up once and then back, and then recovering. For the second set I ran up and down twice, and for the third set I ran up and down three times before a rest. The length of rest time varied between thirty seconds and a minute. My father was joining me, and was a little more breathless than I, but he was nevertheless fit and in good shape (he had mostly been running on treadmills, and it had been some time since he had been running around these fields. I could not care too much for his suffering though; it was a pleasure to have him out here training with me). I indicated that we would repeat five sets in this manner.

What I failed to inform him was that I meant we would do five sets and then re-evaluate. He did, unfortunately, fall into the trap of assuming that I meant it to end there. As we made that fifth climb of the fifth set, he accelerated and left me behind as he pounded the earth and rocketed to the top. From a cardiorespiratory perspective, my breathing was back to normal by the time that I reached the base of the hill. This was the result of the effort going into the climbs being compensated for during the recovery of the descents. Hence it was quite easy for me to suggest, at this point, that we really should not call it a day so soon.

My father stuck with me to the seventh set, and then allowed me to continue by myself. I paused briefly to release some tension in my muscles, thanks to one very specific self-myofascial release and muscle-activation exercise, taught to me by my dear friend John Hardy. I then raced through the eighth set. By this time, as a surprise to me, things had changed. On the fourth, fifth and sixth sets, lactate had been building up in my thighs during the last one or two climbs of each set. From the seventh onwards, there was no noticeable lactate build-up at all. I put this down to my easing into a rhythm, with improved cycling of the lactate back to my liver for conversion back into glucose (a process that simply requires sufficient oxygen to reach the muscles). Hence, as my breathing became easier and more settled, so my body became more efficient at recycling lactate, and the associated burning sensation dissipated.

I was disappointed, in a way. I wished that I had been struggling. The hill was just not steep enough or long enough, but it

154

was the best that I had available. I wanted to be struggling in training, and that was the whole point of it all. The more that I struggle in training, whether mentally or physically or both, the less I would struggle in the main event. If it were not for the fact that there nevertheless had to be some training stimulus taking place for the hills, then I would have resolved that it was all a complete waste of time.

What I did like, however, was having my father watching me from the base of the hill. During the eighth set I had called out my instructions, those being for him to put some extra layers on as he was just standing in the cold. I did not want him to leave from boredom, so I informed him that I would combine the ninth and tenth sets, and that I would appreciate it if he kept count for me.

As I descended following the first climb I exclaimed that I had changed my mind. This would be a set made up of twenty-one 'laps', rather than nineteen. There was no alternative for me. One of my favourite strength exercises had always been twenty-rep squats, and I would always do at least twenty-one, just so that I could tell myself that I still had energy left over, so next time I would have to go heavier. Hence, I knew from the outset that finishing on nineteen climbs would be ridiculous, twenty would be obvious, and to me twenty-one was the natural conclusion.

What I liked the most about my father overseeing my training was that I felt as if it was straight out of childhood. As if he were stood with the other parents whilst I played cricket, or football, or rugby. But now it was just the two of us. It seemed perfectly fitting to me. Running can be such a lonely sport, and never more so than in training, so now it was both my father and I here enjoying it. It was great; it was special to me. By the time I had three laps left we had agreed that we would both run round to our proper starting point at the car park. By the time I had two climbs left he had been well and truly badgered into joining me for the last run up and down the hill.

I knew that his legs had been hurting, and that he had taken a long break from training due to issues in his knee, but he was as fit as a fiddle and he had managed over an hour of training with me so far on this occasion. I would have been happy for him to sprint up and beat me, but he made no such attempt, and it would have been rude of me to try something similar. So we ran up together, stride almost matched to stride and step to step, and we descended together. Then we headed off to complete half a lap of the field before finishing.

In many respects it could not have gone any better. I was fitter for hills than I had thought, and possibly fitter than I deserved to be. I could only suppose that my volume of training on the flats had at least some carry-over, especially with my new, more bioenergetically efficient means of hill running. It obviously meant a great deal to me on a personal level too. Now I could show my dad that there was something that I was good at, and even though it had taken thirty years for me to find it, here at last it was. I even bought him dinner that evening. He might have appreciated it a bit more if he had not been so tired, with legs so such stiff they were already threatening punishing DOMS (Delayed-Onset Muscle Soreness). But, as I kept reminding him when we were out there; it was his own bloody fault for never teaching me to fish.

I felt no ill-effects from the hill-training session, but I did suffer with an awful cold. This was one of those occasions when simply everyone seemed to have a cold. I am never usually bothered, as one naturally strives to be an individual and not follow the herd into the realms of ill-health, but I had little chance of avoiding this one. My pre-race anxieties combined with a high volume of training affected my immune function.

When I went for the medical checks and so on I stayed in a B&B where they kept a cat. Ordinarily that would not have affected me, but on this occasion it did and so an allergic reaction caused further issues with my immunity. The final, predictable, nail in the coffin of my health was the vaccinations. I recall having three, which by itself would have induced a significant strain on my immune system. All these came together with pitiless effectiveness, to ensure that I would feel ill from a day or two after the vaccinations, and continue to be out of sorts for the start of the race. Terrific.

* * * * * * * * * *

During the final few weeks the excitement grew, as did the urge to keep active. I was restless, always. I loathed sitting still, and in part I loathed myself for feeling that way. I wanted to sit down on the sofa and do nothing. I wanted to sit there and watch television and drink coffee. But I hated that too. I looked at the clock constantly. Every minute I sat there I became more and more agitated. The truth of the matter was that I was exercising so much that my body anticipated it, and expected it. I would consider doing about half-an-hour of boxing to calm the feeling down, but I knew that it would not work. I knew that the only thing that would work was hour after hour of endurance running. I just needed to be on my feet, moving swiftly, gliding, and flying over grass and tracks, in woodlands or along riverbanks. And I needed to be out there, out in the open air feeling the wind rush past my face as I run on and on. I am either running or thinking about running, but it is more than simply thinking; it is *needing* the run and feeling an urgency and restlessness about it. I would be agitated and fidgety, unable to simply lie back on the sofa and take it easy.

It almost seemed as though the jungle was calling to me now, or at least so it was in my mind, for the images of being there filled my dreams and waking thoughts. An excitement had been welling up inside me. Two months ago the jungle was still the memory of my previous visit. Now, though, I could feel it. I could feel the air, hot and saturated, warming my skin. I could see those trails, wrapped and suffocated by trees, hemming me in and obstructing my already painfully slow running up the hills. My energy was sapped and my temperature was boiling. I felt so hot, so tired, sweating, aching, and mad. And throughout this vision I wanted one thing more than anything else in the world. I wanted to be out there, doing it. I wanted to be suffering as I see myself suffering. I wanted to feel alive, and know that I was doing something that was special to me, something to make me feel greater than myself. I just wanted to run.

Extreme Physiology:
Exercise in Hot and Humid Conditions

The Jungle Marathon presents a unique challenge to its competitors. Of all of the extreme environments in which we can perform physical activity, the hot and humid jungle is one of the most challenging, perhaps second only to high altitude climbing (i.e. to summit Mount Everest without oxygen).

Many Jungle Marathon competitors may have participated in other multi-stage, ultra-endurance adventure races around the world. It cannot be stressed strongly enough, that the jungle environment is unique. Mile for mile, it is likely to be the toughest adventure race in the world. Exhaustion, due to poor heat management, is the single biggest factor to prevent competitors completing the JM, followed by physical injury (i.e. muscle damage) and external physical factors (serious bites, stings, infection, etc.). The humidity encountered in the jungle severely compromises our ability to cool ourselves, the consequences of which can be disastrous.

The Physiology of Temperature Regulation During Exercise

Heat gained during exercise must be matched by heat lost, in order to preserve the body's core temperature of 37 degrees Celsius. If the core temperature rises above 38 degrees, then the athlete will begin to feel tired and performance will decline. If this rise is not corrected, then the athlete will become too exhausted to continue. Ultimately, the hypothalamus in the brain will cause the individual to collapse, so as to prevent them from causing further damage.

Heat gain is affected by external factors such as the ambient temperature, wind speed, humidity, solar radiation, ground thermal radiation, and clothing. Internal factors that affect heat gain include the metabolism and muscle activity. The greatest concern for the endurance athlete in the jungle is the combination of prolonged exercise in a hot and humid environment, with little or no wind. Sweating is compromised by the saturated air, which severely inhibits our ability to lose heat.

Depending upon the intensity, physical activity increases metabolism 5-15 times above normal resting levels. Approximately 70-90% of the energy produced is heat, which needs to be dissipated to maintain normal functioning. The proteins and enzymes required for life processes begin to slow down when the cells approach 40 degrees Celsius.

Heat is usually lost in our breath and via the skin. The heat in the core of the body is taken to the blood vessels near the surface of the skin, from where that heat is then transferred into the cooler outside air. ***The problem in the jungle is that the outside air is hotter than our skin temperature, which means that our body's normal mechanisms to cool down do not work!***

The only means by which the body can cool itself during exercise in a hot environment is via sweating, and this mechanism is far less effective if the air is very humid. Sweating works by moving water from the blood and glands out onto the skin. From there the water evaporates into the surrounding air, and the energy involved has a cooling effect on the skin. The problem is that if the air is saturated, then there is nowhere for the sweat to evaporate to. If the body cannot cool itself, then the core temperature will rise and exhaustion will very quickly ensue.

The body attempts to maximise cooling by increasing the rate of sweating. The body produces sweat in an attempt to cool itself, but there is a very limited effect. In this case, not only should the athlete be concerned about the amount of heat that they are gaining through exercise, but they should also be concerned about the amount of water that they are losing through sweat.

The sweat comes from liquid in the blood. The blood carries plasma, which is more than 90% water, along with various nutrients and waste products, in addition to cells (red cells, white cells and platelets). When we sweat, we begin taking some of that water away, and we have to compensate for it. The blood is naturally 'topped up'

161

by water that exists in and around the cells of the body. When this happens the cells will be less 'healthy' and will no longer be able to function as well as if they were perfectly hydrated. Water regulation is managed by the electrolytes, such as sodium, which are lost in varying concentrations in the sweat. Sodium, potassium, chloride and other electrolytes, are all kept within very particular concentrations within and without the cells of the body. If water is lost from the blood, the cells, or the spaces in between cells, then this will affect the concentration of electrolytes in those areas. To help prevent imbalances, electrolytes are lost in the sweat to maintain internal balance (homeostasis).

Unless the lost water is replaced, the volume of blood in the body will decrease. This has serious repercussions for the whole cardiovascular system. Our heart rate is determined by how much blood our heart pumps around the body each minute. Because there is less blood, the heart has to pump faster to compensate. If one is used to exercising at a particular workload (i.e. speed), then the heart will now have to beat faster to be able to maintain that workload, or else one will have to slow down in order to maintain the usual exercising heart rate. If exhaustion is usually achieved at a particular heart rate, then it will be reached much sooner if blood volume is reduced.

So, we are at risk of exhaustion as our temperature rises above 37 degrees, and we are at risk of exhaustion due to an increasing heart rate. Not only this, but more and more blood is being directed to the skin, so as to aid cooling. In doing so, blood flow to the working muscles, as well as the organs, is declining, which creates an additional limiting factor to performance. This increased blood flow to the skin has also been found to decrease blood pressure, and to further increase heart rate in an effort to compensate.

The increased heart rate is an attempt to maximise cooling whilst still preserving other requirements, which in our case includes exercise. However, the attempt by the heart to preserve the total amount of blood pumping around the body each minute eventually fails, and this value, our cardiac output, begins to decrease. Our heart is beating faster, but it is still not sufficient to meet requirements for exercise. *As a general rule, heart rate will increase by four beats per minute, for every one percent increase in dehydration.*

Some studies have found that exercise in a hot and humid environment leads to decreased oxygen availability within the muscle cells (as one might expect if blood volume and heart rate have decreased, because they are transporting less oxygen). In turn, the body has to rely upon less efficient means of energy production. Endurance runners use oxygen to produce energy, and tend to exercise at a level that limits the production of lactate. Lactate is produced during exercise from the breakdown of carbohydrates, when not enough oxygen is reaching the muscles. Associated with this process is the burning sensation that develops and often promotes feelings of muscular exhaustion. This anaerobic energy system is particularly inefficient, using a lot of carbohydrate to produce a little energy. If we are not getting sufficient oxygen to our muscles, then we will exhaust our carbohydrate stores far more quickly than if we use the more efficient aerobic systems.

163

Furthermore, because the muscles are becoming hotter (due to the failing cooling mechanisms), the cells become less efficient and cannot effectively utilise the nutrients within them. Thus, it takes even longer to convert nutrients into energy, and those nutrients are then used less efficiently and so yield less total energy. This, in turn, further contributes to the exhaustion of energy supplies and a decrease in performance.

Ultimately, it is core temperature itself that predicts when we stop exercising, regardless of the level of intensity. Endurance athletes have been found to tolerate higher core temperatures than other people, but during an event such as the Jungle Marathon we are truly pushing ourselves to the limit.

Heat acclimatisation results in improved efficiency for losing heat. Someone that is acclimatised will sweat less overall, will have a lower salt concentration in their sweat, and will lose heat more effectively than someone that is not acclimatised. Studies have found that in the absence of acclimatisation, it is the level of aerobic fitness that best predicts how efficiently someone manages their heat loss (specifically, the studies reported improved capacity for heat loss in the subjects that had the greatest weekly running mileage).

Managing Hydration

Maintenance of normal levels of hydration (euhydration) is essential for optimal exercise performance. This allows for effective heat

164

dissipation, via increased skin blood flow and sweating rate, and maintains blood volume (and therefore blood pressure, heart rate and cardiac output).

Effects of Dehydration:

- Decreased sweating rate at a given core temperature
- Decreased skin blood flow at a given core temperature
- Decreased maximal sweating rate
- Decreased maximal blood flow
- Increased core temperature at which sweating begins
- Increased core temperature at which skin blood flow increases
- Increased core temperature at a given exercise intensity

(List adapted from research article by Casa (1999). See Appendix for full reference).

Our capacity to perform endurance exercise becomes significantly reduced once our body has become dehydrated to 2-3% of total body weight. Dehydration must be avoided by matching fluid consumption with fluid losses (primarily urinary and sweat losses). Some athletes have attempted to 'hyperhydrate' in an attempt to increase their water stores and prolong exercise. Early studies that supported this were generally flawed, as they tended to compare hyperhydrated subjects with dehydrated ones. Hyperhydration is only a transient state, as excess water is quickly removed from the body. Maintaining normal hydration is far more effective during prolonged exercise than attempting to hyperhydrate beforehand.

Athletes can lose anything from 1-2.5 litres of water per hour during exercise in the heat. ***With such a huge amount of variation between individuals, it is strongly advised not to consume fluids based solely upon general recommendations.***

Fluid replacement needs to be based upon individual requirements. The goal of fluid replacement during exercise is to maintain a level of hydration within 2% of normal body weight. Thirst is generally not perceived until an individual has already reached 2% dehydration. Studies have shown that athletes that remain effectively hydrated will have lower core and muscle temperatures than those that are dehydrated. Efficient fluid replacement during prolonged exercise reduces carbohydrate usage, improves cardiovascular function and temperature regulation, and improves athletic performance. Following exercise, any water deficit should be compensated for within two hours of finishing. This will allow the cells to work optimally again, and facilitate effective recovery.

On an individual level, each athlete must learn to match his or her own fluid intakes with fluid losses. This can normally be managed by measuring changes in body weight. Typically, the amount of fluid ingested should be 25% or so greater than that which is lost, so as to account for subsequent sweat and urinary losses. Even if such calculations were made in advance, the novel environment of the jungle would create different requirements to those associated with other climates. For this reason, each athlete should be attentive to his or her own needs, and seek advice if they are not confident that their strategy is effective.

Beverage Composition

Fluid-replacement beverages should contain 6-8% carbohydrate, in the form of glucose and/or glucose polymers (such as maltodextrin). Beverages with a higher carbohydrate concentration are not recommended as they slow the rate at which the fluid empties from the stomach. The blood is maintained at 6% glucose, which is necessary to maintain the energy requirements of the brain, and for the transport of glucose to other cells where it is needed for energy. Consuming a drink with the same percentage of carbohydrate as the blood allows for quicker absorption, so promotes hydration whilst simultaneously supplying the body with energy.

The primary electrolytes lost in the sweat are sodium and chloride, with potassium, calcium and magnesium present in smaller amounts. The sodium concentration in sweat dictates how much water can be lost from the cells. Hence, maintaining optimal sodium levels is essential for maintaining the correct volume of water in the cells and in the blood. One adaptation to high sweat rates is that the sodium concentration of sweat is reduced, thus helping to preserve optimal water levels throughout the body. This adaptation takes three days or so to occur.

Consuming water on its own further dilutes the blood's sodium concentration. This can ultimately have disastrous consequences, such as hyponatraemia. It is important to appreciate that hyponatraemia, which is potentially fatal, can simply result from the replacement of sweat with water alone. *Hyponatraemia does not necessarily follow the consumption of water in excess, but simply the replacement of lost water without sufficient sodium.* Hydration is managed most effectively when lost sodium is replaced, and for this reason alone it is essential that some is present in a fluid-replacement beverage. If someone is intending to drink only water, then it is imperative that they make other plans to take in sodium too. This is most important during the first few days, after which the amount can be significantly reduced.

So, uncompensated sodium losses have a negative affect on cell and blood volume, and increase the risk of hyponatraemia. Conversely, ingesting sodium will preserve cell volume and function, preserve blood volume, and promote hydration and temperature regulation. Furthermore, decreased sodium concentration in the blood leads to the thirst mechanism being switched off. If someone does not take in sufficient sodium, then even though they are becoming more and more dehydrated, they will not feel thirsty. The reverse, therefore, is also true. Someone that manages their sodium intake effectively will have an optimal thirst drive, will consume more water as a result, and will be better hydrated than someone that does not. Salt consumption of between 0.3 and 0.7 grams per litre (equivalent to 0.1-0.3 g/l of sodium) can be sufficient to offset sodium losses from sweat, and to reduce the risk of muscle cramps and hyponatraemia. This amount should also be sufficient to stimulate thirst and increase fluid intake, and should not do any harm.

The inclusion of the other electrolytes, namely potassium, calcium and magnesium, is often superfluous for the majority of activities. The levels of these minerals will usually be replaced by a normal post-exercise meal. However, their concentrations would certainly fall during the number of hours spent exercising in the Jungle Marathon. The potential danger for the athlete, comes from the precise balance of electrolytes required in the blood and cells of the body.

Sodium exists in balance with potassium, and the levels of these need to be kept constant in order to maintain homeostasis (balance) within the fluids of the cells and the tissues in between them. An overdose of any one mineral, such as sodium, could have disastrous consequences, not just for performance but for health as well. Hence, for athletes participating in endurance exercise over many hours, particularly in an environment such as the jungle, a balanced electrolyte formula may be far more healthy and effective than water or water plus sodium alone. This further emphasises the importance of replacing *lost* water, *lost* sodium, and *lost* (other) electrolytes. By overdosing on one, performance and health may be catastrophically compromised.

The kidneys are responsible for managing water-balance within the body, and these are the organs that may be damaged by an excessively high electrolyte concentration in the blood. Furthermore, the different minerals are involved in the body's acid-base balance, and a disturbance to this balance can affect both cellular and organ function. Even if the athlete chooses not to care for his or her health, the fact that affecting acid-base balance can promote muscle cramps, spasms and dehydration, as well as other markers of performance over a period of days, is of particular relevance.

It is recommended that any fluid-replacement beverages be tried in training prior to the race, so as to discern which ones the body deals with the best. Some may have particular ingredients that cause stomach discomfort. Fluid consumption during training increases the weight of the stomach, which in turn increases the stress on the supporting connective tissue, and can lead to a stitch. Due to the necessity to consume fluids during the race, it is recommended that they be consumed in training, as this will strengthen the connective tissue and reduce the likelihood of a stitch during the event.

Conclusions

Endurance exercise in the jungle presents some unique challenges to the athlete, far greater than those experienced in most other environments. The key is to prevent core temperature from rising too far. Once it has risen more than a degree, everything becomes less efficient, including how one cools oneself, how the cardiovascular system functions, and how the muscles work and produce energy. Only a small level of dehydration is necessary to begin this process, and the effective maintenance of body water levels is essential for managing body heat, optimal health and exercise performance.

Back to the Jungle

We arrived in Santarem during the night. Following a bus ride along dark roads, we reached Alter do Chao and made our way onboard the boat. This year's competitors had missed out on the views of the Amazon from the plane. By way of recompense, however, we had been treated to a half-day excursion around Rio de Janeiro between flights. The heat had been magnificent and the sky was a rich and pure blue. From a church in Rio we had clearly seen the statue of Christ upon the hilltop, and had made haste to catch a train to the site. Once there, to prove that fortune does not always favour the brave, we all stood in thick cloud. It had been during the ride up that the clouds had commenced their little jolly. They were carried on winds that brought the most refreshing vapour to us on the train. Stood at Christ's feet, we had all been poised, waiting for that one glorious moment when the grey shroud would melt away and Jesus would be revealed to us. It was not to happen, and all of us left with similar shots of an unidentifiable solitary mass, covered in dense, dismal cloud.

The best part of our time in Rio, as a matter of fact, had been lunch. Naturally the opportunity to gorge ourselves on the superb and fresh buffet food was a pleasure in itself. The restaurant had been particularly grand, although the three-person lifts did have to perform a number of trips to bring us all up to the first floor (we had been unable to discover a staircase, I promise). What I enjoyed most of all though, was the company. It was so wonderful that we had only met each other during the journey, and yet we could sit together and converse and laugh and jape as if we were all friends that had known each other for years.

I had leapt upon Vicky and Karen at Heathrow, and it was fantastic to see them again, returning to their roles in the medical team. Kyle was back as well, and I met Andrew, James, Ben and Freddie, all representing the medical team. The athletes were easy enough to recognise at Heathrow, too. I introduced myself to Mayhem and Nobsey first, then Steve from the previous year, some Danes, and so it went on. I recall that I was strolling around the terminal building greeting every stranger in race gear; the competitors were not a difficult pride or coterie to recognise.

Onboard the boat I found some space on the starboard side and prepared my hammock, the ropes having to be crossed over the ropes of other hammocks as we all took whatever room was available. It was during this process that my old friend John appeared at my shoulder to greet me, beaming grin and all. I was shocked to see him for a moment. I knew that he would meet me on the boat; we had been discussing this race and its build-up via texts, emails, Facebook and Skype for months. Somehow, in becoming so absorbed with getting myself to the boat and sorting my kit, it simply struck me as absurd that any friend from the real world should be with me on a boat in the Amazon. The amazement passed and reality returned; we shook hands and exchanged manly hugs and banter as I made myself at home. John had flown out from Dubai earlier, and had been one of the first on the boat and so was nicely settled in already. We chatted until we were defeated by our need to sleep, although in truth the battle had lasted only minutes, and we duly retired to our hammocks for the night.

As the boat set off along the Rio Tapajos I felt bafflingly calm. I enjoyed the warm night's air, the humidity, and the gentle rocking of the boat as I drifted off to sleep. I was overjoyed to see John again after many months of us being in different countries, and I carried a wondrous excitement for the race ahead. I knew that I could do this; I knew that I would not be fast enough to win, not by any means, but I knew that I could manage myself well in the environment and carry myself across the distances required.

My only concern, in all actuality, pertained to my health. As the physiologist it was expected that I could not fall ill through dehydration, because I apparently knew so much about it. But, as I could only tell myself at the time, one can never know how the body will respond to endurance exercise in such a hot and humid climate (or certainly not without experience). My previous visit involved mostly walking whilst rationing water. This time I fully intended to push myself to the limit. If I collapsed due to heat exhaustion, dehydration or hyponatraemia, then I would never hear the end of it. Such concerns could only be managed, however, during the din of the battle. Education aside, the rest was a matter of awareness of how my body would respond to food and fluid intake, during exercise in the

173

jungle environment. Such matters would be tested in the jungle, and for now all I could do was relax in my cradle as the boat rocked me to sleep.

I awoke, predictably, following the sunrise in the early morning. I tried to hide from it but as others began moving around I had found myself encouraged to do likewise. I headed off to a lower deck for a breakfast of eggs, fresh fruit and a coffee, which I then enjoyed on the upper deck in the morning sunshine. As the sun reached higher into the cloudless blue sky the temperature soared. Men that were happy to be topless for a few hours soon had their t-shirts draped across their shoulders. Hats and sunglasses were on, and the suntan lotion was out. The upper deck carried a slight breeze, as well as the pleasure of the sun, whereas the lower decks were darker, slightly cooler, yet without the breeze. There was such a hustle and bustle down there; so little space with people moving everywhere, that I capitalised on time on the top deck, only retreating below when I needed to cool off in the shade.

Beneath a small canopy that offered marginal shade on the top deck sat a team of athletes from Guernsey. Julian had rallied the support of several of his staff at Schroders (current and former), and here they all were, doing their best to do what we were all doubtless attempting to do; to not think about what we had gotten ourselves into. The whole team were in visibly high spirits, as Julian presided over what might have been his flock, exuding a palpable confidence that spread amongst them and either filled them with motivation or dread. It was far too early for me to see anything through the smiles and laughter, but I had a feeling that if Julian was going to finish, then the rest of them were going to be finishing too. In coming here they were raising in the region of £115,000 for Headway Guernsey and the Rainbow Trust. John, Anthony, Nick, Brian, and Michael, along with their illustrious leader, had been training for about a year for this race, building up to around a hundred kilometres a week of running. Not too bad at all, considering Julian was the only one with ultra-marathon running experience. Brave, brave men; such little experience combined with the stress of all those sponsors and their boss. At least if I buggered up the race I could just skulk off and nobody but me would know. In any case, they were maintaining a brilliantly positive perspective on their ambitions, and I found myself envious of their shared camaraderie and common ground.

Just before midday the boat came to a stop, and some of us took immeasurable delight in hurling ourselves overboard and into the cool waters of the Rio Tapajos. The waves were calm yet a fairly strong current persisted; we had to work respectably hard simply to remain alongside the boat. Still, the bliss of cooling off in the river, even if some effort was required, was wonderful. We climbed back aboard before we had allowed ourselves to work too hard.

The boat continued to the shore of Itapuama and we disembarked onto the beach and progressed to the huts. This was the same as before; the army took the hut at the back on the left side, whilst the majority of athletes headed to the hut to the right. John and I headed left to a third hut, and tied our hammocks up there. Angus, joining us from Australia as part of the support team, tied his hammock up adjacent to ours.

I was wearing my Karrimor sandals at this time, and was less than pleased with my reintroduction to fire ants. They teemed everywhere, but appeared only to bite if the skin conditions were right, due to particular combinations of temperature, natural oils and sweat, presumably. I suggested this because neither Gus nor John was affected at first, whilst the little bastards were eating me alive. Perhaps they had just been missing me. I recalled meeting with these during my first visit, and one does become desensitised after a while to the myriad species vying for some flesh and the opportunity to cause irritation.

We had just about made ourselves at home, when the time came to untie our hammocks and take all of our food, medical and survival equipment over to the administration/dining hut for kit checks. We collected our race numbers and route books at the same time. That completed we tied our hammocks up again and John and I went off for a stroll along the beach. The afternoon temperature was dropping and grey clouds had hidden the blue sky. Further on, black clouds were looming and the sound of thunder from some miles away across the river threatened a downpour soon. It is the rainforest, I reflect; they do happen.

On our journey we met a few other competitors simply taking some exercise, including Daryl: back for another year and looking as wickedly strong and fit as ever. I had been reliably informed that he had arrived some weeks ago and spent his time charging up and down the steepest climb in the Amazon for hours on end. But then I had also been reliably informed, by the same chap in fact, that I would be wearing Skins with embedded ice crystals, so one cannot trust all the gossip in these events. I nevertheless made a point not to be too surprised or disappointed when he finished ahead of me. I was certainly glad that he was here; bloody good chap that he was and splendid and intelligent company too.

The clouds arrived above us and the heavens opened. John and I sought refuge from the rain beneath a tree, and whilst there perused various nooks and crannies for signs of wildlife. We took some mean satisfaction in tapping a spider's web to see the resident come dashing out for nothing but our offending twig. The spider was neither as big nor as exciting as we had hoped.

When the deluge subsided we headed back, as the evening light was fading and more rain was on its way. I had the distinct pleasure of seeing an old friend at the administration hut; it was the bombeiro that had previously pointed a revolver at my head. He spoke hurriedly to a Brazilian girl that posed as his translator: "The jaguar hunter!" Oh no. Oh ground that has been so faithful to me all these years please swallow me whole at once. He had arranged for the same girl to thank me at the end of last year's race for 'rescuing him from the jaguars'. I distinctly recall, however, that it was *he* that was gallivanting off into the thickets and pausing to listen out for the thing. *I* was there purely for the morale of the racers, whereas he was the one stalking the undergrowth for his quarry. This was all very unfair.

The rain returned during the night, testing the roof of our hut beyond its limit. Water dripped through, and John and I clambered from both our sweet sleep and comfy hammocks in order to erect our own shelter from our bashas. Gus appeared to be sleeping deeply as, in our mutual good natures, John and I ensured that our bashas created a roof that protected all three of us. I am fairly sure that Gus was aware of what we were doing, but that he pretended to sleep in order to avoid conscription to the shelter-building party.

The morning came and I delighted in what I anticipated being my penultimate shower until after the race. Today was the briefing phase of race preparation. I had missed out on this last year because I had far more exhausting activities to occupy my time. Gil Serique was on hand to act as the rather animated and whole-heartedly fervent translator for us. The main briefing was given by a soldier, who proceeded to allude to all sorts of wonderful stories about the various inhabitants of the jungle. I had already learnt a little about the various snakes, spiders and so forth, so much of this was revision of detail but with an introduction to fairly useful photographs. The razor grass came out for our inspection; the bane of my woodland wanderings in 2007. A British television crew was on hand, and they lapped up everything that could be taken to be sensational.

Essentially, the briefing covered what could kill us, what looked like it could kill us but probably would not, and what could leave us simply smarting a tad. In the evening it was the turn of the medical staff to give a briefing, to which I had been seconded. Kyle discussed some general medical information, and Ivan focussed specifically on foot care and treatment. He informed everyone that *"...the race cannot be won on the first day, but it can be lost on the first day..."* I liked that. He meant do not play silly buggers and risk becoming written-off for the rest of the week.

When my turn came I pounced upon the opportunity to bore for England on the subject of exercise in hot and humid conditions. Most, but not all, of the competitors had received a particularly long and in-depth article from me on this (remarkably similar to the previous chapter of this book, as a matter of fact), but this was an opportunity for me to present to those that had not received it, as revision for those that had, and for me to answer questions from everyone. The majority of questions were predictably specific to particular brands and dosages. Answering such questions required some diplomacy, as I could not very well inform someone that the product they had brought with them was god-awful. In most cases I only had to recommend additional salt to their electrolyte solutions and energy drinks. Manufacturers often include too little salt as it affects palatability, but people exercising are more likely to crave salt, so a higher salt content would not have any negative consequences for them (consider that the actual consumers of energy drinks are people wanting 'energy' to get them through their working day, rather than people actually generating a high heart rate and losing salt and fluids in sweat).

One clear consequence of my briefing was that many competitors had resolved to bite into their salt tablets before swallowing. This was for two reasons. Firstly, by breaking the tablet up they would be able to taste it, which would give an indication of how much they actually required salt. If salt tastes fairly plain and quite edible then one has probably become a little deficient, in which case eat up. The other reason was that by breaking it up in the mouth they would stand a better chance of digesting the tablet before Christmas. Solid vitamin and mineral tablets can often not be effectively digested, or even not at all, and so in this instance it is more appropriate to break the salt up. I prefer to use an isotonic electrolyte drink, and then I carry a bag of table salt that I use to supplement sodium intake. But each to his or her own, of course.

Many athletes were also not aware that hyponatraemia is not simply a consequence of ingesting too much water, but rather that it can be similarly induced by replacing normal water losses without sodium. In other words, some people will suffer by consuming many litres of water in excess of their requirements, whereas others will suffer by replacing lost water and sodium with water alone. The concentration of sodium in the blood will be low by both mechanisms, and the outcome (hyponatraemia) will be the same.

The key point that I tried to put across was that salt intake should not be too high, as this may cause imbalances to overall body electrolyte and water composition. It is far more appropriate to use a conservative approach and respond as required. Importantly, sodium requirements drop over the course of the first few days as the body becomes acclimatised, and the sodium concentration in sweat is reduced. What I do not like about salt tablets is that people can take them as if they are Smarties, and if they have the misfortune of actually breaking them all down in their stomachs then they would be in real trouble. Out here the consequences could be drastic, because even blood tests can only give a snapshot of what is happening in the blood; if salt is still being broken down by the digestive system then blood levels could vary significantly over a matter of minutes. That makes treatment incredibly complicated.

It had not escaped my attention that the television crew, which had been so intent on reporting on all of the excitement and awe of the physical dangers of the Amazon, were absent during the evening's medical briefing. I feared an agenda to show the Jungle Marathon for all of its dangers, and to avoid mention of all the efforts incorporated to limit risk and protect racers. Having written that, I must also confess that in my opinion a race such as this is essentially an opportunity for us to be given daily (staged) goals on our journey to the finish line, with water provided to help get us through. The medical and support teams are here, along with various contingency plans, but I feel that the onus should be on the athlete to take care of themselves. This is the jungle for goodness' sake; there is hardly likely to be an exclusion zone for all wild animals, nor wide, paved tracks to ensure runners have no trip hazards and medical teams can reach them in an instant.

I apologise, and I shall now proceed to dismount my soapbox and cease championing the cry of many a race organiser. Races are under a huge threat of extinction due to health and safety controls and athletes that have accidents and blame such accidents on the course, when clearly any responsible race organiser goes to the greatest of lengths to ensure that their athletes are taken care of. The small number of accidents in any adequately risk-assessed race is testament to this. People seem to delight in hailing a run as dangerous, when one really has to question what expectations the athletes have, and how realistic they are. There are always the city marathons, if people prefer greater safety and predictability. The *Marathon des Sables* can appear ultra-safe because the terrain is so easily accessible by 4x4s and helicopters. That is combined with the fact that the MdS has so many competitors that the revenue can finance a vast medical contingent. Such possibilities are out of reach for the majority of smaller races. I prefer smaller races, so I do a little more to understand the areas in which I compete and ensure that I have the most appropriate medical and survival kits.

There. I have now broken up and burnt the aforementioned soapbox, so I can return to the build-up to the race. I promise. Anyway, I forgot to mention that between briefings we had a kiddies marathon, in which the children were gathered up from all the local communities and brought here to Itapuama. This was the first chance that so many children could meet, as travel between the communities is not common, even for the adults. So, we took great enjoyment in seeing all those children talking and playing together, and then later on they had a series of short dashes along in the sand. The atmosphere was joyous, and the Sun had even made the effort of appearing so as to grant them good weather.

Another task had been sorting kit and returning to the boat anything that we would not be running with. We had been self-sufficient since our arrival, so our bags carried a surplus of food for these first couple of days, as well as whatever other luxury items and extra kit we might have wanted. Sometimes one does not know quite what to wear, for example, until actually experiencing the conditions of the event. Nobody ever knows how many socks they will need. John had very sportingly lent me a couple of spare pairs of his Injinji's, as mine had not arrived from the U.S. in time for my departure. The Injinjis are toed socks, which require a little messing about to pull on, but prevent the toes from rubbing against one another, thus reducing the potential for blisters to form between the toes. We packed our rucksacks for the race, and ensured that everything else, save some food for the rest of the day and the morning, was stored back aboard the boat.

As night fell John and I returned to our respective hammocks. The enchantingly beautiful and fair-haired Holly, a teenaged member of the support crew and the daughter of Julian, had replaced Gus. The latter had been despatched to a checkpoint for the first stage of tomorrow's race. It was an acceptable swap on the basis of looks, but Gus did possess the better jokes (and was equally fair-haired).

Holly pretended that she needed to swap locations within the hut, so as to retreat from the thunderous sound of someone's snores. John and I were confident, however, that the real reason was that she was so impressed with our basha-roof and childish sense of humour, that she had simply pounced on the opportunity to be closer to us. Had this ever been true, which in all honesty I doubt very much, then she must have regretted it the moment John sparked into life with a tirade of inappropriate jokes (not inappropriate to Holly specifically, but rather to humanity in general). John and I wiled away the rest of the evening rating those snores on a scale of one to ten. They rarely fell below a triumphant six, and occasionally exceeded a thunderous eight.

Stage I: 18 Kilometres

It was still dark when John and I awoke from our slumbers and made a start on preparing ourselves for the race. We were to begin racing at 06:30, shortly after sunrise. The generators had sparked into life at 04:50, giving us ample time to breakfast, shower, and organise our kit and clothing. Athletes scurried about, tending to themselves similarly, and gathered like insects around the best sources of light for their personal administration.

It was time for another ritual; just like that first training run. The clothing goes on in a particular order, because that was what was in my mind and it ensured that nothing was forgotten. I had pulled on my Salomon tight running shorts, and wore the same Salomon's standard running shorts over the top of those that I had worn in training. My top was also from Salomon: a black spray-on-looking vest. I had chosen all these because I liked the tight fabrics against my skin, as opposed to baggy fabrics that would create air pockets and attract heat, and which also would have had the tendency to become snagged and torn. I would not require sunglasses when in the jungle; only on the last day along the beach, if at all. The tight materials also helped protect against beasties climbing into my clothes.

The Injinji socks that John had lent me were ankle high and a fraction too small, which meant that when I pulled on my Salomon

XA Pro 3D shoes it looked as though I wore no socks at all. That worked for me though; there would be less material to soak up swamp and creek water, which meant less water to drip into my shoes. With such short socks, I hoped that my feet would be more prone to dry out than if I were in a longer pair. As well as the Salomon clothing, I would also be using their Raid Revo rucksack. I had used their trail running shoes in the desert, and I had been so pleased with them that it gave me some confidence in the rest of their kit too, hence I was trying it all out here. I also wanted to use Salomon because everybody else seemed to favour Raidlight, and I had always strived to be a little bit *outré*, and so it would be with my clothing and equipment too. In fairness I was not alone though; my fellow athletes were sporting plenty of Salomon shoes, clothing and rucksacks themselves.

My medical and survival kits were kept in small dry-bags in the top pocket of the rucksack, along with food and gels for the day, my headtorch, and a large dry-bag to place the rucksack into for water crossings. I had a dry-bag within the rucksack, which acted as a waterproof liner to save my kit from becoming wet. I would use an additional drybag around the outside when negotiating wide rivers, as damp rucksack fabric could take a considerable time to dry. Wet, it would be more easily damaged and it would be heavier too; an important point as so much of my kit had been selected based on its weight. My Platypus water bladder had its own pocket within the pack, and a purpose-made hole permitted the drinking hose to be brought around and secured onto a shoulder strap. I mixed up some energy/electrolyte powder with water in the Platypus and secured the hose in position. The rest of the pack contained my spare clothing (socks), food, and bottles of energy/electrolyte powder.

Once dressed and with all equipment organised into my rucksack, I applied the obligatory sunscreen and took my anti-malarial tablet (Malarone). John gave me some help applying tape to my hips, lower back and shoulders, just as he had done during the good ole days of the MdS. I duly returned the favour. I taped up my first and second toes, as they were the most vulnerable to bruising. My only criticism of the Salomon shoes was that they, like all the other brands I liked and experimented with, were not made in a large enough size. These were a U.K. size 12.5, which is just about right, but I usually favour the space of a size 13.5. When my feet swelled my toes would begin to take a pounding, and then I would be likely to start bruising toes. It is the price to be paid for big feet and a fussy taste in shoes.

Because the initial part of the run included a dash to a short river crossing, many people were going to start in flip-flops or sandals and change once on the other side. Did they not realise that within the first half an hour their feet would probably be soaked anyway? Faffing around during that one section would cost time and save the feet nothing at all.

As the sun rose, out of sight beyond the jungle to the east, the air remained pleasantly cool and still. We headed over to the start line. At 06:30 the race commenced and we charged off across the sand, along and down the bank, and within moments we were heading down into the creek. The crowd of racers had formed a queue as we were brought to a walking pace. I removed my rucksack and held it above my head as I crossed, with the water reaching my lower chest. On the other side many racers were sitting down and removing sandals. They would be drying their feet, pulling on their socks with some difficulty over moist skin, and then pulling on their shoes. So much time lost! The rest of us moved past them and headed up another bank into the jungle proper. We were still walking. I was beneath the canopy now and on the narrow forest trail. Still walking. They were walking out of choice!

I requested to pass and they made some space for me, and with that I was off. Every now and again I would reach a small group of racers at a slower pace than me, and would have to ask if they would be so kind as to make room. They invariably would, although some were less obliging than others. Along such narrow trails it is almost impossible, and quite often dangerous, to try to work out a route adjacent to the path in order to pass others. Hence, those in front must stand aside for those approaching faster from behind.

The trail undulated, a consequence of which was that on the uphill sections more people were likely to be walking or pausing for breath, which gave me the opportunity to pass them. Sometimes I would walk at their pace though, so as to recover from the bout of running that had brought me to them. The temperature had risen with the Sun, but it did not seem to be anywhere near as severe as the previous year. That stifling, choking humidity had been withheld thus far, hence my reason for keeping to a good pace. I wanted to cover as much ground as possible because, when it arrived, the searing jungle heat and suffocating air would hinder my progress.

Stage I

I met up with Jason fairly early on, and stuck with him. His pace was good and it made sense to team up for a while. I was probably faster than him on the climbs, but we shared a similar speed on the flats, and he would disappear off on the downhill sections. It took us an hour and fifteen minutes to reach the first checkpoint. James and Angus ensured we were in good health, and they and the bombeiros helped to fill our water bladders. Jason left ahead of me, as my Platypus took longer to fill and coax back into my full rucksack, but I caught up with him soon enough.

After leaving the checkpoint the terrain was almost exclusively hills. The climbs were gratifyingly tough and forgivingly short. The downhills were dangerous at speed, but it was our choice to carry ourselves along them so fast. Flat sections were virtually non-existent, but then to suggest that everything was a hill would be a matter of perspective. Some undulations were far kinder and subtler than others. Some were utter bastards.

The flat sections that did exist tended to incorporate swamps. This had not been the case the previous year, but resulted from unusually high rainfall in the days prior to the start of the race. The route had been altered to take this into consideration and make it more manageable, but shallow swamps and creeks had to be negotiated in any case. I took some pleasure in seeing the water escaping from my shoes whilst no rubbing seemed to be occurring. Furthermore, whenever my feet entered a creek or swamp, I experienced great relief because of the coolness of the water.

Some razor grass did a good job of lacerating the skin around my left Achilles heel. The open cut was sore and tender, and being so close to the ground it was forever being scraped by roots. At one point a Brazilian competitor passed me and unwittingly kicked a fallen branch into it. Pain surged through my leg more acutely than ever. Until then I could only blame myself; somehow it seemed spiteful that someone else should join in the game of causing me discomfort, by attacking such a vulnerable and tender area. Had he punched me on the nose and stabbed me in the stomach it would have hurt far less.

One factor of the Jungle Marathon that has not hitherto been mentioned is Rod. I had always considered that Rod was that typical special forces chap that could be dropped into the middle of a jungle with nothing but a penknife, and who would promptly snigger to himself and stroll into the nearest pub, even if that were perhaps a hundred or so miles away. Rod was a superb character when I met him the previous year, and I admired him for a no-nonsense approach to everything, including most people.

Another pertinent facet of Rod's character was his perverse satisfaction in striving to make the race as tough as possible. He would manage the river crossings, for the long stretches that lay ahead of us in the days to come, but in the meantime he busied himself by rigging up enforced rope crossings and similar along the rest of the route. One fairly deep creek had to be bridged using two taut ropes; one positioned for the feet and the other for the hands. This was fairly straightforward for anyone with a sense of logic. One stands on the bottom rope, perpendicular to the bank, and then leans forwards onto the other rope. Hence, I climbed on and side-stepped my way across in a few paces, and could not understand what all the fuss was about, and yet many people appeared to be trying to dance on the thing and invariably gave a magnificent display before plummeting into the creek. They must have just been showing off, surely?

The second checkpoint, which was on an incline and barely big enough to swing a small snake, came shortly after that creek crossing, and was womanned by Vicky and Karen (well it could not have been 'manned', surely?). A similar nature of jungle persisted after that and then Jason and I came upon the third checkpoint, manned and womanned by Ivan and Holly respectively. The only things of note that occurred between those two checkpoints were that Jason fell into a swamp, which had not been a premeditated move on his part, and soon afterwards pulled a tree down on top of me. The latter situation had not been deliberate either. Jason stepped onto a fallen tree, which promptly cracked and fell a few inches to the ground, but in doing so brought down a much larger tree on top of me. I had been trapped behind his first fallen tree when the second fell on me. I caught it in my hands and was relieved it was dead and had rotted through. At a living weight it would have probably driven me into the ground like a peg (although one would hope that I would have used my hands to push myself clear of its fall).

From the third checkpoint it was a very simple two to three kilometres downhill and onto the beach for the finish. The last section should probably have been longer, but may have been shortened due to the effects of excessive water where the trail should have been.

Jason and I crossed the line, hand in hand, at 11:00, having worked hard but far from any point of exhaustion. We had managed ourselves admirably, in my opinion, and we had plenty of room to work harder during the second stage. I always feel that I hold a little in reserve during these races. I wanted to spend the first couple of days understanding my fitness levels and abilities. Experience alone would permit me to push harder, and I was reluctant to force the issue out of fear of failure to complete the race, which could so easily follow from burning myself out or making a hydration cock-up or whatever else.

The first day had been a success, so that gave me plenty of time to tie up my hammock, have some food and fluids, and then head off down to the river for a bath and the opportunity to wash my clothes. Many of the stages would finish by a river, and if I could clean my clothes each day then I would feel far more comfortable in them, compared to how I would feel if I left them filthy from the swamps and brushes with trees. I hung up my clean Injinjis to dry for the next day, and threw a spare pair of socks in the bin.

In terms of hydration, my intake of water and electrolytes had been adequate but there was room for improvement. I had only urinated twice during the run itself, and my third would not be required until the evening. During a race such as this, urination should be frequent and it should be colourless. Mine was coloured sufficiently to suggest that I was between two and three percent dehydrated (urine colour charts are available on the internet but due to copyright reasons I am unable to include any here). Over the next couple of days I would need to vary electrolyte concentration, to see how it would affect hydration, palatability and performance.

On a brighter note I had no blisters, although the skin under both first toenails had become bruised, but I had expected that. The number of downhills, combined with their steepness and the twists and turns, had encouraged those toes to be squashed into the tough front of the shoe, far more than would have been the case along flats. Tomorrow I would ensure that the lacing system was pulled sufficiently tight, so as to prevent my feet from using whatever space they had to move forward and back. Decreasing impact stresses on the longest toes would help prevent the blisters worsening, or at least slow their development.

Quite impressively, some razor grass that was hanging from a tree had caused three parallel cuts along my neck, which many people likened to claw marks. I conceded to the bombeiro that I had indeed been arsing about with jaguars again. In retrospect I could not actually recall when I had cut my neck, and so the cuts there were news to me. One has so many cuts and scrapes in the jungle that should anything actually draw blood, then it is but one event amongst a hundred, and I had no idea when or where this had happened. How it had happened was simply a matter of logic (as I was sure that nothing exciting had actually clawed at my throat).

The afternoon was spent applauding and cheering the other racers across the line, and all of us congratulating each other. I enjoyed spending some time with Mayhem and Nobsey, Holly, Angus, John and various members of the medical team. I also met

Dan, another fine Australian chap here as part of the support crew. During the early evening I went for a stroll with a couple of Danes, both named Per, and one of whom had joined us for the first 100 kilometres of the race the previous year, but had ultimately attended as a photographer. He was here this year to run the full course. He was the chap that informed me that I looked like a nerd. Anyway, we strolled along the riverfront to investigate some astonishingly vast webs that John and I had come across during a previous wandering, and were fortunate enough to observe and hear a number of monkeys in a distant tree.

Later on we were given a briefing by Shirley, regarding the nature of the second stage of the race. Shirley alluded to another day of numerous climbs, with three particularly impressive hills to focus our minds. Thanks to the rains we could also expect plenty of mud and swamps to move across. How delightful.

The evening was spent with friends. We each chatted about our own adventures from the day, and listened intently to the stories of the others. The sunset was as spectacular as could be. In point of fact, emerging from the jungle and reaching the finish line, it was fairly difficult to think much about the day that had passed at all. It seemed as though the day's race finished upon the threshold of paradise; that blue river, the white sands and the tropical heat. To experience that with newly found friends made it a far deeper and more meaningful experience than I could possibly do justice with mere words. However, I shall nonetheless have a frenzied stab at it: It was uplifting, pure, righteous, gushingly wholesome and wondrously heavenly. These constituted what I might someday reflect back upon, within that mental log of important experiences, as more *good times*, and the happiest of times. Not bad for a footrace through the rainforest.

Stage II: 25 Kilometres

The night had passed beautifully for me. I love sleeping in a hammock; it feels as though I am floating. There is a trick, of course. One has to make certain that the ends are tied sufficiently far apart to ensure that the hammock is fairly flat. If it sags excessively then once it has some weight in it then it will sag still further. The consequence of this is that one sleeps as comfortably as if in a trouser press. The more level it begins the better. Further, by sleeping across the hammock, along the diagonal, it feels flatter still, and far roomier.

Some, however, might have tied their hammocks perfectly and yet still experienced a poor night's sleep. A couple of trees fell down during the night. Hammocks had, in some cases, either been tied onto those trees or else were positioned along the path the tree took to the ground. Nobody was hurt, but it is never good to have a troubled night amidst such a mentally demanding race. I was fortunate enough to have slept through this undisturbed. The gravity of the matter, as it were, only occurred to me as I listened to the banter of my fellow runners the following morning.

I was using a Special Forces hammock, which had two layers so the centre could be used for storage (or for me if it became cold). The two layers could also be spread apart to make an exceptionally wide hammock. It was not as light as the more popular Hennessy hammocks, but I preferred the more traditional style of mine. The Hennessy hammocks require entry from beneath, via a Velcro hole, and many an hour can be wiled away listening to Velcro tearing apart and arses thudding to the ground.

The race commenced shortly after daybreak. We started heading back the way we had come at the end of the previous day's run. The open ground was water-logged, but with almost a hundred runners all wanting to make good progress, we avoided the best ground if it meant we could get further ahead. We knew what was coming. We reached the other side of the flat, where the narrow path began at the base of a particularly steep hill. We were forced to a walk. The walk became a climb. We waited; those above us waited for those above them. Somewhere someone would be delayed whilst negotiating a particularly slippery or steep section, and that had a knock-on effect for the rest of us. My advice to future runners; sprint off that start line and stay ahead going up that initial section of trail; just do not trip on the fallen trees that litter the ground before the climb!

As the hill flattened, many of the athletes were moving at a fast walk. I was becoming jumpy with anticipation of the run that I wanted to lurch into, when I was suddenly shot in the back of the head. A fallen tree trunk lay across the trail at chest height. I ducked beneath it but as I stepped forward and rose, my rucksack connected hard with the trunk, and something was knocked with force onto the back of my head. I could not discern whether it was a sting or a bite, but the explosion of pain was incredible; I had never known anything like it. Out of a natural reaction my left hand shot up and my hand clasped around it. Whatever it was had a fairly hard and brittle skeleton or carapace, I could not tell which, and it was perhaps an inch or so in length. I had crushed whatever it was in my hand as I detached it from my head. My arm and hand extended out to the side quickly enough to ensure that it was flung clear of me, before it could sting or bite again. All that I had to go on was the feel of it. Obviously not a snake, but then it could be a small spider, a small scorpion or a very large ant.

There are many ants in the Amazon. Some of the largest can cause a person to collapse from paralysis and suffer fever-like symptoms. I hoped that if it was an ant then it had not been one of those. A scorpion seems unlikely because whatever it was fitted so easily into my hand. A Bullet ant, perhaps? It had not wanted to let go, that was for sure. There were reports that would come later of someone that was bitten by one, and a second person had been unable to pull it clear because of the ferocity and strength of the bite. I think that the ant had to be killed and pulled apart before the head came free. Adrenaline had permitted me to ensure that whatever it was came free from my head; I was certainly beyond thinking at the time. A Bullet ant was the most likely culprit, but the pain, even after the villain had been disposed of, was horrendous.

I had not slowed during this, out of the fear of shame of causing a fuss or inconveniencing my fellow racers. Besides, we were only walking and the whole thing was over within a second, from bite to release. I attempted to shake the pain off as I gathered myself to a run. If it had been something poisonous, then my running would have the poison acting very quickly, and I could be laying on my back and frothing from my mouth in no time. Hopefully the worst that would come from this would be discomfort. I hoped. It was a concern for some time, mostly because of the pain. It hardly dissipated and my head throbbed relentlessly for hours afterwards. Welcome to the jungle.

It was a long, tough leg to the first checkpoint, comprising of some good and tough climbs. I greeted Angus and James at the checkpoint and James obligingly checked my head for fang or pincer marks. I was flabbergasted to hear that there was no visual evidence to account for the agony in my head. How unfair. I would have expected a pulsating boil, developing nicely beneath two vast, gaping stab wounds at the very least. Nature can be so cruel sometimes.

I made progress away from the checkpoint: passing some athletes and joining others for sections as I went. I met up with Sophie from England, and three Americans; Rob, Kevin and David, who were entertaining us with renditions from the American Rock Hall of Fame. It was great; it broke up the day brilliantly to find myself enjoying such an enthusiastic singsong. They attempted to cease every now and again, but others would heckle and demand for more. Along a steep and slanted descent we went; across a narrow creek and back up the next hill.

I reached the swamp first. Sophie and the three American chaps were right behind me. A section of water was perhaps two metres across; too far for me to risk a jump from such soft ground. A rotten log to my right bridged it perfectly. It took my weight and I edged my way across. The ground on the other side was 'interesting'. It was saturated and disturbingly boggy. With some steps my feet would sink a few inches; with others they might descend as much as a foot beneath the surface. I tried to keep close to the trees and exposed roots; anything to give me purchase and lessen the likelihood of getting both feet trapped in deep mud. I would be unlikely to lose a shoe, but it would be hard going to make progress. A foot became stuck on one occasion and I promptly fell over, making matters considerably worse.

As I moved on, perhaps a quarter of the way to a rise that marked hard ground about fifty metres from the creek; the others arrived at the log. Sophie was over first, and she waited for the others. One of them was stung; he declared as much as he stood there perplexed. His friend joined him, and was promptly stung too. Then they were both calling out that they were being stung, and then it was all of them. They must have disturbed a nest. *"Wasps!"* I called out, *"Run!"* I made a mental note that if anything ever stings me that I must not stand there in observation of the fact, but rather make progress away from the area as swiftly as possible. Most things here sting or bite in defence, either of themselves or their territory. By moving away from their area in either instance the threat is removed, and the need for defence is equally diminished. Unfortunately, wasps are demanding of significant distances between their aggressor and their territory; and they will pursue someone a good distance from their nest. In such a situation you might be running for a mile before they lay off their counter-attack.

I made for the hill as quickly as I could, calling back and encouraging the others to run too. If I was stung by just one of them then it would attract others. There was nothing to be done but create distance between ourselves and the nest. I was tired enough from my flailing in the mud but had to push myself to run up the hill when I reached it. I was exhausted; hot and panting. This was not how I would have desired to run in this race, but the circumstances dictated otherwise. Again, welcome to the jungle.

I emerged from the hills onto a high plantation. Without the protection of the canopy the heat soared the moment I left the trees. It became uncomfortably hot and I was forced to walk to save myself from overheating. I turned a corner and happened upon the second checkpoint. At last! Vicky and Karen were there to greet me and we organised my water between us.

Whereas I had been moving swiftly and efficiently through each checkpoint of the race thus far, I was now too hot and needed to cool. Taking this opportunity to do so in the company of two of the medical staff seemed to make the most sense. I lay on my back on top of my rucksack on the floor, beneath the cover of the small building. I ate some food and drank plenty of fluids. Vicky and Karen would check that I was doing okay, and I confessed that I had become a little too hot and would not risk moving on until I felt more comfortable.

The boys arrived and left. I moved off with Sophie and enjoyed a chat for a while. We walked, which was fine for me, although Sophie regularly invited me to pass. I was reluctant to push myself though. In the midday heat I needed to look after myself. I had become sufficiently uncomfortable for it to warrant concern. There was nothing that I could have done to prevent it, other than to have moved slower, and that would have been unnecessary. It was perfectly acceptable, in my view, to push myself to the point that I felt uncomfortable, and then to recover. In the heat of the day, however, it had taken longer than I would have liked to return to a comfortable temperature. All we can do is be aware of our condition and manage ourselves accordingly.

After a while I felt confident to run again for a while, and bade Sophie a good journey. I met up with Rob and David not far from checkpoint three. Rob was lying down by the side of the trail, and I took the opportunity of a brief rest. I sat down next to Rob, and it did not take long to appreciate that he was not doing well at all. He was too hot and feeling quite out of sorts; not well enough to continue on just yet. Cooling off in the shade was a good decision, but he appeared to be passing in and out of consciousness. Another runner arrived and I asked him to let Ivan at checkpoint three know that there was a runner in need of assistance. Ivan duly arrived and I headed off. We had not been more than three hundred metres from the checkpoint, but had no way of knowing because of the density of the jungle trees and due to the checkpoint being at a lower elevation.

I reached the checkpoint, greeted Holly and Rod, and topped up my water. I then put my rucksack into the dry-bag and jumped into the creek. It was only five metres or so across, but it was too deep for me to want to carry my rucksack above my head. I had not rested at the checkpoint because I had rested sufficiently just before it. I climbed out of the creek, strapped my rucksack on, and headed off along the trail. I met Dan just beyond the creek; he had walked in from the finish and assured me that it had taken him and his companions (soldiers) more than two hours to reach this point. Deep joy. It was a relentlessly hot day, or at least I hoped it was. If it was not then my internal thermostat was totally buggered up.

Per, the Dane who was competing this year for the first time, caught up with me when I had once again slowed to a walk. I was simply too hot to run. Or rather, I knew full well that if I ran, then as my body heated up I would be unable to cool. I felt that I was already on that brink; operating at the highest temperature that I could safely manage, above which my health had the potential to spiral out of control. I did not know how *real* that feeling was; I had never pushed myself that hard. It was more the fear of the unknown that made me desire to move slower and with greater care of myself. I had made good progress today, but I would be moving much faster in a couple of days' time once I had become better acclimatised.

Per and I walked on together. After a while even at our walking pace we felt hot and fatigued. We stood on opposite sides of the narrow trail and promptly collapsed down onto the ground in unison. We lay atop our rucksacks and ate, drank and relaxed for about a quarter of an hour. That was longer than we felt we needed, but that was why we *knew* it had to be about right. Cooling down takes so much longer, because the body is so inefficient at it out here, so more patience is required than might be acceptable when training at home.

The trail was flatter in this final leg than it had been for any of the race up until this point. We reached an area that I knew to have been the campsite the previous year. But there was no sign of the finish banner, nor other competitors. In fact, we did not have any trail markers here either. We were near a settlement, so local children might have removed them, or possibly some runners that wanted to make it more 'interesting' for the rest of us.

Per and I dropped our rucksacks to the ground and split up, checking all possible routes off the site for footprints. After a delay of a few minutes we picked up the trail, gathered our kit, and continued on our way. The trail led down a hill to a creek where I had bathed during my first visit. Some fallen logs lay strewn across the trail, and mindlessly I allowed my shin to connect with one as I made to climb over it. The pain was far from pleasant, but as it was a familiar pain, unlike the morning's bite, I accepted it and shook it off without fuss. I moved to climb over another log and did exactly the same thing with precisely the same area of shin. That really did smart, and this time I grimaced and growled through gritted teeth.

On the other side of the creek, we progressed along a good distance of path before we encountered an impressively steep climb. This presented us both with a good challenge, as we had to check for secure footholds and avoid loose ground before we could scramble higher. We reached the top, after which we had flat ground thereafter. The heat seemed to be increasing. The path widened and we were exposed to the naked Sun, unprotected by trees as we skirted the borders of plantations. Eventually, and most definitely not before time, we came in sight of the Tapajos. The community buildings came into view, along with a football pitch, and Per and I ran together across the line, hand in hand as we did so.

Per announced that he was off for a wee and a wank, and I announced that I was going to collapse. I walked past the first tree, because I did not want to appear too weak, and promptly laid down against the second. This was conveniently located next to a massage couch, where Freddie was tending to the walking wounded. He kindly checked up on me, and I confessed that I would be content to remain here until I felt comfortable enough to put up my hammock. A moment was spent admiring the haematoma on my shin, developing nicely from the one-man log-kicking championships earlier. The logs had definitely beaten me though.

I lay there, taking on more water and gradually regaining a more civilised body temperature, and saluted the other runners as they came across the line. This was really most impressive. I lay there, my top off but draped across my shoulders, my back on top of my rucksack and against the tree, and I was drinking water from a water bottle (I carried a water bottle as a reserve, with the mindset that if I emptied the water bladder, then I would have to be careful and ration out this final 750 millilitres to the following checkpoint). I was simply too hot to want to put up my hammock. Having run and walked for half the day, I begrudged ten minutes of effort to organise my sleeping arrangements.

I did eventually feel healthy enough to move off and find an appropriate site for the hammock, ensuring that there would also be space for John to tie up somewhere close by as well. Once that step was mastered, I decided to head off to see the medical team so that they could tend to my feet. Beneath the first and second toes on both feet I had blood-blisters that had swelled and were putting pressure on the nail-beds. This made them exquisitely sore, and I needed an expert opinion before I commenced playing silly buggers with a safety pin and a cigarette lighter.

I was having a chat with Freddie when Kyle appeared. Kyle had a trafiner: a pen-sized implement with two connected wires protruding from the edge that, at the touch of a button, became red hot and can efficiently burn through nail. Freddie seemed more than pleased to have a play. Although my second nails were bruised, I was experiencing no pain from them, so I would leave them for now. The more damage I cause myself, the more that I have to deal with. Making more holes in me than necessary also increases my risk of infection. Watching the trafiner's burning tip touch the nail and begin to burn through it was a respectably squeamish affair for the first hole. Obviously burning through the nail itself did not hurt, but I feared for the tender skin beneath. The metal proceeded through and the blood and pus was released. The relief was magnificent. Nor was there any pain, as there was sufficient distance between the top of the blister and the skin beneath. Both nails were drained and I then taped them up, thanking Freddie for his superb work, and Kyle for the use of his red-hot implement.

Stage II

Rob arrived shortly afterwards and in a very poor condition. Two outdoor showers were available here, and Rob was sat beneath one to aid his cooling. Unfortunately Rob's condition deteriorated. He was brought into one of the community buildings and laid down on top of a massage table. He was pale and his face appeared waxy. Freddie, Kyle and Sally (support staff) tended to Rob, and I assisted as best I could. Rob took in two I.V. bags and promptly projectile vomited more than any man has ever projectile vomited before. I had been stood next to Freddie as I held the I.V. bag, whilst Freddie replaced the old one. We could not move out of the way because of what we were doing. The vomit hit us both square in the legs, quite clear in colour and as warm as might be expected. We did not react or attempt to move away at the time. Then, carefully, Freddie and I delicately and gingerly moved out of range just in time for the second round.

Whilst the medical team was busy tending to Rob another competitor arrived. Roy was a big Canadian lad, and he was in agony. He had also been attacked by wasps, and as a result of such a high number of stings, he was paralysed down one arm and a part of his neck. The giant lay on the floor, squirming in pain and kicking out, as Kyle rushed to his aid.

Once all had apparently calmed down I went off to take a shower and to (finally) have some food. I had become so preoccupied that I had been neglecting myself. Their need was greater, obviously, but now was the time to look after myself. Even this proved difficult. Many other athletes were either suffering from diarrhoea or were forcing themselves to be sick, or else just wanted advice on their food or hydration strategies. I was surprised at how many people thought I would know precisely what they needed to do. All I could advise was the most universal information, and when it was with regard to their stomach problems, I had no means of knowing what the cause was, so could only give an indication of generalised positive courses of action.

At this point, anything that I could do to provide relief for the medical team would probably be appreciated, and if it was hydration-related then helping people now was better than having them deteriorate later on. The person that was putting his fingers down his throat was not being the most sensible. He felt sick but that did not mean that he should have encouraged it. His body was still trying to do something with the mess in his stomach, and it would no doubt relieve him of the contents when good and ready.

As for me, I was still dehydrated and hungry from all my rushing about since the end of the race. I still had not managed to eat anything. Jeremy came in next and was soon in the medical building. He had been suffering from severe muscle cramps, which were a potential consequence of a significant water and electrolyte imbalance. The muscle cramps generated muscle spasms, which were so strong that Jeremy was hyperventilating as his body attempted to oxygenate the muscles. His hyperventilating then compounded the problem within the muscles, exacerbating his cramps and spasms. His whole body was being affected by the cramps, as he curled up and his legs, stomach and arms all contracted rigidly and spasmed uncontrollably. It took some time before he could lay flat and appear to be in any degree of comfort. Kyle spoke with him throughout, comforting him and talking him through what was happening and how he could help himself. Kyle's manner and professionalism was impressive to say the least.

Jason came in next; my running partner from the previous day. When I saw him he was lying on the ground and Freddie had inserted an I.V. tube. I held the bag, allowing Freddie to tend to those more in need. As soon as the fluid began going into his arm, Jason appeared to have a breath of life go into him. I knelt down at his side; my arm outstretched aloft to hold the bag, and chatted with him about what was going on. All of the runners that received I.V. solutions experienced stomach cramps, and Jason was no different. At least by this stage I could talk him through it and I did what I could to help him relax. Jason was back to normal in no time and was soon making his way off to tie up his hammock and have some food.

By the time I got back to my hammock I decided to take a Dioralyte to aid my own rehydration. It helped enormously and I joined John, Sally and Paul (another competitor and Sally's lesser half), for food and banter. My legs were being inundated with flies, which simply adored the numerous lacerations to my lower leg. I had not felt any pain to alert me to the cuts, so I gave them a good spray with Betadine, which seemed to help keep the flies at bay for a short while too. It was great to see the two Australian support guys, Angus and Dan, before I turned in for the night, but they were soon dispatched off to their checkpoints for the next day.

Amidst all the activity of the afternoon we had also been treated to some torrential downpours. They had not lasted for long, but had produced small water channels in the sandy ground, and a large lake beneath my hammock. As I lay in my hammock in the evening I found three ticks nuzzling into my skin. One was on my leg, another on my chest and the last one on my shoulder. I prised them off and returned them to the wild from whence they had come. This was an issue with the heavy rain; it brought such critters into drier areas where they might not normally venture. A little hungry and a little thirsty, but in good company and recovering at last from a tough day, I drifted off to sleep.

Stage III: 43.8 kilometres

The start was expected at the break of dawn. This would be a particularly long and hilly day, perhaps the toughest due to its combination of distance and a few good climbs. In contrast to the first two stages, we would have plenty of flat sections, thus giving us an opportunity to stretch our legs and enjoy a good, hard pace. After today, the onus would be on distance rather than climbs, so in my mind I considered that any fears of not finishing should be quelled by the end of this stage.

We awoke at 04:30, in the dark once again, and began organising ourselves for the off. The morning air was certainly fresh and cool, and with a mind focussed on preparation, the early start was never unpleasant. Just to put this into some sort of context, I am the sort of person that prefers to work extraordinarily late and then sleep through mornings. When I have absolutely no choice in the matter, then I tend to be of the opinion that if I must experience a morning, then I shall do so in the frame of mind that if I do not disturb the morning, then the morning will not disturb me. I am not, by even the most forgiving and generous stretch of the imagination, a morning person, yet I struggled to get out of my hammock not one bit. Had I awoken to a torrential downpour, then I might well have permitted the others a few hours' of headstart as I waited for the skies to clear.

211

My first duty was to tape my first and second toes, taking meticulous care to ensure that minimal stress would be placed on the nails during the run. Next I dressed, untied my hammock, mosquito net and basha, and packed everything away into the Raid Revo. The faintest hint of light splashed across the black sky as I was breakfasting. The suntan lotion was rubbed in next. I had given up on my one hundred percent Deet insect repellent by this stage. The mosquitoes seemed to regard it as a marinade.

I strapped John's back for him, and permitted him to Vaseline his privates without my interference. It was bad enough that he always insisted on reaching his hand into his crack in full view. It was almost enough to put me off my breakfast.

By this time, as the start of the race was expected to be near, we heard whispers around the camp that it would be delayed. There was some predictable frustration at such a possibility. Whilst I endeavour to be as understanding as possible, even I found some irritation in this. Breakfast, for example, had been timed to ensure that my blood glucose levels would peak during the start of the race, and be maintained for sometime afterwards. An hour's delay would mean that I would start the race feeling hungry, which, although manageable, would be an inconvenience I could do without.

I found Freddie, who was looking knackered, and discovered that he had been working through the night. Both Rob and Jeremy had taken turns for the worst having returned to their hammocks. Both had been evacuated to hospital, via the river, in the middle of the night.

I was stunned. Rob had appeared to be recovering steadily all evening. When I last saw him, he had been standing up, talking, coherent, and much improved from how he had been when he had arrived at the camp. A problem with severe heat stress is that the body can begin working against itself. The brain's hypothalamus contains the temperature control centre, for maintaining the body's homeostasis. When the body becomes cold, then muscles generate heat by shivering. When core temperature begins to rise, sweating commences and energy levels drop. If heat stress is so significant that it interferes with that control system, then the body can be shivering to generate heat even though core temperature is already elevated. The effects can be disastrous.

Hearing that Rob was in a coma in hospital was heart-wrenching. As in the Lakes, any taste for a run today was lost. I would run, if the race went ahead, but it would be with a sour taste in my mouth and with no enjoyment to be gained from completing this next stage. Rob was not someone I had known before meeting him on the trail yesterday, but there is a sense of brotherhood (well, siblinghood really) amongst racers in these events. These are all great people and it can hurt considerably to think of a fellow runner in distress.

Freddie and the rest of the medical team appeared tired and dazed from their having been helping people throughout the night. Given a hospital and all the staff that they would normally expect, they would manage and doubtless show no external signs of stress. Out here though it is back to the grass roots, and they were all doing far more work individually than they would be doing ordinarily. Furthermore, one becomes so tired in the jungle environment just by existing; hence people that live in these climes are far more likely to have afternoon naps than the rest of us at home. The medical team were not as acclimatised as the locals, were jet-lagged, and had worked through a long day and then all night. It was now the morning and they still had not slept. They had all worked incredibly hard. In addition, yesterday was an exceptional day, with the temperature and course taking their toll on the competitors.

On reflection, it seems most likely that so many casualties materialised from yesterday's stage because of the heat. The first day had been fairly mild, and the athletes had managed to push themselves hard and move quickly over some impressively challenging terrain. During Stage Two the temperature had soared into the mid-thirties, which, with close to a hundred percent humidity, had severely compromised the ability to cool for those of us who were unacclimatised. As our core temperatures rose we faced an incredible feat to prevent overheating, and this was compounded by the associated risk of severe dehydration and electrolyte imbalances.

Shirley called us to an impromptu briefing, with Freddie and Vicky at her side, and announced that due to insufficient medical cover we would not be racing today. Jeremy had been released from hospital and was making a steady recovery, whilst Rob remained in a serious, perhaps critical condition. Freddie reiterated the importance of awareness of heat stress, and with that, somewhat deflated, we prepared ourselves for a full day at the camp.

Stage III

One competitor had the audacity to complain to me that it was such a pity the stage had been cancelled, as if that was the most important thing in the world. I bludgeoned him to death with my mug and pounded his head into the ground, and then that look in my eye passed and I snapped out of my dream. I quipped something that it was a shame about Rob, and then conceded that once those considerations were taken into account, then somewhere down the line it was indeed a shame to not be running. As mentioned, even if we had sufficient medical cover I had no taste for a run today. I tied my hammock up again and went back to speak with the medical team.

There were, predictably, various complaints about the lack of a run today. Maybe it is just me; perhaps I am too sentimental or overly sensitive or whatever, but I could not help but have my concerns with the medical team and the casualties. One of the medical team was in a state, thanks to a competitor snapping at her and accusing her of being at fault, for letting Rob continue past a checkpoint, when he had clearly been struggling. Everybody had been struggling! It is down to the runners to manage themselves, not for the medical team, which is only here to help; to govern everybody's right of passage. They are here to patch up wounded soldiers, not to act as the gatekeepers.

Granted, if someone arrives that clearly will not make it to the next checkpoint, then they should be detained until their situation improves or they are retired from the race. Having seen Rob myself, I know that there was no way that anyone could have done more than she did. In these situations, some misinformed imbeciles pride themselves most highly for finding someone to waggle their self-righteous finger at.

The truth, as ghastly as it may seem, is that the only person responsible for Rob's condition was Rob. One can blame anything from a lack of experience in these conditions to a lack of fitness, or to a poor hydration strategy. Ultimately, Rob made the decision to come here and compete as he wished to compete. He recognised his own internal warning signs too late for him to be able to manage himself safely through the race. The very real danger is that Rob's condition was now regarded as critical, so there was a risk that he might not pull through.

One of the swiftest and apparently fittest competitors in the *Marathon des Sables* died in his tent during the 2007 race. He was one of over seven hundred and fifty competitors. Less than a hundred dropped out that year. Bernard, a family man a few days shy of his fiftieth birthday, passed away into the night having been one of the fastest competitors across the line on that day's stage. Who was responsible for his being there other than himself? Had a greater number perished then questions could have been raised regarding the safety of the race, but this was not what happened. The onus has to be on the individual, and I would hope that Rob would agree with me on that.

Various people pulled out of the race today. Many had seen or heard about Rob and Jeremy and decided that they could not risk themselves any further. Often, such a decision was based on vicarious experience, rather than personal experience. Rob and Jeremy were

Back to the jungle. The huts at Itapuama

Tying up hammocks and mosquito nets at the base camp

The sun setting beyond the jungle on the far side of the Rio Tapajos

The first major river crossing

A steep descent into a small creek. Although a delay to progress, they give a welcome opportunity to cool down

From creeks to swamps: Mud and roots force a walking pace until the ground firms up further along

Above left: The widest section of road encountered, combined with stunning views in first few kilometres of the long-stage

Above right: John having just completed the first long and gruelling river crossing

Below: Following a steep descent after checkpoint four, it is swampland and then an ascent to drier ground

Above: ~30 kilometres of white sands for a final stage to the finish line in Alter do Chao

Below: A very happy sprint finish: Locals, competitors and support crew cheer each of us over the line

both regarded as supremely fit and healthy. If they had been hospitalised after two days, then what might the remaining stages have in store for those that perceived themselves as less capable? In reality, the only person that can know how they will cope is the individual, and then only during the event itself. We had all worked hard yesterday, and most of us were now recovered or at least on the mend.

I knew how much I had struggled yesterday, and how I regularly conceded to the oppressive heat of the day and slowed or rested. I could have *run* faster, but to what end? Those who had made it through yesterday without becoming ill, simply needed to repeat the subsequent stages in a similar manner. For those of us who had become ill, we had to learn our lessons, seek advice if required, and put it all down to experience for the following days. To quit the race on account of seeing someone else become ill seemed very peculiar to me. Did they have such little confidence in themselves that they had to make such drastic assumptions? Did they consider that their training and fitness was inadequate? There were some that talked of quitting because they had families and responsibilities, but they had those before they came out here. So much seemed to be a matter of coming here with unrealistic expectations, following a lack of research into the risks and realities of exercise in the jungle. Perhaps I am being too harsh; too unfair. It all just seemed incredibly drastic and unnecessary. People could always take things easier and learn more from this experience for a better attempt the next time.

Naturally I received some snide remarks about how my article and briefing had clearly been useless, but fortunately this came from only a few imbeciles that had fingers they still felt compelled to wag. Although I went through the day in a most dismal melancholy, my heart was lifted by a high number of athletes that thanked me for the article and briefing. They would often tell stories about how one particular piece of advice had been tweaked to suit them, and how they had managed themselves through the day triumphant. I was happy because they were so grateful, and aware that a learning experience may have influenced their success where others failed.

I was busier than ever, with runners approaching me for advice and assistance. I would quite often be led off to someone's rucksack, where they had kindly laid out all of their food, energy gels and bars, and various tablets, powders and potions. It was a pleasure to feel useful, and I would finish and then search out those I had given advice to previously, to see how they were getting on. Sometimes food and hydration strategies need to be fine-tuned once another day's worth of experience has been gained.

One of the Danes was suffering terribly with diarrhoea. He was reluctant to take an Imodium for it, as, like me, he preferred to take care of his organs and limit his intake of pharmaceuticals. I approved of his charitable considerations towards his liver, but suggested that this was the right time to take something. Granted, if it cleared up in twenty-four hours, then that would be the best possible outcome. However, if it did not, then he would be doing himself no justice by running for the next few days with, well, the runs.

The remainder of the day was spent playing cards and engaged in banter with the other athletes and support teams. The

218

television crew did leap on me for my considered opinion of the events that had passed. Expecting to be quizzed on physiological matters, as they had discussed with me, I was instead faced with a barrage of medical and pathology-related questions. On those I could only reiterate what I had gathered from the medical team, but it was not my area of expertise at all. In the end they did not use any of it anyway.

I reflected afterwards that I had been far too chipper; illuminating them as to how this was a simply marvellous event, and that anybody with a high level of aerobic fitness could stand a fair chance of getting through. I refused to concede that it was a dangerous event for Britishers, as it was not. Like many things in life, the JM is a dangerous event for anyone who is unprepared, unfit or inexperienced, or combinations thereof.

Oh dear. One of the runners, a fast lad who was ahead of me on the tables, was becoming frustrated with his hammock's rain-cover. Why, oh why, do people do this to themselves? With no space at home I had been tying up my hammock, mosquito net and basha in my research office. It had taken an age for me to be satisfied with the arrangement of para cord, and holes cut in the mosquito net through which I fed the hammock's ropes. All of this had to be done so that when I came out here I simply unrolled the mosquito net and hammock as a single unit, and the basha could then easily be tied up above them.

I knew that the time spent fine-tuning the details, and learning the skills in the comfort of the office would mean that I had no such issues to worry my race-focussed mind out here. This poor chap was gathering himself such an amount of stress, all because he could not get the cover's orientation correct, and all of his ropes had become tangled and knotted together. Having just accused me of being an arse for my inability to play cards, I felt ever so slightly smug for his sufferings. And no, it is not that I cannot 'play' cards, it is just that I become so bored and distracted that I have no care and easily make gaffes that people assume are my means of cheating, but it is nothing nearly so callous and calculated. I would find it more entertaining to watch wood bow. Anyway, I showed him a better method for preventing his ropes from tangling, and went back to my place at the card table.

John and I had made firm friends with Holly. For some unfathomable reason she tolerated our company and was even gracious enough to laugh at our awful jokes. In turn, we were naturally grateful for the distraction of someone as young, fresh and with ambitions outside of the usual race and work-related ones. She was embarking on a 'year out' before commencing university, and would be off to Costa Rica and then Australia in the coming months. I had never been permitted a 'year out', but I am so happy in my life and feel that I am approaching where I want to be, that I cannot possibly have any regrets. Anything done differently would mean my not being in the position that I now find myself. I have a great job, wonderful friends, and a fulfilling way of life. I still envied Holly for her passion to explore and have wild adventures, which I am convinced is a rare a wondrous thing in a woman so young.

Stage III

Jason had kindly asked me later in the day if I was well. I had been looking deflated having dwelt on the events of the previous evening. He was certainly grateful of my assistance and the banter, for when he had been coming-to in the medical building. I suppose that the whole thing had been something of an emotional drain. Ordinarily I might not have been fazed, but there was an element of shock for my thought process, having been taken from focussing on the race to attending to casualties.

In the evening Shirley announced that stages three and four would be combined, but with a fair alteration of the route, to ensure that we would reach the site we needed to for the commencement of the long stage the day after. Stage Four is generally quite an easy day, intended to give athletes a rest before the long stage. We would be foregoing a portion of that, so as to ensure that we were still on target for a two hundred-kilometre-plus race, and staying at the camps we needed to. Later on I spent some time chatting with Nobsey and Mayhem, Per, and Paul and Becky. Paul had been my companion during the support visit the previous year, and was here now as a competitor with his other half, Becky, the fastest woman in last year's race. I went to bed at 21:15, late by comparison to previous nights, and anxious for what the next day might bring.

Stages III and IV: 45 Kilometres

I awoke at 04:45 and repeated the usual routine, before heading over to the start line with the others. Kyle had returned from the hospital and gave us another briefing on the dangers of heat stress. Rob was still in hospital, whilst Jeremy was now recuperating onboard the boat.

I edged towards the front of the racers at the start line. The track was wide and flat; the fastest ground we had had to run on thus far. As is usually the case, many people congregate at the start line to enjoy the spirit of a sprint start, but promptly slow to a gentler pace or even a walk within the first fifty metres. I could see this happening today, and reckoned I ought to be closer to the front to save me having to queue behind slower runners.

The countdown commenced and we were off. A number of us accelerated quickly ahead. To my delight one of the girls declared, "I can't believe how fast they're moving!" That gem was going to feed my motivation until at least the first checkpoint. We were still weaving in and out as we dodged passed slower runners. Many had set off too fast and when reality hit home they appeared to find themselves confused and bewildered and ambling along, but had reached quite an impressive distance from the start.

There would be no line of competitors queuing to pass the others today. The track was sufficiently wide to allow passing to take place quite easily. This was the first time that I had been able to run at my training pace. Until now, due care and attention to the branches on the trees, and the debris and roots on the ground, had caused me to reduce my stride length and pace considerably. This morning I could fling my ridiculously long legs out in front of me and stretch and stride and leap and bound along the trail.

I joined in behind Alistair and a Brazilian. Alistair, another English competitor, had maintained a position far ahead of me during the race until now. Following the good start, I was finding that our paces were more closely matched, and I hoped for a moment that I might be able to spend some time with him on the trail. That moment did not last long. I was having to boost my pace just a fraction above my training speed to keep up with the both of them. Long-term I knew that it would never work out.

As if the gods desired to underline the point, Michael, a German, hollered out to me from behind that I had just lost my water bottle. *Arse, bugger, bollocks, fuck!* My reserve water bottle had been kept in the rucksack's side pocket, and held in position by the weight of water. I knew today would start fast so I began the race with that one empty and only having water in the Platypus. I ran back and picked up the bottle as Michael and a string of other runners passed me by. I turned on the move and jogged after them, as I fumbled to shove the bottle back into the pocket, and strap the rucksack on. I was back to my running pace as I pulled the straps tight. I moved past that line and was on my own; Alistair and the Brazilian were long gone now.

I arrived at the first checkpoint in only twenty-five minutes, much to the surprise of Angus. I had hardly touched my water, so none was replenished. In the cool of the morning air it was no warmer than my late afternoon training runs in London. Well, perhaps it was, but I had certainly felt fresh at the time, and had not begun to sweat much or feel thirsty. Managing needs means managing personal needs; not forcing oneself to drink when not necessary, and not drinking too little because someone said 250 millilitres of fluid every fifteen minutes is a good guide. The best guide is oneself.

The checkpoint was just beneath the canopy, as we had come off the wider, dirt track, and found ourselves running through the jungle again. The trail was nevertheless far wider than what we were used to, or perhaps it was my imagination in my newly found sprightly state. There were plenty of open areas around communities too, meaning more open flats to run along. Speed seemed to be everything to me; I wanted to make as much progress as possible while the going was good. As soon as the midday heat approached, it would start taking its toll on my performance.

I came running around the corner of one community area and found myself on a dirt road by the Tapajos. The second checkpoint was close now. One of the television crew ran along with me and gave me an interview on the day so far. I was impressed he could keep up for a while, because I was still keeping to a good speed. Once again though it was a lost interview; discarded to the editor's room cuttings or erased into a cyberspace graveyard. I think that having described the easy temperature, open, almost humidity-free air, and the wide tracks that my line which concluded, "it's just like running around Hyde Park" was the chipper and smug nail in that ones coffin. My inane grin and genuine, heartfelt happy-to-be-here-ness probably helped nothing either.

I reached the checkpoint approximately an hour after leaving the previous one. Shirley, Karen and Vicky greeted me, and a few locals were out to applaud us into their community. A couple of Brazilians who I had not seen until this point promptly appeared along the trail behind me, and then disappeared up the hill beyond the checkpoint. I had stalled myself in topping up the little water that I had taken from the Platypus, and in my exchange of pleasantries with the team. Shirley informed me that a stinker of a hill was waiting for me just where the trail disappeared into the jungle. She was not fibbing, although I have found that the gradient of a hill is very much a matter of opinion and state of mind. The more tired, hungry and fed-up one might be, the more imposing the climb.

I moved past the Brazilians on the climb up, which in all actuality was not too grim, but simply the first climb of the day. The Brazilians did not seem too enthused with my progress, and so accelerated past me. They had far too much energy for my liking. The path from that hill was the familiar, narrow, undulating trail that I had come to experience during the easier parts of the first two stages. Hence, I was comfortable to run up many of the hills, rather than to walk, climb or cry my way up.

Fallen trees often blocked the trail, forcing a climb over or under, and these always slowed pace. Care had to be taken if going under to ensure that nothing nasty was ready to introduce itself as my new best friend. When going over, care was necessary due to the risk of slipping or the trunk falling. Ants often swarmed over such trees, necessitating a second look before placing a hand down for balance.

Despite a narrow trail, once again, I was satisfied with my average pace. I was making good progress amidst the gathering heat of the morning. I arrived at an area of swampland maybe two hundred metres across. Far down beneath the canopy, the light struggled to penetrate, which combined with the cooler, fresher air, to make the swamp appealing to all but by still-dry feet.

The water here was deep, dark and murky. As I made my way across the muddy ground to the edge of a channel, I removed my rucksack and held it aloft as I dropped down into the water. It reached high up on my chest, and I gently waded along; a fallen tree to my left to grab for should the world's biggest anaconda try to pull me under. I climbed out at the other end of the channel, hugged some trees and gingerly moved my feet around on the roots, and then had a further, deeper section to wade through. I was of course grateful that no anaconda-based adventure occurred. I was also grateful that leeches did not favour this region of the Amazon; otherwise I might not have had any blood left for crossing such an area.

I reached the third checkpoint at the top of an incline and out in the open. Ivan was there along with a bombeiro (my jaguar-hunting friend). The latter filled my Platypus as Ivan informed me that I was in twelfth place. Not bad, considering I had been around thirtieth after the first two stages. I left the checkpoint with Michael, who was the fastest non-Brazilian runner, overall. Our paces were disjointed and did not work together; we were faster than each other over different ground, and before long he moved ahead and off down the trail.

I soon came onto a plantation. Despite it only being 09:20, the temperature was scorching and an almost unbearable heat burned my face and skin. The jungle is humid, but that is relief compared to the unprotected, naked attack of the Sun in these exposed areas. I was reduced to a walk as I felt my temperature soar, with attempts to run during the short sections of shade doing little to raise my average pace here. I resolved to walk until I was back under the canopy. I was carrying a bandana with me, although I had not been wearing it. In vile truth I had still been feeling a little sick from before my departure to Brazil, and the bandana had been used as a handkerchief. It had been cleaned each night though, along with all of my clothing, and so I now drenched it in water from my bottle and placed the *clean* garment on my head. The relief was nigh-on orgasmic, although disappointingly not cooling for any more than two or three minutes.

The jungle was ahead, with Freddie manning the fourth checkpoint just beneath the canopy. It was 10:15 and I had fallen into seventeenth position, care of my little walk through the plantations. I filled up my Platypus and headed off. I was beneath the canopy for only a kilometre before emerging back out into the open. It felt like running in a sauna. I was prepared to half-walk, half-run the rest of the way, but children came out of their homes by the plantations to clap and cheer me on. I honestly could not bear to walk in front of them, and managed a sort of vaguely bearable jog/shuffle instead.

227

I reached the end of the community area, which was where the campsite had been located at the end of stage three the previous year. The route continued past that and down to the river, where the fourth stage had commenced. I fumbled to put my rucksack into the dry bag. Rod was on hand, managing the rope that stretched to the other side of the river, more than two hundred metres away, and declared that as much as he would love to help me it would have been inappropriate and I was on my own. Fair enough.

I shuffled into the water, held the rope, and happily collapsed on my back. Good progress might have been made with an adapted front crawl, but in all honesty I simply could not be bothered with it. I lay on my back, the dry-bag as a buoyancy aid resting on my chest and held in my right hand, the rope in my left, and I used a variation of the breaststroke to reach the other side. I had learned this stroke from my lifeguard training, and had been surprisingly quick through the water with it, and it used very little energy, care of my gangly arms and legs. I relaxed on my back, kicking my legs as I reached my left arm along the rope to pull me along, pausing after each kick and allowing my body to drift along on the surface, only kicking again a few seconds later as I slowed. The cool water of the river was so heat-quenchingly refreshing that I wished the river crossing had been extended by a mile.

The mind does wander, of course, and there was a sort of checklist being ticked of all the inhabitants of the river that potentially could inconvenience me. There would be caimans and piranhas, snakes, electric eels, stingrays and those giant catfish. None of them were likely to take the faintest interest in me, as long as I did not kick them or decide to start playing dead. There would be at least a hint of blood entering the water from my various scrapes in the jungle, but even though that might alert piranhas to my presence, they would not be inclined to introduce themselves unless I was already in real trouble. Piranhas can be soppy like that, which is to my benefit here.

I left the water and made my way up a slope to where Shirley had arrived and was sat upon a log. I sat next to her as I took my rucksack from the dry-bag and put it back on. We had a quick and pleasant chat, and I thanked her for the race and promised her that I was in my element, loving every challenging, thermometer-cracking moment of it. Another runner arrived at the far side of the river, and so I took that as a sign to leave and head for the finish, not too many kilometres away now.

From the river it was a wide, sandy road to the next community, which would be the campsite for the end of stage four; and the current amalgamated stage. There was no protection from the sun and in the heat I was feeling fatigued from my efforts. I half-jogged, half-walked for a few kilometres. As I neared the settlement the sound of music filled the air and came to greet me. Shakira? Curiously, and in difference to my usual taste in music, which favours Handel, Bach, Tchaikovsky and such like, and well, okay, that also tolerates the Chilli Peppers, indie, and some rock music, I did not mind this at all. Ordinarily of course, anything that can be described as 'pop music' would have had me vomiting with a tremendous enthusiasm. On this occasion, however (and one can only suppose

229

that it was an effect of the heat), it actually spurred me on to accelerate. I ran as fast as I possibly could for the last kilometre into the community, and sprinted across the finish line (magnificently, in my opinion). I shall never forgive myself, I can assure you.

It was shortly after 11:00, and I made my way to the area where athletes were tying up their hammocks. This was the campsite with the million colonies of fire ants, all awaiting their chance to consume runners alive. I had a chat with Daryl for a while, which was great. Daryl understands how his body responds to exercise and the heat and so on, and it is quite a breath of fresh air to hear him telling me what works for him, rather than asking for my opinion on it. As it happened, I had practically doubled the concentration of my hydration fluid in the Platypus, and found that I was experiencing my best (optimal) levels of water and electrolyte balance as a result. How I felt, the colour and frequency of urination, and even the way the drink tasted, all suggested that I had things in far better order than I had during those first two days. I had tried drinking plain water today as well, just as a test to see if I needed to adjust the concentration of my energy/electrolyte drink, and the water tasted ghastly, whereas I was craving the hydration formula. Not bad at all.

I left Daryl so that I could find somewhere for my own hammock. I promptly found an area on the edge of camp where the trees were of a good width of trunk and about the right distance apart. The problem was that there were not enough for John and any others that would be joining us. When John arrived, we organised our camp area a little more centrally, although still at the mercy of the ants.

Sally, Paul and Holly joined us as well, making it quite a cosy little camp. We put a basha down on the ground, and used it as an ant-free surface to lie back on, as we basked in the afternoon sun and enjoyed our typical gay banter.

I had my two first toes trafined again in the evening, as the blisters had re-formed. Once again, I enjoyed the company of the medical team for a good chat. A little later Holly came to inform me that a giant spider had been found within the main building. This was where I had escaped the rain with Jo the previous year. I walked around to the main entrance with her as she tentatively informed me it had been referred to as a 'Bird spider?' This was interesting, and hugely doubtful. I would love to see a Bird-Eating Tarantula, the largest spider in the world, but it would be fortunate if out of all the possible species it was that particular one that was visiting us here.

I went into the building and found a tarantula on the wall. This was not a foot-long, 6-inch tall Bird-Eating Tarantula; a species with inch-long hairs that it fires at its aggressors in defence and which act as an irritant. This was a fairly average, bog-standard hairy spider. It was not as big as the one that had ran across Al's foot during the previous Jungle Marathon. A Bird-Eating Tarantula indeed. I was most disappointed. I was content, however, to stand next to it upon a chair and shine a headtorch onto it so as to illuminate it for the television camera. Had I thought that it could jump the foot to my face then I might have reconsidered, but I imagined he or she was far too overwhelmed by their new celebrity status for any of that nonsense. Perhaps wildlife can be this way sometimes.

231

Tomorrow would be the start of the ninety-kilometre, long stage of the race. My concern was not fitness or the heat or hydration. I felt that I had sufficient command of all of those. What I worried for were my feet. They were fairly battered already, and I imagined that after a few hours they would become tender, and stay so until I reached the finish line, sometime before or after midnight. At least the following day would be to recover, as the final athletes came in. After that it would be a straightforward 'fun-run' along the beach to the final finish line of the race.

Stage V: 90.5 Kilometres

This would be it then, a reckoning of my ability to finish this event. So far so good, as the previous stage had been an effective confidence booster, and I was by now feeling noticeably better acclimatised. How long would my feet last before the pain became immense? Would I be whimpering across the finish line at the end of this?

Per had finished no more than half an hour after me yesterday, and I felt that as he maintained a fast walk that I should join him for the initial section through the jungle. I believed that if I walked fast through the jungle, then my feet would be less likely to kick every root and fallen branch in the Amazon, and they would consequently be in better shape afterwards. Once the jungle section was over, the rest would be open tracks, roads and beach until the end of the stage. I was already thinking of binning my shoes for the final stage along the beach, and race veterans Daryl and Becky had both agreed that this would be possible. Fourteens; if only they made good trail running shoes in a size fourteen, then my feet would not be made to suffer so much.

Per was intending to jog some of the jungle trail today, but agreed that we could team up. I wanted him to prevent me from bounding off and tripping up all over the place. We headed over to the river for the start of this true baptism of fire. We would commence with the fresh dawn air, persevere through the hell that lasts from mid-morning to early afternoon, and then battle on through the cool of the evening, tired, fatigued and in need of our hammocks. I wanted to finish in the evening, but knew that my bastard feet would be quick to stall my plans.

My rucksack went once again into the dry-bag. We gathered on the bank, restless, itching to be permitted to enter the water and make our dash into the unknown. I had waited for John at the camp for as long as I could, but he was traditionally last man to the start line, and I could have waited no longer. At least there were plenty of people in front of me; the river was wide enough for us to create distances between each other and move passed the slower racers, but importantly those ahead of me should clear the area of anything lurking beneath the surface. A hundred smelly people running into the river would probably frighten many of the inhabitants out onto the bank. This was a good section of river to cross: two hundred metres or so of flat and calm water.

The air was calm in the dawn light, and the sky clear, foretelling a hot day to come. The countdown ended and we marched into the water. There were too many bodies for me to safely manage a front crawl, and so it had to be a standard breaststroke. There was a rope, as before, but there were too many people around it and I progressed faster without it. Hands and heads met feet in the chaos of the swim. I exited the water and packed my dry-bag away whilst walking. I would have liked to run on this wide, flat section, but Per had to sit down to sort his kit and so I strolled on. It seemed unnecessary to be walking here, but it was all part of the plan; stick with Per, manage your pace, get through the fifty kilometres of jungle, and then have your feet in good shape for the final forty Ks.

Even at a walk I was passing people jogging. A long-distance pace has to burn as few calories as possible, whilst still being energy-efficient and maintaining a speed greater than which would be achieved when walking. I think that my distance pace is fairly respectable, but then I have a good walking speed too. If Becky's looks could have killed then she would have had me frogmarched back to the river, drowned, hacked to pieces by caimans and the remains devoured by the piranhas. I maintain that it had not been my fault *per se*, and there was certainly nothing malicious in my gait or expression. But when I strolled passed her as she ran I could not feel anything other than guilt, and I deserved every bit of the verbal abuse she sent my way. Well, I suppose that had I shouted "Morning!" in my typical facetious tones it might have been akin to pouring petrol on the flames. *Oh no*: I really do think that I did. I am sure she said that she would have hit me if she could have been enthused to run faster. I naturally apologised on behalf of my ridiculously long legs, and then permitted them to carry me onwards.

Per caught up and we both jogged together for a while, much to my relief. We were on a wide track beneath cover, and by the time the trail brought us out onto a wide, solid road, we were entirely by ourselves. A large group of runners had just disappeared down a slope to the front. We walked now, which gave us the chance to chat for a bit. When we reached the top of the decline, which was delightfully long and respectably steep, I educated Per as to the joint-saving enterprise of the controlled deceleration, and we rocketed to the trough, using our momentum to carry us a fair distance up the next side.

This road was certainly wide enough and strong enough to have a couple of heavy lorries passing. It must link plantations and logging areas with some of the towns and ports (possibly). As Per and I chatted about the world in general, my eyes kept searching the ground. We were halfway up the hill when I pointed out that the footprints could not belong to runners, as there were not enough of them. *Arse.* Per headed back down the hill and I continued to its brow. When I reached it there was a good view to the next hill, and no runners in between. There were no markers, and no reasons to suppose that they had taken this last hill so quickly as to be now out of view across the next one, which was a good distance off to the front. I turned and jogged down to Per, and we searched together for markers.

We found one, not far from the base of the hill that we had just charged down. Somehow we had not seen the marker or the thin entrance to the jungle, or perhaps we simply did not expect it to be there. We maintained a very steady jogging pace along the narrow, jungle trail, as we began passing people we had already passed once already this morning. I greeted Becky cheerfully once more. We claimed a desire to add an extra couple of kilometres to the stage, because 90.5 was a silly number. They laughed at us and we deserved every bit of it.

Stage V

We caught up with Daryl, who was also going unusually slowly, and he led us into checkpoint one. James was manning the checkpoint and Daryl took the opportunity for a break, whilst Per and I, having used no water during the mild conditions and easy pace, continued on. We felt a need to ensure that we were ahead of everyone that had overtaken us during our outrageous lapse of attention.

The hills, when we reached them, were long, high, and steep, even by the standards of the first couple of stages. Per and I relished the challenge and overtook plenty of other racers on our way up. Per also noted that whereas many people rested during and at the top of the climbs, we were fit and able to continue without the faintest hint of a pause. He put this down to acclimatisation and good training, and I concurred. It was certainly encouraging. I actually favoured the hills, and felt that I wanted as many as possible. I found them quite comfortable, because none were so high as to make me breathless. It meant that I had a faster average speed than many others that might have been faster than me on the flats, but not able to make good progress on the climbs.

The pace began to cause problems for me. Per's average speed was approximately five miles per hour, whereas my running pace is closer to seven or eight. My walking pace is a fraction over four miles per hour on good, flat ground. Hence I struggled to jog at Per's speed, and so would do a scout's pace; walk a given distance and then jog to catch up. It meant that when I ran I still had my feet connecting with roots and so on, which was going to cause me problems later on. Other than that, the pace being just above a fast walking pace meant that I was making better progress than I had expected.

We reached checkpoint two, and were refilling our water bladders when Daryl caught up with us, somewhat dismayed that we were ahead of him until we pointed out that we had not rested earlier. Out of checkpoint two the terrain was more of what we had just been used to; plenty of hills and winding tracks through close jungle. After that checkpoint, Per and I came off the trail twice as we spotted old markers and took them to be indicative of this year's route. We had not gone far before the trail came to an end, but it was frustrating to have to double-back. We had thought that we had gotten that out of the way with this morning's humiliating balls-up.

The trail flattened out not long after that checkpoint, and the going became far easier. This was most definitely a good thing. Per and I were both on our last dregs of fluid. I had a few mouthfuls left in the Platypus, after which I would be on the reserve bottle. When that happened, it would mean walking easily, and rationing the water as if in a survival situation. I would go from a racing frame of mind to one focussed on ensuring that my water lasted me until the checkpoint. Accurate maps of the trails do not exist, so it is not possible to ever know how far the next checkpoint is (potentially this could be managed with GPS, but the trail winds so much that distances would still be unreliable, especially as GPS can lose signal easily beneath the canopy). We knew approximate distances from one checkpoint to the next, but the reliability of such estimates were questionable, combined with experience of times over similar distances varying by an hour or more over different terrain.

We reached checkpoint three, where the television crew delighted in asking why 'Mr Hydration' had run out of water. I mumbled something about how maintaining optimal hydration was the reason that I had almost run out of water. Had I compromised on my hydration and consumed less fluid, then my water might have lasted but I would have been dehydrated. After my garbled justification I presented my full reserve water bottle and hoped that would stop them asking me anything else. Freddie mentioned that others had similarly depleted their water, and that the distance to the next checkpoint was even greater, so we should monitor our supplies closely.

We paused at the checkpoint to take some food from our rucksacks, and then moved off, eating as we walked. This was such a different game to the *Marathon des Sables*. By knowing the distances between checkpoints there, I could estimate fairly well when I should be in sight of the next checkpoint, and I would consistently be within fifteen minutes of that prediction. Here the terrain was so variable that such calculations were unworkable for me. It was just proving to be one more element that made the Jungle Marathon that little bit more challenging; presenting the runners with more to think about in their personal management and care.

It was going to be approximately thirteen kilometres from checkpoint three to checkpoint four, according to the map book. The distance to checkpoint three had been about ten-and-a-half kilometres.

I had been short of water for the last twenty minutes of a leg that had taken over an hour-and-a-half to complete.

Per and I caught up with Sophie. We had heard from Freddie that she had been keeping up with the lead female runner: a Brazilian who I had seen struggling on the hills during the first day. By now though Sophie was by herself. She had started to feel ill, with nausea and stomach problems. She joined us and we headed on towards checkpoint four as a trio.

There were only a couple of small hills *en route* to checkpoint four. I was relieved when we reached the steep gully down to the creek, where I had rescued Andrea during the previous race, so I knew that we were close to the checkpoint. The way down to the creek was treacherously steep and muddy. I went down grabbing roots, vines and trees for safety, or simply as something firm with which to lower myself down the slope. I slipped and fell twice, although no more than a metre or two each time. Because she was being daft, Sophie was following me and slipped and fell in precisely the same places that she had just seen me trip and fall. Per gave up on both of us and shot up the other side without waiting. I reached close to the creek and promptly stumbled and fell into it. *Marvellous*. At least Sophie refrained from following me in and just stood at the side and laughed at me.

Just as Sophie and I fell into the steep mud-caked wall that represented the trail, Per took a photo of us before disappearing off to the checkpoint. *Git*. Sophie and I scrambled up, although at times I was contemplating using my knife in an ice-axe fashion for greater purchase. We made it, and moved on. Per was back in view ahead and the three of us spread out along the trail for the last kilometre or so into the checkpoint. There were a few more bends in the trail than I could recall from my previous visit, but we arrived at the cut-off checkpoint with plenty of time to spare.

Ben and Andrew were there, along with Roy who had retired from the race after the wasp attack, but was now assisting the support crew. Per received a treatment to his back from Andrew, whilst Ben gave Sophie some attention. Daryl was lying in his hammock, recovering for a while before continuing on. I ate, drank and rested for just shy of a quarter of an hour. Having been advised to proceed together, for the sake of morale and such like, Sophie departed the checkpoint first, followed by me, with Per bringing up the rear. Sophie had left first because she was the slowest, due to her being ill, and I had left second to get Per back for leaving me to die in the creek.

Another steep, deep gully followed. Sophie and I, because it was our tradition, duly fell down most of one side, albeit in a controlled and seemingly expert manner. It simply had not been as graceful as it would have been if we had stepped down instead of slid. On the other side Sophie took an accidental detour, so focussed as she was on going 'up' that she missed where the trail led to the side. On the flat trail the three of us, having been reunited in the gully, spread out once again along the path. Per took the lead. Three-quarters of an hour later Daryl appeared and ran passed me.

Approximately eight kilometres from checkpoint four we emerged from the jungle onto the wider, community trails that lined the plantations and linked them and the communities together. We were in and out of cover for a while after joining the wide trails. That meant that we were exposed to the sun again, but I at least felt better able to cope with this than I had done when out on the plantations over previous days. I had completed the rest of this stage with Judah last year, so I at least knew what to expect. As I jogged, though, my toes felt distractingly tender; a dull ache had developed over the last hour or so, earlier than I had hoped. The nails were sore now, and this would become worse until I could take my shoes off at the end of the stage. I was in for a character-building forty kilometres.

I was heading down a slight incline beneath some tree cover when I caught up with Per. He soon had to stop to stretch his back, and so I took the lead and headed on. His back was in an awful state, mostly because he ran whilst holding his rucksack straps. Instead of his shoulders moving his elbows back and driving movement through the hips, Per had everything restricted between his lower and middle back. The joint between his hips and lower back (sacro-iliac joint), and the vertebrae of the lumber spine, were working through too great a range of motion whilst having stresses placed upon them. Such stresses would normally have been dampened by connective tissue leading to his shoulders. His back became a weak link, and it had been causing him a fair amount of discomfort all day. I could not suggest that he change his running pattern, because that was how he had trained, and so to alter it now would just cause other problems.

I came to the top of a long, steep and sweeping incline, with a narrow ditch cutting its way down through the wide trail. The hard mud surface was fine to run on, and the route ahead was clear to see, and so I dismissed any urge to hold back and instead gathered momentum as I charged down. A few locals wandering up moved to the side of the trail and applauded me as I raced past them. This was a long hill and I was moving faster and faster, waiting to see the bottom where I could run it out. The area was exposed and light, but a couple of trees had branches stretching over the trail lower down. As I approached, a Capuchin monkey ran from one side across to the other. When my eyes looked forward again, I could see where the slope flattened out and checkpoint five lay just beyond the base.

Shirley, Karen and Vicky were womanning the checkpoint. Daryl and another competitor, Steve, were resting there. I topped up my water and checked that there would be hot water for food at checkpoint six, and then moved on. Mark, an American, and Per were coming into the checkpoint as I left. I did not want to rest here, as I wanted to time a hot meal for just when the temperature began to drop in the evening. I wanted to have as much energy for the remainder of the distance as possible. Locals applauded my exit from the checkpoint, which was welcomed every time and met with a wave of gratitude from me. I moved on, taking the first option right, and continued along the wide, open road, on my way to the next checkpoint, some food, and a good rest.

I ate an energy bar on the move, and once finished I broke into a run again. The run was soon brought back down to a walking pace. The oppressive midday heat had subsided, but I was nevertheless beginning to feel out of sorts; no doubt just the result of pushing myself over the distance that I had covered during the day. I could have been further along had I moved at my own speed, but I had been so concerned for my feet that I had accepted being energy inefficient in order to look after them. They were certainly bruised and battered now; I could feel them, swollen and squashed in my shoes. Each step carried with it a dull, throbbing pain, which was at least a relief from the acute, shooting pain that surged up when I kicked roots and so on in the jungle. The road here was as forgiving as could be.

I passed a plantation over to my left, and I stared at the Sun beyond it. I still felt too hot to run, but fatigued with it; far more so than I had expected. It is all in the nature of racing in such conditions. I was getting through it. It was now after 17:00. I still felt hot and exposed to that burning Sun. Surely I would feel it cool down soon?

The seven kilometres to the sixth checkpoint passed quickly and I met Ivan and Angus there, along with a number of children from the area. I began to empty out my rucksack to get to the dehydrated food bags at the bottom. As I would be resting here I wanted to ensure that my food was now organised for the rest of the race. Daryl arrived but moved on within a couple of minutes of my arrival. I had had my doubts about him; first when I had seen him so early on in the day, and again when I saw him in his hammock at the fourth checkpoint. Now he looked fit and strong, indicating that he had been managing himself well, and off he went.

I sat back and requested some hot water for the food. None was to be had. Disaster! My heart sank and I was so disappointed. I was planning my food on the basis that there would be hot water here, which is what I had been led to believe. Ivan informed me that it was too early. A woman went off to heat up some water, but I had to press on. It would have taken at least a quarter of an hour to prepare the hot water. Maybe I would get some at checkpoint seven then. I was so hungry, so tired and so lacking energy that the prospect of the leg to the next checkpoint was not a delightful one. Energy bars simply did not contain enough energy for me to use over this sort of distance, unless supplemented with good high-energy foods as well. I moved on.

Another Mark, an American, had caught up and passed whilst I was at the checkpoint, so I expected to see him again soon, along with a couple of Brazilian runners that had come out of nowhere. I passed Mark after a few minutes, and a few minutes after that I passed the two Brazilians. They were standing around at the bottom of a hill, and they looked dreadful. They had arrived at the checkpoint full of beans, and since then all they had done was walk downhill and yet they looked ready to give up. Moments later I turned to look back down the trail and they were nowhere to be seen.

The uphill that followed was a long, long plod, although not by any means steep. I expected to see others behind me, but when I turned I found that I had the trail to myself. Nobody was within half an hour of me. At 18:30 the Sun was almost set, taking with it my chances of reaching checkpoint seven before dark. I removed my headtorch from the top of the rucksack and put it on. The trail led back into the jungle, although it was a wider passage than usual.

Kamikaze bats flew towards me, swooping down and then changing direction rapidly to escape the light of my headtorch. They were fast. There are vampire bats in the Amazon, but they would be more likely to bite a dog than a person. Any bites would be bad though; the risk of rabies from bats is high, and would necessitate evacuation from the jungle to the hospital in Santarem. I had been offered a rabies jab, but it seemed a ridiculous additional burden for an immune system already coping with typhoid and hepatitis A and B inoculations, along with my anti-malarials.

The trail was on a slight uphill gradient, and as I approached the top I heard voices to my left. The path led around to the next checkpoint. No hot water! It was being organised, but again it would take some considerable time before it was made ready. I was back on a proper road now as well, which ought to make my journey to checkpoint eight fairly straightforward.

James was manning the checkpoint. My feet were in agony, but I was not in favour of relieving the stress by taking off my shoes, as I knew that my feet would not go back in again afterwards. They were far too swollen for that. Besides, the relief would last until my next step, so nothing would be accomplished. I was so incredibly tired as well, ridiculously and unduly so, or so it seemed.

Ten minutes later the two Brazilians arrived, full of beans, and when they saw me they approached Dan, who had also just appeared, and began complaining that they had gotten lost. Hah! They had miraculously gotten lost, wandered off the trail, and yet made up an impressive amount of time on my lead. They did not require rest anymore so they headed off for the next checkpoint. I had no mind to chase after them.

There is a grey cloud that hangs over this race, and it is that brought by local runners that take short cuts through the woods, that are fed by the locals, and that do not carry as much kit as the rest of us (because locals take care of them). When people look at where they have placed on the position table, they often regard position without the inclusion of Brazilian racers. It is unfair on the Brazilians that are doing the full distance each day, and carry all their kit as we do, and are eating only the food they carry with them. The problem is that some of the Brazilians dislike the idea that foreigners should come here and be able to beat them in their own country, so out of pride they cheat to make it look as though we were beaten.

Other competitors reported hearing their position change between checkpoints, as Brazilians had overtaken them, yet they had not actually been passed along the trail. Such reports are commonplace from many of the competitors. I had often seen Brazilians loitering in an area of the jungle, and after I passed them I would find that they had finished ahead of me.

Today, these two had run into two checkpoints full of energy, yet been exhausted when I had seen them out on the trail. When I kept checking behind me on my way to this checkpoint, it was because I knew they had waited for me to pass so that they could head off another way. The trail was so straight that had they been within half an hour of me I would easily have seen them, yet they were nowhere near and impossibly appeared at the checkpoint ten minutes after me. I could work unfairly hard to overtake them, only to have them dart off somewhere and emerge on the trail later on. I would have to work harder and over a much greater distance. Easier by far to concede that we are competing here in different races – theirs and ours – but it should not be like that.

The whole attitude of such people smacks at those of us with some measure of integrity, sportsmanship, and honour. We know it shows nothing to a community when their racer beats a visitor by completing half the distance and carrying half the weight, but they have different priorities. We can only see them carry on with it, although in this instance my irritations were voiced to those unfortunate enough to be within earshot, such as Dan, James and those two Brazilians.

Shirley had organised teams to sweep along the trail and check that people were sticking to the route, and it was certainly no secret that some competitors cheated. The problem is one of diplomacy. What would be fairest to us would be if people found cheating were disqualified from the race. However, if this were to happen, then there is a likelihood that the local communities might refuse Shirley access to their land in order to race through and sleep in. Should that happen, then in the spirit of fairness, we would have given up the opportunity to race here, in which case everybody loses out. We want to race, so we have to accept that there are some games and politics involved, and matters will hopefully improve over time.

I was able to contemplate such things, because I was going nowhere fast. I was still lying on my back in the road, staring up at the stars and enjoying the cool of the night. I informed James that I would give Per twenty minutes to catch up. I needed all the rest I could get. When I arrived I had asked if Daryl had been here. He was pointed out to me but I did not see him, so I asked again and once more he was pointed out to me. In the dark my eyes could not focus and I could not see him, nor did I have the mind to step forward and walk up to the people right in front of me for a better view, for he had been standing right there. He left and moved off along the trail within a few minutes of my arrival. I was actually bordering on delirious, when I come to think about it, but I reasoned that my mind was just presenting me with a tunnel-vision to get through. *Just keep putting one foot in front of the other, and you will get to the finish.*

Per arrived with five minutes to spare, and promptly laid down himself to stretch his back, after which we were off. Alas, not for long though. Per wanted to sleep for half an hour at checkpoint eight, so he ran on ahead. By this stage I was walking fast, and managed to pass a couple of struggling Brazilians (no, not the same ones as before, fortunately), but each step was agony. There was a deep, continuous, throbbing pain that was now simply the state of affairs within the front of both shoes, and I was unable to think that it came from a particular toe. It was just pain, relentlessly and unkindly surging up into my brain with each footstep, and I longed to take my feet out of the shoes. The risk of doing so during this stage was too great though; I might get bitten by something or even just damage myself on a sharp stone. It would not take much to degenerate my city-boy feet into an even worse, pathetic mess.

It was hard not to feel pitiful. I just had to get through it. In a sense I did not even mind the pain; it was actually something else to think about other than why I was so tired. What I objected to, and hence the reason for my self-pity, was purely that I could not complete this stage as I had intended to. The first half had gone fairly well, although I accepted that I would have completed it much faster at my own pace. In hindsight I should have focussed much more on limiting time on my feet (by moving faster), than varying speed or anything to relieve potential impact stresses. It would be written off as experience now, and I had time to think of such things as I shuffled on, moody and annoyed with myself, anxious to reach the next checkpoint.

I caught up with Anthony next, one of Julian's team from Guernsey. He had flown past me earlier but was now struggling. We exchanged banter as we made our way into the checkpoint; we were fit but beaten up fairly well. I think that we would have both been happy for the company at that point. Someone else to talk to can be a good thing, provided the mood stays positive and both are focussed on the task in hand. It would be destructive for people to meet and exchange only complaints and their petty issues. Anthony and I had both been put through it, but we were as irksomely positive and blasé about the whole situation as we could be.

The checkpoint was on a road directly before the Rio Tapajos. It was good to see her again; the finish line was by the river some distance to the north, and I was getting through it. Paul was manning the checkpoint, having retired from racing himself, following that harrowing second day of heat and hospitalisations. Per had only recently arrived himself, and was now just beginning to tie up his hammock. I did not wish to waste time putting mine up, but I was definitely no longer in a rush, which I appreciate is unusual behaviour during a race.

I can only ask for you to understand that I was truly out of sorts. However disapproving you might be of my apparent lack of gusto, this is as nothing by comparison to how truly fed up of myself I was at this point. I was so dazed from my fatigue that I resolved to have a doze before continuing, and I rather fancied the hardness of the ground. I lay down on my back on the earth, my rucksack behind my head, and shut my eyes. I did not imagine that I would sleep, but simply to lie there with my eyes closed and feet pain-free for fifteen minutes would be rejuvenating enough.

"*You lucky, lucky, bastard!*" I was already grinning as I opened my eyes. John had arrived and treated me to his obligatory salutation. Excellent. Well, granted that I traditionally finished a fair way ahead of John, so his arrival underlined the result of my sufferings, but it was nevertheless fantastic to see the silly smiling sod again. I had passed him earlier, not long after Per and I had taken our morning's scenic route, but that was many, many hours ago now.

I dragged my wrecked, ruined, fetid, calloused, stupid and annoying body to its tender, irritating, annoyingly pathetic feet, which hurt (both the process of rising and the ghastly feet). I hobbled with John over to a small hut adjacent to the area where people were sleeping. Finally I had come to a checkpoint with hot water. I sat down to eat and John, incredibly kindly, rushed to help the tired and exceptionally weary Anthony with his food and water. At the time, Anthony appeared to be severely rundown, either through fatigue or illness, or a combination of the two. He was sat frozen in position, impressively incoherent, and I felt sure that he would take a considerable time to recover. I was beyond doubt that he would collapse at any moment, hence John's efforts to ensure he could at least get his hydration and energy levels heading in the right direction.

John and I made ready to leave. Per would remain to sleep, and planned to catch up with us later. I felt sure he would. We went on. John was in surprising and enviably good health. His walking was fine; he looked as if he was simply out for a stroll around town, and I could have deeply hated him for it, were it not for the fact that I relied upon his company now so much.

As I went on, the pain in my feet became subdued as the shock of walking again subsided. I felt convinced that my issues were more to do with my general health than my feet. It could not have been the heat, because it had not been particularly hot today, and I had not once felt the oppressive, debilitating heat of earlier in the race. On the contrary; I had felt fitter than ever. Although the lack of a high-energy meal when I needed it the most caused problems, again it could not have been sufficient to make me feel so devastatingly shattered. Nor could I put it down to the cumulative effect of the race so far. A virus? Possibly, but I felt in good health until the last few hours, so it was unlikely.

Whatever was making me feel so awfully weary it changed not a thing. Come what may, I would be reaching the finish line, albeit much later than I had imagined, and in a state far more exhausted than I would have liked. Thirteen kilometres to checkpoint nine; this was to be a long, long stretch by comparison to the last few legs.

Predictably, perhaps, those thirteen kilometres were monstrous. For me it was the most arduous and challenging leg of the day. The ground conditions were good, the terrain was fine and the hills now held no comparison to what had been covered earlier in the jungle. It was purely my own state that forced things to be such a drain of energy. There were demons with me here in the Amazon, and they would be malicious and cruel in their attempts to take my victory away from me. My nightmarish trudge continued through the darkness.

The trail continued along the road for a while. Locals would take it in turns to shepherd us along. As John suggested, perhaps they felt that the bright cyalume trail markers were for their benefit rather than ours. I just became frustrated with these people, as much as they thought that they were helping. We had covered about a hundred miles through the jungle, and now that we were on a road with glowing markers, beaming out in the darkness to highlight our way, I considered it ridiculous and annoying to have people walking with us. I am sure that their intentions were good, and it was mostly my own dark mood that desired of someone to vent its frustrations upon. Perhaps it was just that typical male pride issue, when it comes to these matters: "Captain Cook did not require directions and neither do

I!" With stoic fortitude and a grossly misplaced sense of confidence we press on and find our way in the end.

Thankfully we were soon guided down to the beach, where we were as we should be; together in a world of our own; our own day's histories making us what we were in our minds then. And at this time; this reunion of two souls battling their demons through this self-inflicted and very personal hell on Earth, a change came. Out there on the beach a moment of perfection transpired. Away from all signs of civilisation once more, and this paradise that I knew so well showed herself in a new way. I could feel the powdery white sands underfoot, as the beach paradise and calm sea-scale river were illuminated beneath an astonishingly bright full moon. And there I was; the crunch of the sand (for the nature of the grains felt as such against the rubber of my shoes), the sound of the gentle waves lapping the shoreline, and the blackness of the night sky punctuated by the sheer brilliance of the moon.

I had all of this; this whole world and for a while all of my pains and fatigue were made to feel so sweet; so pure and right to me. Had I been brought here then I would have appreciated what I could see, but to actually feel it as I could now, to experience it as though all of my hardships had been to bring me here, it was this that made it so magnificent. The great big juicy sticky red cherry on the cake, of course, was having one of my best friends here to share it with. Such an experience of beauty, of magnificence, of wonder, of achievement and of the sublime to such magnitude is something that comes rarely in this life. The moment means all the more for its precious rarity; both then and even now when I come to write of it.

Pain and tiredness left me now. Such emotions were dispensed to be carried upon the calm breeze that cooled my face and moved silently in the night air. Even then I wondered how anyone else might know this feeling. How could someone unfamiliar with such physical stresses possibly know how one feels as the result of such ardent adventure and perseverance through adversity? How could anyone outside of our runners or racers niche experience such things or grasp how one can be affected? This perfection we find when hell transforms into heaven? Perhaps you think me ignorant or arrogant for considering such questions, but I know in my heart that this is the most beautiful moment in endurance racing that I have ever experienced. It was home and it was the stuff of dreams. I am glad for anyone who has felt such things, and I hope that everyone does, and the more often the better.

As we moved along, John's silhouette ahead of me, my enthusiasm waned slightly as I remembered that the trail would lead us off the beach, although I could not recall how far ahead. For the time being, John and I treated ourselves to the luxury of a break, and we laid down in the sand and gazed up at the sky. The markers had disappeared; we no longer had the glow of cyalume sticks to follow, and for miles now we had been following footprints that we could not guarantee were from runners. As we lay there we observed figures emerge in the far distance. Runners, perhaps? Some came from where we had just come from, and then others appeared from the direction in which we were heading. They were support crew; the cyalume sticks were cracked and shaken into life, and then hung onto trees to light our way. John and I returned to our feet and continued on.

John had been trying to lead the way with keeping our spirits up by singing Python's *Always look on the bright side of life*, as per our final stint together in the desert race. I was so atrociously wiped out that I could not even sing with him for more than a few verses. I really was so far from my familiar self.

The route took us along narrow paths, past community buildings, and we were once again shepherded by the locals. We were then back out onto the wide dirt roads. The journey was punctuated by a brief return to the beach and a river crossing. Despite a width of no more than ten metres, the water was deep and we had to swim as wading was impossible. As we walked in, John told me to stop playing silly-arses and shuffling, as swimming would be far safer to avoid upsetting the wildlife; I duly complied. It was not like me to need someone else to slap sense into me, but tonight was one such occasion.

On leaving the water I remained cold for sometime. I alerted John to this, mostly to ascertain how he was feeling, and to see if it had actually become that cold. It had not; my body was not regulating temperature properly. I began to shiver, my body ignorant of the warmth of the night, as I attempted to recover from the temperature drop of the water. We were getting through it though. At some point, this night would end and I would have a day to recover. Just a fun run along the beach after that. *Just this night to think about; to get through.*

Wet and tired feet plodded along a dirt road. A few kilometres passed and we arrived at checkpoint nine. We did not remain at the checkpoint longer than the time it took us to fill our water bladders. Just seven kilometres remained between here and the finish line.

The road undulated cruelly. The hills were continuous and seemed never-ending, as is always the way in such circumstances. I had to rest on the side of the road at one point. The pain in my feet was as nothing; just a nuisance of no consequence. It was the fatigue trying to beat me. I was not tired, in the sense of needing to sleep. I simply desired to stop moving; to lie back and remain, using no energy and permitting my body to recover. It made no sense to me still. I even encouraged John to carry on by himself if he wished. *'Don't wait for my John; I'm done for. Save yourself...'* When I was prepared to move off again John encouraged me to rest for longer, which again was kind and generous of him. But I knew that the rest was not really helping. I needed to stop completely, and that would happen once we passed beneath that finish line.

It was actually the sight of a headtorch coming along the road behind us that spurred me on. I had already lost so many places that to lose one more would have been inconsequential. However, in my mind, enough was enough. *No more fucking about, Hinesy; move your arse to that finish line. You've got to finish the game. Seven kilometres is laughable!* Even on that terrain I could have run it in half an hour. I dreaded to look at my watch. Eventually a path led us off to the left and, with relief, we made our way for what I knew was our last time back to the beach.

We crossed some water channels and were soon in sight of the lights of camp. Contrary to all measures of sense we broke into a run to get us over the line. Having held hands as we finished, John and I exchanged a hug, as Gil came up and gave me a much-needed hug as well. Without John so much of that section from checkpoint eight would have been far more horrid than it had ever threatened to be. I never fully lost my sense of humour, but I lost all ability to express it and help John out. He carried me those last twenty kilometres, and during that time I experienced both my darkest times of the race and a true and beautiful paradise. It was now 04:30 and time for bed.

My headtorch had given up its will to live, long before I had come close to doing so. I staggered over to where everyone had their hammocks up and made my way along until I had passed almost all of them. The odd solitary hammock could still be seen out on its own further along. When I reached the next couple of inviting trees, the ones with 'come to bed with me branches'; I put my rucksack down and tied up my hammock. I sat up in it for a while, contemplating the next course of action. The basha would have to go up too, even though it was already feeling warm and dry, and I was sure that there would be no rain. I was just equivalently sure that if it did happen to rain, then I would not enjoy having to move from my slumber to put the basha up later. I sat because even the smallest movements seemed to be so unfathomably energy-sapping. The basha went up and I secured the six guy ropes to roots. I had not brought pegs to save weight, and there was always something to tie the para cord onto.

Next I had to remove my shoes and socks. This was the moment that I had both looked forward to and feared. What would my feet look like?! Removing the shoes was painful, and my feet were tender. I placed the shoes upside down on a fallen tree trunk, and then did likewise with my socks. Ordinarily I would keep them in my rucksack or hammock to protect them from habitation, but I had a feeling I would not be needing them for the last day. I still planned to run that barefoot, and savour the joy of allowing my feet to run comfortably and uninhibited.

I sorted my kit and retired beneath my mosquito net. John arrived and put his hammock up parallel to mine. Anthony came over the line not long after that, and then found us and tied his hammock up with ours. I was too tired to eat, which was stupid in retrospect, but I actually could not bear the thought of food. At 06:00 my incredibly slow and deliberate preparations were completed and I fell asleep. I awoke with the hustle and bustle of the camp, and an already impressive heat, at 08:00. I pretended I was not there and that the morning was only happening to other people. I snoozed until 12:00.

I sat round in my hammock; my feet hovering above the ground as I gently swung. All was not well, and I was still unusually and unexpectedly lethargic. In my shorts, the shorts that I wear around camp rather than to run in, I kept two days' rations of toilet paper, folded up in a small, sealed, waterproof freezer bag. I headed

259

off with a view of returning lighter. I decided against the latrine, as it was teeming with monstrous black ants, and this would not have allowed for a relaxing experience.

As I walked I decided, in the interests of efficiency, to expel some trapped gas that was simply begging to be set free. I did so. I followed through. *No!* Oh for goodness sake what have I done to deserve this? My anus had spat at my shorts. I reached the rocks that I had considered in my mind to be just perfect for a turd burial site. I pulled my shorts down, squatted, and my arse exploded. I had not had diarrhoea so terrifyingly horrid since I was a very young boy, an episode I still recall well because my parents had taken my sister and I shopping that day, and the whole fiasco had caused us all much irritation and inconvenience, not least myself of course. I was ill, and this explained a lot. I must have been carrying this through half of yesterday; little wonder I had been in such a bad way.

I wiped and polished and headed straight to the river. Somehow a couple of Danes had managed to choose a spot to sit not more than a few metres from where I entered the water. I hoped that my cream shorts had not betrayed the fact that I had, well, shat myself, and gave them a cheery wave and self-satisfied grin as I lay down in the river. Annoyance after annoyance; the river was shallow for a long way, too far for me to expect to easily find a deep section. I removed my shorts, and gave myself and my shorts a good clean, before putting them back on and heading to my hammock.

I sat in my hammock for a while, both Anthony and John could see that I was out of sorts, and I confessed that I must have picked up a stomach bug. People are known to have stomach problems as a result of consuming gels and so on, but I had never experienced that and there was no way that food itself could have been responsible for this. It had to be an unfriendly bacterium; I was hoping that it was not worse, such as a parasite or something that would not pass soon. I tried to eat but I was struggling. I returned to my personal toilet twice more.

After the first visit I went out into the river with my soap. I would give myself a good clean, and do likewise with all of my clothes. As I lay there, basking in the Sun and my miseries, Holly came gleefully, elegantly, and poetically dancing into the water to join me. *Bugger.* I had seen her earlier and she had wanted to come out to have a wash. I was fairly glad that I had not used my soap on the clothes when she asked for it. So there we were; she the outstandingly beautiful, young, fresh Aphrodite and me; the haggard, sick, gravy-farting, dismal excuse for a human being. And thus, with us both duly representing the Yin and Yang of the world, I considered the universe to be in perfect balance.

Naturally I confessed that I was in fine health, suffering not at all from the previous day's leisurely efforts, and was unequivocally glad to see her again and for her company out in the river. The latter point was true, of course. It was wonderful to have her out here, as to me she was a shining beacon of happiness and joy that had somehow been kept pure and innocent of the follies of the rest of us. Being with her helped me to forget about the previous day, and to simply focus on the here and now. Here we were rocked and carried by the waves, the sand on the water's bottom, the beach with its tropical palms and the jungle trees. The sky was as blue as could be in a cloudless sky; the air hot and water cooling and perfect. I thought of all such things as I so deeply hoped that my stomach's misdirected vengeance had been sated.

The athletes were all queuing up now to receive coconuts; their surprise gift for completing the long stage. One of the bombeiro's, Peneforte, was cutting the coconuts open with his machete, as I watched from the water. I had no stomach to drink from the coconut, so I watched the queue end and Peneforte return to the boat. I would have loved to have tried a fresh coconut, but for the ominous feeling within me. Holly and I headed back onto the beach and I went to hang up my shorts, tight shorts and running vest to dry on a tree, before returning to my hammock for a rest. I was now wearing my running shorts, in the absence of further spares.

As the evening grew near I felt compelled to enquire of John if the sand, sea and sky were indeed all hints of purple. He informed me that they were indeed not. Shit; that will be my eyes then. Ben came to my rescue with a Dioralyte, which tasted rancid to me, and I had no desire for liquids, which was madness considering how dehydrated I had now become. I sipped on the half-pint of Dioralyte for three-quarters of an hour, and then started on my own water, and attempted to have some food. Ben had given me a couple of Imodium tablets too. The prescription was along the lines of 'one should be fine, whereas two will have you sealed up until you are ready to shit bricks'. I took two and wondered whether or not it would be enough. I rested in mortal fear of flatulence.

I felt better for the fluids, and mildly more human. Everything from the previous day was at least making sense now, although I still accepted my error in moving too slowly to begin with. Having said that, I still could not have wanted more from the last twenty kilometres, than the hardships overcome whilst in the company of my good friend John. There were moments during that night which could not have been bettered.

It was dark when I headed off to check on my clothes. With the poor light from my headtorch I struggled to find the tree, although when I did I found that my clothes were still soaked. I walked off and promptly kicked a thin, broken tree stump, not more than a couple of inches in diameter and protruding four inches above the ground. The pain was excruciating, agonising and instant. It shot up to my head and burst into stars behind my eyes. I was wearing flip flops, and the big toe of my right foot had connected so hard and painfully that I imagined immense soft tissue damage. My hand held a tree as I looked to the sky and stifled a scream into as manly a growl as I could muster. I might have been inclined to curse, but I knew it had happened because the *odds* were against me. I was still not entirely myself, as I was still struggling to reach a euhydrated state, and my concentration was suffering as a result. I had been staggering around, with very few of my remaining wits about me, as I groped in the dark with the pathetic light from my headtorch. With so many tree stumps along the beach, it would have been more surprising if I had not stubbed a toe on one.

I had to try to move the toe. Even before looking at it I had to know if it was broken or the bone had been damaged. It moved perfectly. The relief was both wonderful and unexpected. I looked down and held the dismal light close to the toe. It looked grim. Where my big toe was there was what appeared to be half the tissue of the toe on the outside, as if it was a really fat, juicy sausage that had burst through its skin in the frying pan. Blood covered it and ran down the side of the flip flop and was making a red pool in the sand. The tree stump looked no better, as my blood was on that too. I limped back to my hammock, and showed John, entirely irritated that his camera had packed in. I did not want to go to the medical tent because I wanted to limit movement to save sand getting into the wound. The team was busy though; almost everyone seemed to need medical care.

John went off to request that someone take a look at me when they had the chance, and after a while Karen came over; her hammock was also up with ours. She was also suitably impressed, but explained that I should clean it and then get to the medical tent, because there were just too many people waiting for them. Fair enough; I should hardly expect bed service for a cut toe. I drank some water, and occasionally shone my light on the red, purple mess that pretended to be my toe. Off I should go; I needed to check in with Ben anyway on account of recovering too slowly from my stomach problem.

Stage V

Incidentally, I had by now decided that the cause of my stomach bug must have been the hot water used for rehydrating my food at the second camp. Because the water was heated on a fire, it had not always been hot enough to kill off all the bacteria by the time I went for food. Because of the extra day, I had spent so much time eating and drinking hot beverages, that there were doubtless plenty of occasions when I had helped myself to water that had not been heated for long enough.

Hence, I had probably become infected from the water. That would make sense, because so many people reported stomach problems of a similar nature after we left that area (and we were there for two nights). There were other ways that I could have become affected, such as from insect bites, but that seems unlikely because this illness was focussed so much on the digestive system.

I hobbled off to the medical tent. Ben was treating someone but greeted me and informed me that he had heard I had been beating myself up. I confessed that I had been feeling particularly rough anyway, and then promptly and vigorously stubbed my toe, but maintained that this was purely 'attention-seeking', which met with his approval. I sat down next to Ian (Mayhem) Mayhew and Per, and I stared at the mess. Others showed their support by getting their cameras out and taking photos. I looked at it, and it was a ghastly, horrid mess. I kept looking at it. I looked at it some more. I looked at it until as if by magic my whole foot acquired a pins and needles sensation that rushed up to my knee. *Oh for goodness sake man; pull yourself together*. I laid down and elevated my foot, which brought instant relief and I felt immediately normal, but chose to enjoy my more comfortable position. I recognised that it was just a stress response, induced by my being so put-off by the sight of the thing, but it was annoying. Particularly as Mayhem was mocking me for it, which I deserved.

Ben came over and cleaned the wound with water. There was nothing there. The wound had clotted anyway, so the water removed all the dried blood. As for the 'tissue', which had made me think that half my toe was gone, that was just the remains of the tree stump that had been thrust into the skin. Once that had been washed away all that remained were three rather sore but innocuous cuts. A few plasters were all that was necessary. What an arse. I would still have to bandage it and seal a waterproof freezer bag over it to protect it during the morrow's run; but there was certainly nothing to worry about. I should not even have bothered matron with something so pathetic in the first instance. I suppose it had just been that final straw, at the end of a couple of days during which an awful lot of straws had been laid on this camel's back.

I remained in the tent to chat with the others. Per, the photographer from the previous year, was busy having a toenail removed, which was almost as painful for us to watch as it was for him to endure. His face howled of the excruciating agony of it all. Holly joined me and brought me some emails. I had quite a few for a change; including from a number of the previous year's competitors who had been following my progress online. Andrea kindly reminisced over her rescue from the gully the year before. If she could see me now she would probably have addressed it to the biggest wimp in the rainforest. Still, at least my presence here in the tent had been useful. I was still carrying a fairly well-stocked first aid kit, which saved the medical team delays in getting supplies from the boat, as I had a few bits and pieces to tie them over.

I went back to my hammock to sleep. I was feeling marginally more human, but was still dehydrated and by now was feeling fairly hungry too. I did not care though. I was in no state to be able to race tomorrow. I had no objections to waking at ten o'clock, four hours after the start. I would still be able to walk the last thirty kilometres to the finish line. I was beyond caring now; I would finish the race and that would be that.

Stage VI: 30 Kilometres

John woke me at 04:30. At 05:00 I crawled out from my hammock and tidied everything away. I cut up a plastic bag and dressed my toe, using the plastic as the final sheath, and taped it onto my foot to hopefully prevent sand from getting in. I would do today's run with John, and I could think of nothing sweeter after his help in getting me through the long stage. I had not eaten my breakfast, because I could not possibly have been sicker of the taste of rehydrated rice pudding with cinnamon. In any case I still had no appetite, but accepted that I could make it through a thirty-kilometre run on whatever reserves my body had up for grabs. Nevertheless, John proceeded to throw food bags at me continually, including cashew nuts, Haribo sweets, and whatever else he could find to offer me. It was a real privilege to have him here looking after me.

I went to collect my clean clothes and discovered that my shorts had been stolen. My running clothes had been left, but the shit-specked shorts, which over their many years had faded and become almost see-through when wet, had gone. I thought that their new owner, who must clearly have a need for them far greater than my own, was welcome to every bit of them.

I gathered my rucksack and headed off to the medical tent, which was where the water was kept. The countdown began and the race started without me. The greatest consistency in this race has been John's tardiness for making a start line on time, hence I was late but still ahead of him. I filled up my Platypus and sauntered over to the line. John followed on. Five minutes after everybody had set off, John and I stood where the start line had been, prior to it being taken down by the organisers, and we gave ourselves a ten-second countdown before setting off at a steady jog.

As planned I was running barefooted. I had binned my Salomons on the way to collect my water. They had survived well over a thousand miles of training and over a hundred miles in the jungle, and with that I decided that they deserved to stay out here, to die in glory rather than to return to England to fade away. Well, and they were heavy, obviously, and by now my rucksack was as light as it could be. There most certainly were not any spare socks in there; that was for sure.

We ran along a short stretch of beach and then up a steep sandbank perhaps twelve feet high. We descended over the other side, and had already caught up with the tail-enders. Next came a short section of water, which saw an end to my carefully but imperfectly protected toe. I sent John on ahead as I removed the dressings and replaced them. Everyone I had just passed now overtook me, but I ensured I passed them again moments later. I ran on along the firm sand at the front of the beach, whilst enjoying far better health than I had done during the previous two days. I was able to stretch out and run without fear of tripping up on roots. I ran as I had not run before during this race. I moved up the field of runners, elated to be able to run fast, even on sand.

I had passed the Geordie, Cookie, and Becky along the way, who had been running with John, to Cookie's cries of "will somebody please kick his fucking legs out!" at the sight of my bounding passed them. That was a nice shout for my motivation, and prompted me to sprint as John followed on the pretence of fulfilling the role of 'he that would kick my legs out'. John and I returned to a civilised jog and continued on our way. I was deeply happy to be able to run fast again, even if to the comical irritation of those not yet recovered from the long stage.

By the time we reached the first checkpoint, John was already becoming fed up with my pace. I was trying to push us too hard, and he had already gone beyond his training distance of four miles. As James went off to collect some more tape for my toe, I encouraged John to make a start so that I could catch him again. James secured a better dressing and John and I left together. John was in favour of taking the direct routes over higher sand, rather than the longer way around the water's edge, which was fine until I realised he did it to permit a walk on the incline! I was keen to crack on and run, and before long it became clear that we were doing each other no favours.

John was looking pale and sweaty, and my legs were bothering me from the restricted pace, so as I descended down a sandbank I stretched out a little, and then checked back. John gave me a nod of acknowledgement and I carried on. A few seconds later and I looked back to see he was twenty metres behind. Thirty seconds later it was a hundred metres or so, and I began tormenting myself about what to do. He is my friend so do I run with him, knowing that I might resent him for the awkwardness of sticking to his pace, or do I leave him, displaying ingratitude for all his help?

I knew that if I tried to run with him that it would not work. We walk at the same pace, and we can run together for a good few miles, but we cannot run a long distance together. My training runs had been considerably longer than his, and if I limited myself to his fitness level, then I would feel that I took an easy way out. John would understand; he was knackered and should be enjoying himself at his own pace. I was sure he would understand. I stretched out and accelerated along the beach.

I soon found myself on my own, but then reassuringly began passing runners again. I sprinted passed Mayhew and Nobsey on my way into checkpoint two. I filled my Platypus, put on some sunscreen as I had not had the time earlier, and continued on. I wanted to get today done quickly not just because it was the last day, but in an attempt to reach the end before the Sun reached its zenith, bringing as it would a formidable heat onto the unprotected beach. It was hot enough already, and it was only 08:00.

It was an easy run along the beach to checkpoint three and Ben. I had moved past Sophie on the way, and she had not cared much for my lanky legs either. Out of checkpoint three I made the mistake of following the route of the firmest sand around the water's edge, rather than taking the direct route across the softer sand. This cost me such a distance, and about three places at the time, that it had been an unquestionable error on my part. But still; one lives and learns.

I reached a section of rocks that Daryl and Becky had warned me of, suggesting that it might be a challenge without shoes, and I slowed to a walk to negotiate the area. I was so focussed on where I placed my front, left foot that I paid no attention to the rear right foot, and as I brought it forward it promptly came into contact with a rock. Another mind-bursting shot of pain, over though in an instant. I looked down to see the third toenail on my right foot had been raised along one edge with blood seeping out from beneath. I knew that it would get caught and that sand would gather beneath it, wedging it up and causing further pain and soreness. I could think of only one solution, and could benefit from the adrenaline surge that had accompanied the impact pain. I bent down, took a deep breath, and grasped the edge of the nail between the thumb and index finger of my right hand. I then pulled and tore the nail away from the nail bed beneath and the skin at the front of the toe. The pain was not as great as you might imagine, and the procedure was over within five character-building seconds.

I walked on over the rocks, the nail still between my two fingers, and I then rinsed the toe in the river. As I continued, Gil came into view ahead and was taking photos. He called for me to walk into the river to get around the majority of rocks, but I could see plenty of rocks in there, and would have been far more likely to have had another accident if I attempted that route. I made my way past Gil and gave him the pleasure of a few good shots of my bloody and nail-free toe. Once on the other side of the rocks I broke into a run once again. I carefully placed the toenail into the zipped hip pocket of my rucksack, mostly because I had always been quite attached to it of late, and did not want to dispose of it just yet. Perhaps I needed time to mourn.

The nail bed routinely filled with sand, and every now and again I would attempt to rinse it out in the river, but the blood had congealed around the sand and it was now all held in place. It would take some efforts with a knife back in England to get it entirely sand-free. I left the toe for the time-being. It was less than nine kilometres to the finish line.

A muddy section created an interesting change to the sand, and was followed by a water crossing. I passed one of the lead runners here, who stated that he had run out of energy and was craving some energy gels. Mine were in the top of my rucksack so I invited him to take a few, which he gratefully did. In those situations a small gesture like that, which meant nothing to me because I would not be requiring them after the day, can mean so much to someone in need. It is not worth entertaining the idea of keeping them for a rainy day. Besides, I was promised a good drink in exchange for each one.

As for me: I had no energy in my legs and was beginning to get hot. The temperature was on the rise and my core was duly following suit. I had the heart for today's run though, in the cardiovascular fitness-sense. Because I had been stretching out and running at what I considered to be a fast training pace, I was feeling that my heart and lungs were full of energy. My legs were heavy, but they would carry me to the end, and that was all that mattered. I walked for a short while in order to permit a good run for the last kilometre or so to the finish.

Following a water crossing I picked up the pace again. I could see the tall hill that stood isolated in front of Alter do Chao, and I could see the old pier and beach huts. I passed Paul and then a couple of others as I turned right to follow the wall that runs along the front of the town. There was one other runner in front of me, and I greeted him politely, almost apologetically as I passed him too. I had the final two hundred metres to myself, after which steps would carry me up into the centre of town and the finish line.

I reached the steps, locals and support team and other racers lining the barrier of the wall and cheering me on. Steps! Brilliant; it reminded me of the steps that lead from the north bank of the Thames up to the Millennium Bridge; the closest thing to a steep hill that I had in the majority of my training sessions! I bounded up the steps as fast as I could, accelerated towards the road, slowed as I took a split-second to check for traffic, and then sprinted the ten or so metres to the finish line, full of speed, energy and elation as I reached the end.

Shirley was on the line to hang my medal around my neck, and the area was filled with athletes and the support and medical teams, all cheering and applauding. I thanked Shirley sincerely for everything. I was tired but paradoxically felt wondrously alive. Vicky and Karen came over to give me a hug, as did Holly, and then almost anybody else anywhere near me; whether I knew them or not.

The medals were big and bulky; made locally from clay and far more meaningful than the usual dull metal affair, which could have been knocked up anywhere in the world. As wonderful as the medal was, however, I could only manage to keep the weighty medal around my neck for a couple of minutes before I had to remove it; the stomach problem really had wiped me out, and even now I was feeling the effects.

Nothing, however, could possibly detract from the joy of having finished this incredible race, this toughest of races and this greatest of races. I had loved it. From beginning to end I had adored this race; I loved it for its hardships and I loved it for the moments of immeasurable and incomparable beauty. I loved this race for the friendships forged, for the personal care and attention of the medical team, and for feeling such a part of it all, for being welcomed by so many people and for being made to feel wanted and helpful. As people came up to congratulate me our mutual joy and happiness for each others successes simply added to the feelings we had for ourselves.

I laid down on the floor, in the shade of a raised area that almost looked like a bandstand, which was where the medical team had based themselves. I drank some sugary drinks, and then went down to a market stall that provided the runners with fruit, care of Shirley. I was particularly happy to be able to speak with Rob, who had recently been released from hospital, and although a little shaky was out of harm's way and on the mend. I wandered back to the finish line to balls up a television interview John was giving, by giving him a bear hug on camera. There was no ill-feeling for my having taken off earlier on, and we both made our way to get some drinks. John had loved the race as much as I did, which made everything a greater joy still.

Epilogue

After the race my first attempt at eating did not go so well. I managed some fresh fruit, which was glorious, but I could only pick at the cooked food that was on offer. I mostly lay about and consumed copious volumes of the guarana drink, whilst dreaming of a return to normal well-being. Later on we made our way to a hotel in Santarem for a banquet and the awards ceremony, whereupon my appetite returned and you will be delighted to know I enjoyed the pleasure of food once more.

We enjoyed a half-day stopover in Manaus, which was worth a look around and so Ben and I did just that. Later on, Sophie and I celebrated having the most minging and godforsaken of feet, both of us having lost a toenail on the last day (although she had ruined hers at the airport, which was cheating).

Following my return to England my big toe became infected; this was the one that met with the tree stump shortly after the long stage. The infection was deduced from the most pungent, horrid and ghastly of smells, along with an appearance that slowly but surely my foot was leading me into zombiedom, or perhaps leprosy, but in either case it was not welcomed. After a week of failing to recover, or rather a week of further degeneration into zombiehood, I resisted no more and visited Soho's drop-in clinic. A nightmare of a nurse then thought

I must have had a stress fracture, for no reason other than 'because people that run long distances get those'. This was despite my clearly having walked into the clinic with no obvious difficulty. She seemed quite disappointed when all she could find was the infection, and duly prescribed me some antibiotics. A week later and the infection had cleared up beautifully, although the toe remained swollen for a while afterwards.

Another battle promptly ensued, which was that between my healthier toe regions and my dying-off toenails. The nails had bitten the bullet care of those tight shoes, and were now just waiting to drop off. My next big event was already planned, and this was to be something of an outrageous distance event; a race that had never been finished in fact, and I could stand no delay to my training, just because my feet were not in good shape. To have run with such sore toes would have been impossible, or at least led to some silly compensations to offset the pain, and so I pulled off the three offending nails within a fortnight of my return. With that accomplished, my mind was then focussed on the next big thing, and any opportunity for post-race depression was to be offset once more.

As for my reflections on the race itself, I know that I speak for others as well as myself when I state that this is very much a race to return to. At the end of the support visit, when I watched people cross the line, there was a sense that this event was so unbearable that many of the competitors were simply relieved to be through it. In 2008 though the mood was different. Many of us enjoyed the ride and compared it favourably with races we had completed before.

278

Epilogue

The jungle is such an amazing environment, filled with constant sounds of nature, and with such diverse and contrasting landscapes. As a result, the mind and senses seem over-burdened to absorb all that is taking place. During a run, this captivates the mind and draws focus, making it such a fascinating and exciting race that there really is nothing that can compare in such a way.

It is far more my personal circumstances, rather than any other factor, that keeps me from competing year after year. As a lecturer now, I am bound to the academic calendar, and the Jungle Marathon falls within the first month, October. Hence, and much to my continuing disappointment, I am not involved in the JM to the degree that I would like to be. Even if not as a competitor then I would happily return year after year as a member of the support crew. I shall strive to make myself available to competitors and staff for whatever help I can give, and I continue to maintain regular email contact with Shirley.

The Jungle Marathon is an amazing race. I recall my return home from the *Marathon des Sables* and contemplating, rather dejectedly at the time, just how few people in the world had finished it. I considered that there were not many people that I could share the experience with. But then, even within the United Kingdom there were thousands of people that had crossed that finish line. Successful finishers of the Jungle Marathon number in the hundreds worldwide. To have completed this race is a very special achievement indeed, and the incredible environment in which it takes place makes it even more precious. The scale of the race means that with so few competitors, everybody comes to know everybody else, and great friendships can be forged. Hence, although there were more than ten times the number of competitors in the MdS, I made more than ten times as many friends during the Jungle Marathon.

There are certainly plenty of other similar races in the world, in both deserts and other jungles, but there is nevertheless something wonderfully unique about the Jungle Marathon. It has become something of an enigma in the world of ultra-endurance adventure racing. It is the race that simply has to be done. Whereas I see that the *Marathon des Sables* presents itself as the rite of passage into the world of these races, it is the Jungle Marathon that seems to me to be the real proving ground. I have never heard of any similar race to be held in such high esteem, and with such respect given to those that have finished. There seems to be an edge in the voice when people talk to those relaying the details of their most recent adventure race. It is almost as if they are itching to get to the bottom of a very important point. What they are saying may be very interesting, but how does it compare with the Jungle Marathon?

Shirley would deny that the Jungle Marathon is the toughest adventure race in the world. However, I am certain that the hot and humid climate of the Amazon presents the most difficult environmental conditions, mile for mile, than anywhere else. Some may wish to disagree, but the body manages itself far better in the hot and dry climates of the deserts, and is able to survive extreme cold far better than it can extreme heat. In this sense, the equatorial jungle regions represent the most challenging environment for the long-distance runner. As for the course itself, all that would be required to find a more difficult race would be for a greater number of steeper climbs, or any other approach that makes the going harder. Such a race may appear over time, after which the JM could lose it's probable title of the toughest race of its kind. At the time of going to print though, I am certain that the Jungle Marathon is the most gruelling individual, multi-stage, ultra-endurance footrace on Earth. Until a more demanding race comes along, this is certainly the one to complete to prove one's worth as an adventure ultra-runner. But then, I adore Shirley's Jungle Marathon, and have enjoyed the time of my life racing out there, and cherish the growing friendships I have made. No individual on Earth could be as heavily biased as I am, to favour the Jungle Marathon as I do. So take my words as those based upon biased opinion, albeit an opinion I know I share with many others on the circuit.

With this tentative recommendation though comes the severest of warnings. All of these smaller races, of a hundred competitors or thereabouts, are confined in the level of medical and emergency support that they can realistically provide. I would not want anyone to attempt this race that was not confident of their ability to take care of themselves, even if they were less sure of their actual ability to finish. In other words, whilst a grey area may appear in confidence to reach the finish line, none should exist in terms of knowing how to take care of oneself and stay as safe as is reasonably practicable. Plenty of people live in jungle regions, but few race through it. Dehydration and hyperthermia can become life-threatening, and in an environment so close and with so few people along the trails, it is essential that everyone that goes out to the Amazon has an awareness of how their body responds to heat stress, and knows how to take action accordingly.

Naturally, I hope that I will be able to stay involved in the race, and that I will be able to return, either as a competitor or as support crew, over the coming years. I love the Amazon and the great friends I made there, many of whom I am sure I shall keep in touch with for years to come. For some time after my first visit there were 'Reply all' emails being sent amongst over thirty contacts. Now, thanks to Facebook, we all know how each other's training is coming along and which races people have lined up. The camaraderie of those involved in these events is greater than I have witnessed anywhere else. The sense of wishing to help and support other athletes and crew is overwhelming.

I have met people in some races that actually wanted others to fail so that their position would be higher, whereas in the Amazon I saw people too dejected to continue when a friend dropped out. Similarly I saw people giving food that was not spare to those that needed it to get through the day. Competitors stopped along the trail to help those that were suffering, and the greatest of efforts was always made to help struggling comrades through. Perhaps that in itself is indicative of how challenging this race is. There is something inspiring that may be felt when experiencing someone else's hardships with them, and giving something up to aid them through to a triumph at the end. I have of course seen examples of such behaviour in other races, but never to such a degree because further help was always so easily attainable, and in any case simply demonstrates why I believe that many of us runners are the true salt of the earth.

The Jungle Marathon represents the toughest of ultra-endurance adventure races, but it represents the greatest of them too. For most, the Amazon is such a formidable environment, but it is the place of dreams as well. It is an area of wild landscapes and tropical beaches. It is home to some of the last wild cultures on earth. Its nature is untamed and aggressive, yet it is a home that feeds and provides for its inhabitants. Realistically, of course, it is a place that is being destroyed by deforestation, and Jungle Marathon competitors represent a portion of the eco-tourists that bring money to the region without harming the land. In that sense, if in no other, perhaps I (even 'we') have a moral obligation to support the race and save a dying part of our world.

Supporting and competing in the Jungle Marathon has been the experience of a lifetime, and it has been an absolute joy. I am grateful to those that recommended it to me, and similarly I hope that those whom compete themselves having read this book, bare me no grudge. The route and locations may change from year to year, but the general terrain will remain the same and the spirit of the race will persist. There will be trials and tribulations throughout, and there will likely be times of severe anguish and anxiety, later melted away by moments of wondrous astonishment and the deep joy that can come from seeing the surroundings and situations with fresh eyes.

The Jungle Marathon

The Amazon can be a terrifying, belittling, and unnerving place, but for the very same reasons, it can be a wondrous, adventurous, and fulfilling place, filled with beauty and of areas still unaffected by industry; a true paradise. To run through such an environment, competing in an ultra-endurance running race, bringing together such a challenging pastime in such arduous conditions, and through this all to gain personal triumph at the end, is nothing less than the achievement of the sublime.

A year later, and another group of competitors are preparing to head out into the jungle. I am envious that I cannot be with them, and I long to be once again drifting along the Rio Tapajos, or lying in my hammock after a hard day's run, or relaxing and cooling off in a creek or river. I miss the leaf litter under foot and the close jungle trails. I want to feel that heat, burning me up and keeping my mind racing with considerations of hydration, electrolytes and energy expenditure.

When John and I were discussing our race histories, we agreed that the Jungle Marathon was by far the most fun, as ridiculous as that might seem. The scenery changes every few paces, and it is never possible to see more than a few tens of metres ahead, once beneath the canopy. There are hot, narrow trails; the air is humid and difficult to breathe, whilst the streams and creeks are cool, crisp and fresh. Fallen tree trunks must be climbed over and swamps of saturated black mud must be waded through. The jungle bites and stings, and it cuts and it burns; but it is also one of the most beautiful places I have ever seen, or been privileged enough to experience.

Epilogue

In the evening, when the banter of nearby friends in hammocks comes to rest, then the Howler Monkeys in the trees take over. They cry out their alarm calls such that all may know that darkness follows. Then it is the loud, continuous noise of the cicadas. It fills the night and resonates perfectly with the jungle air. Above it all, a brilliant white moon sits in a starlit sky above the impossibly wide and calm waters of the Rio Tapajos. The water is black in the night, and its waves gently lap the sands of the beach, just a few metres away from us at the jungle's edge. And when the morning comes, just before first light, then we will be awake; taping our feet and eating our breakfasts; preparing for another great day of running through the Amazon Rainforest. I cherish that moment when I stand proud and focussed near the start line; my best friends close by. When the running starts, as the Sun is rising in a pale blue sky; then the world comes alive, and could not possibly be more striking, more meaningful, or more poetic.

The Jungle Marathon exists because we exist: we runners that want to push ourselves and see a world of adventure as well as one of fitness and training and lifestyle choices. Simply to be a runner is all that is required. An adventurous spirit will help with maintaining the interest. Training frequency and mileages must invariably increase, and we must learn to tune-in to the feedback of our bodies: our temperature, our breathing and our muscles and joints. Then, it is time to see how we fare in novel environments and in the company of likeminded people. It is both easier and harder than most people would imagine. In terms of what needs to be achieved from training, then it is straightforward enough to be considered easy. If the training has accomplished what was required, then the completion of the race will be easy, at least in such a sense as physical fitness and ability. Balancing everything; managing ourselves through it as we might like to do and still gaining some element of satisfaction from it; that is what is difficult. To sink rather than swim in such an event can be the result of one wrong decision: one misinterpretation of how our body was truly faring. But, perhaps for us to experience the sublime, then this is a part of the challenge to be relished.

Whatever hardships existed in the Amazon, they were of no significance when I consider the joys that came from being there. I can well remember the acute soreness of my feet, during the final half-marathon to the finish of the long stage. I remember the anguish of my deteriorating health and its consequences during the subsequent day. What I remember most of all though is that tunnel-like view of the jungle when dashing along the trail, of friendships formed and of the banter with those I met along the way. I remember a glorious run along the beach at the very end. Most of all, my one perfect memory is that of staggering out onto the white sand beach near the end of the long stage, and feeling the cool breeze and seeing the bright moon up in the sky and the river at my feet. I remember being there with one of my best friends, and I remember taking time out to lie back on the sand and take it all in.

If I were given the choice between sitting here and writing this, and being back out there with tender feet pounding a jungle path, then I am afraid to say I would happily be on that trail. Now, in point of fact, I must end this final rant and head out to Epping Forest on the outskirts of London. As is so often the case nowadays, another race looms. It will not be as grand or as exciting as the jungle, as it is a paltry triple-marathon along England's southern Jurassic coast, but it ought to keep me spared from trouble for the best part of a day. I shall be running with John B, whom I met in the jungle in 2007, and Sophie from 2008. As for this evening's two-hour run in the forest: I would not have it any other way.

"Security is mostly a superstition. It does not exist in nature, nor do the children of men as a whole experience it. Avoiding danger is no safer in the long run than outright exposure. Life is either a daring adventure, or nothing."

- Helen Keller

Appendix

Planning and Preparation

You can never have too much information about the place that you are going to. Unfortunately, with the Amazon, there are very few useful maps available. I attempted to find some prior to my visit, but the best I could manage was to trace the route of the boat with Google Earth. Because of the thick jungle canopy, and the fact that the hills although frequent are not particularly high, there is currently no good means that I am aware of for exploring the topography in advance. Maps simply show that the area is green. An indication of topography, however, is available in the map books issued to competitors before the start of the race.

The Amazon rainforest is the largest equatorial forest in the world, and contains thirty percent of the world's remaining forested land. One tenth of the planet's plant and animal species live within the Amazon. The Amazon River itself is over 4000 miles in length (6577 km), and has over 1100 tributaries. It is reckoned to carry 20 percent of the world's fresh water. The Amazon Basin has no land above 1000 feet (300 metres) in elevation. If you are fortunate to be at the harbour in Santarem during the hours of daylight, then it is possible to see the *Meeting of the Waters*, where the deep blue waters of the Rio Tapajos meet with the milky, sediment-filled waters of the Amazon. The language used by most in the region is Portuguese, and few locals were able to converse in English. Gil, the photographer and local guide, was used as the translator on the many occasions when it was necessary.

The temperature tends to hover around the low- to mid-30s Celsius during the day, with humidity between 85 and 100 percent. Temperatures in the high 30s are virtually unknown, and there is a yearly average of 27C, with temperatures being consistent throughout the year. Because the race takes place during the dry season, it rarely rains more than once a day (during the wet season it may rain continually). The rain usually lasts less than an hour, but is torrential and will test the knots on any basha/hammock-cover. Along the trail, the path can quickly become a muddy stream, making progress almost impossible. There will always be a temptation at such times to move off the trail and progress around it, but doing so increases the risk of injury from plants or attacks by insects, wasps, and so on. The rain also brings out tics, so it then becomes necessary to increase the frequency of personal checks. Using a buddy to look for tics on the back and other out-of-sight regions is recommended. When the Sun is out, it will begin to feel hot from shortly after 8 in the morning, hence on most days the race starts at sunrise or shortly thereafter. At nighttime, the temperature may become cool, but never cold (it very rarely drops below 10 degrees Celsius).

The nature of the land varies with weather conditions. Swamplands shrink and expand, and the rivers and creeks rise and fall. Where trail has been cut, trees may fall down overnight, creating fresh obstacles. Sometimes the route will be adapted at the last minute to avoid sections where the swamps or trails are too dangerous. Mostly, however, these sections must simply be accepted as a part of the nature of the area. If you go to the jungle, then these circumstances must be expected and dealt with to the best of your ability (most often with patience and extreme care). Swamps vary in depth, and one unlucky step can cause you to go from swamp a few centimetres deep to over two metres. Use exposed roots and fallen trees for support, and be aware that they may be home to more permanent jungle-dwellers. Strive never to disturb what is overhead, as branches may connect to wasp nests, and wasps rarely enjoy their important work being disrupted.

Risks of injury from animal life are plentiful but unlikely to materialise. In the rivers there are stingrays, electric eels, piranhas, caimans, snakes and giant catfish. When entering water, be sure to shuffle, so as to give nearby creatures the chance to move out of the way (stingrays, for example, dwell near the bottom and are likely to sting if a foot crashes down on them from above). Beware the candiru! This miniature catfish is known to swim up the flow of urine until it becomes lodged. This is incredibly painful, and the relief obtained once a soldier has chopped a chap's member off with his machete could only be welcomed in the short-term (deaths have allegedly followed 'lack of treatment', although I am unclear if this would have been due to pain, stress or physical damage; the fish do not just sit there). Avoid urinating in water, whether it be river, swamp or even a puddle, at all costs. Curiously, it seems that women are not similarly afflicted, although I would not recommend urinating into water just in case.

On land, risks are from ants, caterpillars, scorpions, spiders and snakes, mostly. Various plants are spiky and/or sharp, and may easily lacerate the skin. Jaguars and wild pigs can be dangerous, as they tend to be territorial, but are unlikely to attack humans. Making yourself big and shouty might help, but similarly it might not. Running is always a bad response when confronted with a carnivore, because instinct tends to switch them into hunting mode, and they will give chase when they had no intention of doing so previously. Climbing a tree might help, but you would need to be quick, and you would definitely lose some places in the race. Being big and shouty is the only advice that I have come across. The trails are mostly too small to be able to give anything a wide birth. When dangerous animals are reported along the trail, competitors are held at the previous checkpoint, until it is deemed safe to continue.

In all cases, defence is firstly about avoidance. Do not place your hands onto any jungle surface that you do not need to. Keep to the trails, and avoid lying down anywhere but in your hammock. I accept that I may have laid down on the floor, as did many other competitors, but we all knew we would have had only ourselves to blame if anything had gone wrong. Most dangerous animals will attack only in defence, either of themselves or their territory. Some snakes can jump three or more metres, if the mood takes them, so do not antagonise them under the impression that you are swifter than them. With snakes, the first bite is usually reactive and a warning, and so contains less poison than a second bite.

I had tried to familiarise myself with many of the snakes of South America, but it is particularly challenging because the patterns found in North America are different. There is a system for recognising a Coral snake and distinguishing it from a non-poisonous relative, which works in North America but not in South. If you have the time to learn the various types, then this may become of use should you be bitten and need to inform someone of the offending species. But, a snake bite is unlikely; a bite from a poisonous snake is less likely still, and the risk of a lethal bite is minimal. Should you be bitten, then once out of harms way it is essential that the wound be treated as if it were a fracture, i.e., totally immobilised, in this case to limit the movement of blood (and poison) around the area. An emergency whistle is a part of the survival kit required by all competitors, and a distress signal (six blows) should be given until help arrives. The first person to reach you should then head for the nearest checkpoint and alert staff.

The snakes to watch out for are the Fer de Lance, Bushmaster and Coral snakes. The Fer de Lance (Bothrops atrox) is of a brownish colour with pale geometric markings. It grows to 4-6 feet (1.2-2 metres) in length. Some relatives have a more reddish colour, and some live in trees. The Bushmaster (Lachesis muta) has a large head, is pinkish-brown in colour, and marked with dark brown triangles. It averages 6-8 feet (2.0-2.6 metres) in length, and is typically nocturnal. Coral snakes are deadly but not aggressive. They usually reach 1.5-

3.0 feet (0.5-1.0 metre) in length, and have a banded skin of red, black and either white or yellow.

Leeches are not likely to be found in this region of the rainforest. Insects will be attracted to sweat, and are likely to sting and bite as they banquet on your salt. The armpits and groin are particularly vulnerable and should be protected. Insect repellent tends not to be useful here. Ants, particularly the small red fire ants, are an irritant but not particularly dangerous (unless in vast numbers). The bites create a localised burning sensation, and as these ants mostly inhabit the ground it is the feet and lower legs that are most susceptible. It is imperative, however, that they should not have access to the face, because should venom reach the eyes then blindness can result. Bites from the larger black ants can be amazingly painful, and should be avoided wherever possible. One species of black ant; the Isula or Bullet ant, which I have only seen as solitary individuals, are extremely large (up to 5 centimetres) and can leave their victim shivering from fever and intensely ill. The affected area can become paralysed for up to twenty-four hours. Bullet ants can often be found on lower areas of trees and within hollow trunks. Most ants, scorpions and spiders, have the capacity to leave their victim in pain, but are generally not lethal (there are, unfortunately, exceptions).

Disease threats are numerous. These include various amoebic and bacillary dysenteries (something my long-stage of the race could have benefited without), Yellow Fever, Blackwater Fever, Dengue Fever, Malaria, Cholera, Typhoid, Rabies, Hepatitis,

Tuberculosis, Chagas' Disease, Onchocerciasis and Leishmaniasis. Vaccinations against Cholera, Typhoid, Hepatitis, and Tuberculosis should all be up-to-date. Rabies is a risk, although within the jungle it is the bats that are the most likely carriers. I chose against vaccination as I knew that I could be transported to a hospital within the required 24-hours.

I used Malarone for protection against malaria. The mosquitoes in this region are resistant to some anti-malarials, and as this can change it is important to check beforehand. Malarone is expensive, but is easier to take than some others (some need to be taken before and for many weeks after). Malaria can lay dormant in the liver for years after infection, so it is essential that any flu-like symptoms are taken seriously, and any doctor examining you is informed that you visited this region of the Amazon. With regard to the other diseases mentioned, avoid drinking water that has not been boiled (Puri-tab if necessary), and protect your skin from insect bites. For the latter, I wore long shorts and a shirt when not racing, but I soon gave up on the insect repellent, which at 100% Deet appeared to do nothing but melt my camera and sunglasses. Fortunately, there were not many mosquitoes around the camp areas, although this would be dependant upon local climate (I was on the boat during my support visit and saw clouds of mozzies there so thick they could be seen from the shore).

Infections are a much greater risk in the jungle than elsewhere. The humid environment delays clotting, further increasing the risk. All cuts, however slight, should be treated at the end of each day's stage at the latest, and not ignored. Any illness will limit your ability to complete the remainder of the race, so it is essential that health and hygiene are tended to as priorities. Wounds should naturally dry out well once out of the jungle and at the camps. I would typically wash, clean wounds, and then spray them with Betadine. I did not see the worth in covering wounds, as they needed only to be dry to be safe. In any case, there were not enough plasters on the planet to cover all the stupid little cuts I earned during the Jungle Marathon.

Details of recommended vaccinations can be obtained through G.P. surgeries or dedicated travel health centres. Many such places can be found on the internet (in London, for example, there is **www.masta.com**, which is based close to Oxford St.), and one can often visit without an appointment. It may also be useful to know that some G.P. surgeries add an extra charge for issuing certain pharmaceuticals that are deemed 'private prescriptions'.

Any infections contracted in the Amazon need to be assessed as early as possible. I suffered flu-like symptoms following my first visit, and although I made the effort to see a doctor, which I would not have done ordinarily, I accepted it when they shrugged off the idea it could be related to my time in the Amazon. This was a mistake, and I should have pressed further for a blood test. As malaria can lay dormant for years, it is important that appropriate action is taken should indications occur. Following my second trip, one toe became infected, and despite spending a couple of weeks cleaning it thoroughly and doing all I could do reduce the infection, it was a losing battle. After one week of antibiotics there were no further signs of infection.

Clothing and Equipment

This information is purely included as a guide. I can only refer to the kit that I used, and how that worked for me. Another person could use the exact same clothing and equipment and have a very different experience. Hence, personal experience is the best guide, but I have included what I used as I appreciate many people may like it for comparison or inspiration.

Clothing

The jungle is hot, sticky, and sharp. I selected clothing that was minimal, so as to allow clear transfer of sweat from my skin to the air. The items were also made of tight fabrics, as I feared that loose-fitting clothing would snag and tear easily on sharp tree spines and such like. Because I had been impressed with Salomon's kit in the past, I wore their running vest and shorts. Beneath the traditional-style running shorts I wore their tight shorts too. These functioned as the base layer, and because of the fabric they were still comfortable when wet from sweat, swamps and rivers. Most importantly, perhaps, I had selected that style of shorts because they would remain tight to the skin and save inconvenience should any smaller jungle inhabitants wish to experience the environment of my nether-regions. Although amusing, this is an important point, as many insects and creepy-crawlies enjoy the warm and moist atmosphere of the anus. The number of bites I received in lines around the base and top of the shorts was testament to the number of critters frustrated by my successful efforts to keep them at bay.

I wore some short Injinji socks throughout the race. Their being short meant that they did not hold water for long, and therefore did not drain water into my shoes. The Injinji style also meant that my toes did not rub, and hence I derived no friction-based blisters. As at the *Marathon des Sables*, I wore Salomon's XA Pro 3D GTX. These are great shoes because they give so much support and protection. I would probably aim for a model without the Gore-Tex in the future, as it is not really useful in the jungle environment. Importantly, they now make them in a size 13.5, which would have saved my feet had I used those instead of the size 12.5 that I crammed my feet into when I raced. The ground is uneven and strewn with branches, roots and so on, so the grip of those shoes was superb. I am sure that normal trainers would have increased the likelihood of slips and falls.

On the last day I used a bandana to protect my head, and wore a pair of Julbo sunglasses. Neither were necessary prior to that day because of the protection of the canopy, and I could have managed without the bandana (it became hot after the early morning, and the final stage could be completed before the hottest part of the day if run at a good and consistent pace). I used a Stormlite Compass Master M1 watch, because I could not afford a good Suunto or

Garmin. The most useful feature of the Stormlite was the skin thermometer, which although not wholly accurate due to the combined effects of skin and ambient temperature, was nevertheless a very useful guide. I would strongly recommend a watch with a thermometer for this event, and having plenty of trials before the race to familiarise yourself with it (the temperature at which you begin to feel exhausted, is the main finding of interest).

After the race I had my 'dry kit' available, which comprised another pair of shorts and a lightweight, long-sleeved shirt. I also had a pair of very cheap and very lightweight flip-flops. It is particularly pleasant to change out of running shoes at the end of each stage, and open sandals, etc, are useful for protecting the feet whilst allowing wounds to dry.

Equipment

I used a Raid Revo 30 rucksack, mainly to keep my Salomon theme consistent, but also because most people tended to use Raidlight's, and I had wanted to be different. As it happened, there is now a growing number of people at these events that favour Salomon's kit. Other manufacturers are also on the rise and experimenting with adventure racing gear. The rucksack should be as light as possible, especially as heavier fabrics may become a nightmare should they become saturated. I used a large drybag to put the rucksack into for river crossings, and there was additional space to trap air and so functioned as a buoyancy aid.

I used a Platypus water bladder. Some people like Camelbaks, but I have seen too many with broken seals to ever wish to use them. Platypus actually followed suit, and made a version with a 'zip' lid. I tried it once, and the lid did not work particularly well and the seal for the hose ripped the first time I attempted to use it. Hence, I prefer the original Platypus, with a screw-on hose where the bladder is also filled-up from. It takes longer to use than the newer version or the Camelbaks, but I find them more reliable.

Sleeping Equipment

A hammock, mosquito net and basha (waterproof cover) are a must. All need to fit together as a unit. I used a Special Forces jungle hammock (bought from E-bay), which was durable and had two-layers, and which I had fully intended to use again after the race (and subsequently have). I had to buy a number of mosquito nets before I found one that worked passably with the hammock, although that still required some gaffa tape. I would use the same again, but for many the Hennessy hammocks will be more appropriate, as they are far lighter than the kit I used. A silk sleeping bag liner is sufficient to sleep in. I tried sleeping only in clothes during my first visit, and found that it became sufficiently cool some nights for it to be uncomfortable. The silk liner I used during the race was warm, pleasant to sleep in, and ultra-lightweight. My top tip is to use Deet insect repellent on the hammock ropes. I used this in areas where ants were in high concentrations and yearned to explore the hammock in more detail. Although the Deet was apparently useless against mosquitoes, I found it very effective at preventing the ants' progress along the ropes.

Other Equipment

A specific first aid kit list is issued each year, along with other important information for racers. As this is liable to change, there is no reason to include it here. However, I would like to mention that in my experience, gauze, tape and Betadine came in the most useful. I used Strappal zinc oxide tape, because it has a good adhesive, and is elastic enough to function as a support tape if required.

A survival kit is also required, but as the essential contents may change with time, I will not give specific details here. However, an emergency whistle is a part of the kit, and something that I always wore around my neck (since it would probably be of no use in my rucksack). A small hunting knife was gaffer-taped to a strap of my rucksack. Whilst it might be tempting to look the part and wield a mighty machete, it is going to be far too bulky and heavy. I used a machete during my support visit, where it was used for cutting through undergrowth when clearing the paths. Competitors will not be required to do this and so it would represent a redundant burden. A small knife may give some piece of mind, being no doubt longer and sharper than fingernails, but mine remained secure on my rucksack strap and was only used for first aid and general, mundane and unadventurous tasks.

I stored everything within variously sized Exped Drybags. These are ultra-lightweight and very robust. I love Expedition Foods (**www.expeditionfoods.com**) for main meals. They have an 800 Kcal range that is far superior in energy to most dehydrated meals. I had some beef jerky as well, which I added to the Expedition dinners, as the solid meat tasted good and slowed digestion (staving off hunger for longer). I also used their breakfast meals in the mornings, and only wish that I had taken advantage of the variety they had on offer. For the rest of the day I used Powergels and various energy bars.

I used the Electrolyte drink powder from SIS (Science in Sports) in my water bladder. Although the electrolytes and carbohydrates make this a superior blend to many sports drinks on the market, I do not approve of the sweeteners that they use. I have an associate now that can make energy drinks to order, and I am happy to make recommendations (see **www.infinitnutrition.eu** for more details). I carried a small bag of table salt, as this could be used to top-up on sodium if I felt it necessary. As it was, I managed to tailor the concentration of my energy drink sufficiently to not require it.

No 'calorie' requirement can be given, because calories themselves are a fairly redundant concept. The energy that your body burns during a day or activity can be measured in calories, as can be the energy contained within food. However, they are not equivalent measurements. The calories in food are measured following combustion, i.e. processes that do not occur in the body. The body uses enzymes to break food down, and so the energy derived from enzymatic processes, and the energy derived from combustion (as per the label on food), do not tally. I recommend buying lots of different foods, and experimenting in training to find how much, which brand, and which types of foods your body utilises the best for energy. I appreciate that this may seem contradictory, as I have just recommended Expedition Foods 800 Kcal range, but until a better system comes along we must simply assume that an 800 Kcal dehydrated meal will provide us with more energy than a 250 Kcal one. An 800 Kcal dehydrated meal will not furnish my body with as much useable energy as 16 apples each containing 50 Kcal, however in an event such as this we are confined to the practicalities of weight, bulk and the perishable nature of most foods.

During the first couple of days at the base camp, you will have your main kit bag with you as well as your racing gear. Hence, you can make final decisions then about what you wish to take and what you can do without. I would strongly recommend that you take plenty of food for those two days, as it does not do to begin the event having already been surviving on race-rations, and the additional energy can probably only be a good thing. Unless you travel before the scheduled race flight, however, you will be unlikely to have access to shops in Brazil before the trip to the base camp.

In an environment such as the Amazon jungle, hygiene is incredibly important. A toothpaste and toothbrush are a given, and a bar of soap (preferably biodegradable / environmentally-friendly) is useful for cleaning yourself and your clothes. There are showers, creeks or rivers available to wash in each day (please take the utmost care in creeks and rivers, and do not bathe alone). I took a small packet of sunscreen with me, but really only used it on the last day, as that was the only stage in which I was exposed to direct sunlight for any significant length of time. Had I been slower on the third stage, so as to be exposed to the sun for longer, or faster on the long stage, and so exposed to the sun earlier, then I would have required some on those days too.

Insurance

The Jungle Marathon is an ultra-endurance adventure race, involving over 200 kilometres of racing through the Amazon jungle. The heat can soar into the mid-thirties with 100% humidity. In addition, there are risks from wildlife that can never be controlled. Furthermore, the course involves moving along tracks that are cut afresh each year, and so the ground is covered in trip hazards and obstacles. The landscape is hilly, with many extraordinarily steep and slippery sections. Far be it from me to doubt the Post Office travel insurance package, but I would strongly recommend confirming that your policy covers you for this event. I used Dogtag insurance (**www.dogtag.net**), as they have specific cover for extreme sports.

Travel

Generally, travel is arranged via the registration process for the race. Should you wish to travel earlier, or not via the U.K., then Brazilian airline TAM, flies to Santarem. Flights are not generally direct, and often involve stops and transfers at Rio de Janeiro or Sao Paulo, then Manaus and/or Belem. Because the airlines tend to work in a circuit, if you choose a flight that runs in the wrong direction, then there could be up to ten or more stops! From Santarem, travel to Alter do Chao is possible by road (approximately half an hour) or by boat (over an hour, depending on the type of boat). Bus or taxi from the airport should be the simplest form of transfer. There are hotels in both Santarem and Alter do Chao, but as the latter is by far the more pleasant, beautiful and relaxing, I would recommend this over Santarem.

If you choose not to travel on the scheduled flight, please ensure that Shirley is aware so that you are informed of when and where to meet the main boat down to the base camp. Visas are not required for British nationals in Brazil for visits of up to ninety days. In some areas it is necessary that the passport has at least six months remaining on it, and stay duration can be reduced to thirty days for men travelling alone, due to immigration attempting to cut-down on travellers involved in the sex-trade. When first entering Brazil (most likely either Sao Paulo or Rio de Janeiro), you will have to collect your baggage and go through customs and immigration, before checking-in for your next flight.

As with all such events, it is recommended that you wear or carry as much race kit as you are legally permitted to take onboard. Race shoes should be worn, and clothing should be in your race rucksack, along with your post-stage clothing, spare socks, sunglasses, headgear, survival kit and medical kit. Some of the survival and medical kits will have to be taken in the checked baggage, as must much of the food. A customs form will need to be completed to show whether or not food is actually being taken into the country. I am not aware of the permissions required for dehydrated food, energy drinks, gels, bars, and so on, although as the key threat is fresh food, this should not be a concern. I would recommend checking before travelling.

Checked baggage may go missing during the numerous changes, and so the less luggage checked-in the better. Should the worst happen, then the baggage may be recovered and sent on to Santarem within a day or so, in which case it is likely that Shirley would arrange for it to be brought to you. The most important thing is that you get to the boat on time. Other racers will always help out when food and such like is lost, and most of us bring far too much anyway, so as to permit last minute changes and so on (we might not know what we will feel like eating, until we have arrived and experienced the climate for a couple of days, and even then will still take too much for the first two days of the race, just to make sure).

Communication

Satellite telephone and an email service is available, at a charge, to all competitors. Updates of the stages, including competitor rankings, are also uploaded onto the race website. However, a beach and a boat on the Rio Tapajos are not the most stable environments for satellite communications, and faults and disruptions do occur. In 2008, Andreas, the German computer boffin responsible for communications, spent many hours travelling away from the site and into Alter do Chao (possibly further) in order to facilitate the passing on of emails and the website updates. I would suggest making loved-ones, followers and fans aware of this prior to your departure, for fear that they might otherwise think you are ignoring them.

Miscellaneous

This appendix should have answered most common questions likely to be had by potential racers. The Jungle Marathon race website, **www.junglemarathon.com**, will have additional up-to-date information for competitors, and more is supplied on the registration forms.

Training

Because training for an event such as this is so individual, it is not possible to give specific advice. So much depends on existing fitness levels, experience, diet, sleep, stress and recovery ability, that there are simply too many factors to take into account. I would expect that anyone intending to compete in this race, is already well experienced at devising and adapting their own training programmes.

For my training, I built up to running between fifteen and eighteen miles, six consecutive days a week. The onus was very much on the continuous runs, as in order to reflect the requirements of the race, I needed to know that I was fit to run good distances from one day to the next. The six-day weeks would occur no more than once a month, and generally I would run four or five times a week (sometimes three), over distances varying between fifteen and twenty miles (occasionally, but rarely down to eleven miles). If I felt that I needed extra rest then I took it, and I always managed a pace that I knew would not tire me for the next day.

Key features of the training were that I always used a rucksack, and favoured wearing the shoes and clothing I would be wearing during the race. Had I the chance (time and money), then I would have prioritised training in a hot and humid climate, I would have travelled out to Brazil at least a week prior to the start of the race, and I would have incorporated hill-training as the mainstay of my preparation.

Ian Mayhew, an Exercise Scientist with a Master's degree in Exercise Nutrition, designs training programmes for ultra-runners, cyclists, Ironmen and triathletes. He can be reached via his website: **www.gearsandtears.com**

Suggested Reading

On the Amazon:

Bartlett, R. D., (2003) "Reptiles and Amphibians of the Amazon. An Ecotourist's Guide", University Press of Florida, Florida, United States.

Bates, W. H., (2007) "In the Heart of the Amazon Forest", Penguin Books Ltd., London, England.

Blake, P., Sefton, A., (2004) "The Last Great Adventure of Sir Peter Blake. From the Antarctic to the Amazon", Adlard Coles Nautical, London, England.

Emmons, L., (1999) "Neotropical Rainforest Mammals", Second Edition, University of Chicago Press, London, England.

Kricher, J., (1999) "A Neotropical Companion", Second Edition, Princeton University Press, Chichester, England.

O'Hanlon, A., (1989) "In Trouble Again", Penguin Books Ltd, London, England.

Von Humboldt, A., (2007) "Jaguars and Electric Eels", Penguin Books Ltd., London, England.

On Endurance:

Armstrong, L., (2001) "It's Not About the Bike", Yellow Jersey Press, London, England.

Armstrong, L., (2003) "Every Second Counts", Yellow Jersey Press, London, England.

Appendix

Askwith, R., (2004) "Feet in the Clouds. A Tale of Fell-Running and Obsession", Aurum Press Limited, London, England.

Fiennes, R., (2007) "Mad, Bad and Dangerous to Know", Hodder and Stoughton General, London, England.

Hines, M., (2007), "The Marathon Des Sables: Seven Days in the Sahara Enduring the Toughest Footrace on Earth", Healthy Body Publishing, England.

Karnazes, D., (2006) "Ultramarathon Man. Confessions of an All-Night Runner", Penguin Books Ltd., London, England.

Stroud, M. (2004) "Survival of the Fittest. Understanding Health and Peak Physical Performance", Yellow Jersey Press, London, England.

Symonds, H., (2004) "Running High. The First Continuous Traverse of the 303 Mountains of Britain and Ireland", Hayloft Publishing, Cumbria, England.

Bibliography

Armstrong, L. E., Maresh, C. M., Gabaree, C. V., Hoffman, J. R., Kavouras, S. A., Kenefick, R. W., Castellani, J. W., Ahlquist, L. E., "Thermal and circulatory responses during exercise: effects of hypohydration, dehydration, and water intake", Journal of Applied Physiology, 1997, 82 (6), 2028-2035

Avellini, B. A., Kamon, E., Krajewski, J. T., "Physiological responses of physically fit men and women acclimation to humid heat", Journal of Applied Physiology, 1980, 49 (2), 254-261

Blake, P., Sefton, A., (2004) "The Last Great Adventure of Sir Peter Blake. From the Antarctic to the Amazon", Adlard Coles Nautical, London, England.

Casa, D. J., "Exercise in the heat. I. Fundamentals of thermal physiology, performance implications, and dehydration", Journal of Athletic Training, 1999, 34 (3), 246-252

Casa, D. J., "Exercise in the heat. II. Critical concepts in rehydration, exertional heat illness, and maximising athletic performance", Journal of Athletic Training, 1999, 34(3), 253-362

Casa, D. J., Armstrong, L. E., Montain, S. J., Rich, B. S. E., Stone, J. A., "National Athletic Trainers' Association Position Statement: Fluid Replacement for Athletes", Journal of Athletic Training, 2000, 35 (2), 212-224

Castellani, J. W., Maresh, C. M., Armstrong, L. E., Kenefick, R. W., Riebe, D., Echegaray, M., Kavouras, S., Castracane, V. D., "Endocrine responses during execise-heat stress: effects of prior isotonic and hypotonic intravenous rehydration", European Journal of Applied Physiology, 1998, 77, 242-248

Convertino, V. A., Brock, P. J., Keil, L. C., Bernauer, E. M., Greenleaf, J. E., "Exercise training-induced hypervolemia: role of plasma albumin, renin, and vasopressin", Journal of Applied Physiology, 1980, 48 (4), 665-669

Febbraio, M, A., Snow, R. J., Stathis, C. G., Hargreaves, M., Carey, M. F., "Effect of heat stress on muscle energy metabolism during exercise", Journal of Applied Physiology, 1994, 77 (6), 2827-2831

Febbraio, M. A., Snow, R. J., Hargreaves, M., Stathis, C. G., Martin, I. K., Carey, M. F., "Muscle metabolism during exercise and heat stress in trained men: effect of acclimation", Journal of Applied Physiology, 1994, 76 (2), 589-597

Fink, W. J., Costill, D. L., Van Handel, P. J., "Leg muscle metabolism during exercise in the heat and cold", European Journal of Applied Physiology, 1975, 34, 183-190

Fortney, S. M., Nadel, E. R., Wenger, C. B., Bove, J. R., "Effect of blood volume on sweating rate and body fluids in exercising humans", Journal of Applied Physiology, 1981, 51 (6), 1594-1600

Fortney, S. M., Wenger, C. B., Bove, J. R., Nadel, E. R., "Effect of hyperosmolality on control of blood flow and sweating", Journal of Applied Physiology, 1984, 57 (6), 1688-1695

Francesconi, R. P., Sawka, M. N., Pandolf, K. B., Hubbard, R. W., Young, A. J., Muza, S., "Plasma hormonal responses at graded hypohydration levels during exercise-heat stress", Journal of Applied Physiology, 1985, 59 (6), 1855-1860

Gonzalez, R. R., Pandolf, K. B., Gagge, A. P., "Heat acclimation and decline in sweating during humidity transients", Journal of Applied Physiology, 1974, 36 (4), 419-425

Gonzalez-Alonso, J., Teller, C., Andersen, S. L., Jensen, F. B., Hyldig, T., Nielsen, B., "Influence of body temperature on the development of fatigue during prolonged exercise in the heat", Journal of Applied Physiology, 1999, 86 (3), 1032-1039

Hargreaves, M., Dillo, P., Angus, D., Febbraio, M., "Effect of fluid ingestion on muscle metabolism during prolonged exercise", Journal of Applied Physiology, 1996, 80 (1), 363-366

Havenith, G., Inoue, Y., Luttikholt, V., Kenny, W. L., "Age predicts cardiovascular, but not thermoregulatory, responses to humid heat stress", European Journal of Applied Physiology, 1995, 70, 88-96

Havenith, G., Luttikholt, G. M., Vrijkotte, T. G. M., "The relative influence of body characteristics on humid heat stress response", European Journal of Applied Physiology, 1995, 70, 270-279

Hoffman, J. R., Maresh, C. M., Armstrong, L. E., Gabaree, C. L., Bergeron, M. F., Kenefick, R. W., Castellani, J. W., Ahlquist, L. E., Ward, A., "Effects of hydration state on plasma testosterone, cortisol and catecholamine concentrations before and during mild exercise at elevated temperature", European Journal of Applied Physiology, 1994, 69, 294-300

Latzka, W. A., Sawka, M. N., Montain, S. J., Skrinar, G. S., Fielding, R. A., Matott, R. P., Pandolf, K. B., "Hyperhydration: thermoregulatory effects during compensable exercise-heat stress", Journal of Applied Physiology, 1997, 83 (3), 860-866

Latzka, W. A., Sawka, M. N., Montain, S. J., Skrinar, G. S., Fielding, R. A., Matott, R. P., Pandolf, K. B., "Hyperhydration: tolerance and cardiovascular effects during uncompensable exercise-heat stress", Journal of Applied Physiology, 1998, 84 (6), 1858-1864

Maresh, C. M., Gabaree-Boulant, C. L., Armstrong, L. E., Judelson, D. A., Hoffman, J. R., Castellani, J. W., Kenefick, R. W., Bergeron, M. F., Casa, D. J., "Effect of hydration status on thirst, drinking, and related hormonal responses during low-intensity exercise in the heat", Journal of Applied Physiology, 2004, 97, 39-44

Mitchell, J. W., Nadel, E. R., Stolwijk, J. A. J., "Respiratory weight losses during exercise", Journal of Applied Physiology, 1972, 32 (4), 474-476

Montain, C. J., Coyle, E. F., "Fluid ingestion during exercise increases skin blood flow independent of increases in blood volume", Journal of Applied Physiology, 1992, 73 (3), 903-910

Montain, S. J., Coyle, E. F., "Influence of graded dehydration on hyperthermia and cardiovascular drift during exercise", Journal of Applied Physiology, 1992, 73 (4), 1340-1350

Montain, S. J., Coyle, E. F., "Influence of the timing of fluid ingestion on temperature regulation during exercise", Journal of Applied Physiology, 1993, 75 (2), 688-695

Montain, S. J., Latzka, W. A., Sawka, M. N., "Control of thermoregulatory sweating is altered by hydration level and exercise intensity", Journal of Applied Physiology, 1995, 79 (5), 1434-1439

Montain, S. J., Latzka, W. A., Sawka, M. N., "Impact of muscle injury and accompanying inflammatory response on thermoregulation during exercise in the heat", Journal of Applied Physiology, 2000, 89, 1123-1130

Montain, S. J., Sawka, M. N., Cadarette, B. S., Quigley, M. D., McKay, J. M., "Physiological tolerance to uncompensable heat stress: effects of exercise intensity, protective clothing, and climate", Journal of Applied Physiology, 1994, 77 (1), 216-222

Nadel, E. R., Fortney, S. M., Wenger, C. B., "Effect of hydration state on circulatory and thermal regulations", Journal of Applied Physiology, 1980, 49 (4), 715-721

Nadel, E. R., Pandolf, K. B., Roberts, M. F., Stolwijk, J. A. J., "Mechanisms of thermal acclimation to exercise and heat", Journal of Applied Physiology, 1974, 37 (4), 515-520

Neufer, P. D., Young, A. J., Sawka, M. N., "Gastric emptying during exercise: effects of heat stress and hypohydration", European Journal of Applied Physiology, 1989, 58, 433-439

Nielsen, B., Hales, J. R., Strange, S., Christensen, N. J., Warberg, J., Saltin, B., "Human circulatory and thermoregulatory adaptations with heat acclimation and exercise in a hot, dry environment", Journal of Physiology, 1993, 460, 467-485

Nielsen, B., Savard, G., Richter, E. A., Hargreaves, M. Saltin, B., "Muscle blood flow and muscle metabolism during exercise and heat stress", Journal of Applied Physiology, 1990, 69 (3), 1040-1046

Nose, H., Mack, G. W., Shi, X., Nadel, E. R., "Shift in body fluid compartments after dehydration in humans", Journal of Applied Physiology, 1988, 65 (1), 318-324

O'Hanlon, A., (1989) "In Trouble Again", Penguin Books Ltd, London, England.

Pandolf, K. B., Cadarette, B. S., Sawka, M. N., Young, A. J., Francesconi, R. P., Gonzalez, R. R., "Thermoregulatory responses of middle-aged and young men during dry-heat acclimation", Journal of Applied Physiology, 1988, 65 (1), 65-71

Roberts, M. F., Wenger, C. B., Stolwijk, J. A. J., Nadel, E. R., "Skin blood flow and sweating changes following exercise training and heat acclimation", Journal of Applied Physiology, 1977, 43 (1) 133-137

Saboisky, J., Marino, F. E., Kay, D., Cannon, J., "Exercise heat stress does not reduce central activation to non-exercised human skeletal muscle", Experimental Physiology, 2003, 88 (6), 783-790

Sawka, M. N., Francesconi, R. P., Pimental, N. A., Pandolf, K. B., "Hydration and vascular fluid shifts during exercise in the heat", Journal of Applied Physiology, 1984, 56 (1), 91-96

Sawka, M. N., Gonzalez, R. R., Young, A. J., Dennis, R. C., Valeri, C. R., Pandolf, K. B., "Control of thermoregulatory sweating during exercise in the heat", American Journal of Physiology, 1989, 257 (Regulatory Integrative Comp. Physiol. 26), R311-R316

Sawka, M. N., Hubbard, R. W., Francesconi, R. P., Horstman, D. H., "Effects of acute plasma volume expansion on altering exercise-heat performance", European Journal of Applied Physiology, 1983, 51, 303-312

Sawka, M. N., Montain, S. J., "Fluid and electrolyte supplementation for exercise heat stress", American Journal of Clinical Nutrition, 2000, 72 (Supplement), 564S-572S

Sawka, M. N., Toner, M. M., Francesconi, R. P., Pandolf, K. B., "Hypohydration and exercise: effects of heat acclimation, gender and environment", 1983, 55 (4), 1147-1153

Sawka, M. N., Young, A. J., Francesconi, R. P., Muza, S. R. Pandolf, K. B., "Thermoregulatory and blood responses during exercise at graded hypohydration levels", Journal of Applied Physiology, 1985, 59 (5), 1394-1401

Sawka, M. N., Young, A. J., Latzka, W. A., Neuffer, P. D., Quigley, M. D., Pandolf, K. B., "Human tolerance to heat strain during exercise: influence of hydration", Journal of Applied Physiology, 1992, 73 (1), 368-375

Smith, J. H., Robinson, S., Pearcy, M., "Renal responses to exercise, heat and dehydration", Journal of Applied Physiology, 1952, 4, 659-665

Takamata, A., Ito, T., Yaegashi, K., Takamiya, H., Maegawa, Y., Itoh, T., Greenleaf, J. E., Morimoto, T., "Effect of an exercise-heat acclimation program on body fluid regulatory responses to dehydration in older men", American Journal of Physiology, 1999, 277 (Regulatory Integrative Comp. Physiol. 46), R1041-R1050

Vrijens, D. M., J., Rehrer, N. J., "Sodium-free fluid ingestion decreases plasma sodium during exercise in the heat", Journal of Applied Physiology?", 1999 86 (6), 1847-1851

No Shore Too Far

Jonathan Stedall

Hawthorn Press

for Jackie,
as promised.

Hawthorn Press

Published by Hawthorn Press, Hawthorn House,
1 Lansdown Lane, Stroud, Gloucestershire, GL5 1BJ, UK
Tel: (01453) 757040
E-mail: info@hawthornpress.com
Website: www.hawthornpress.com

Cover image © Saied Dai
Wood engraving © Miriam Macgregor
Design by Lucy Guenot
Printed by Henry Ling Ltd, The Dorset Press, Dorchester

Every effort has been made to trace the ownership of all copyrighted material. If any omission has been made, please bring this to the publisher's attention so that proper acknowledgement may be given in future editions.

The views expressed in this book are not necessarily those of the publisher.

Printed on environmentally friendly chlorine-free paper sourced from renewable forest stock.

British Library Cataloguing in Publication Data applied for.

ISBN 978-1-907359-81-1

Contents

Preface

My wife Jackie, to whom these poems are dedicated, died in September 2014 at the age of 64. About a year later I wrote a poem for her that I called 'A Bigger Picture'. Since then others have followed, all prompted by my attempt to come to terms with my grief and by my long held belief that death is a transition rather than an end.

Jackie didn't like the word 'battle' in relation to her illness. For two years she 'lived' with cancer. She spoke to our son, Tom, about 'the extraordinary quality of these days, the precious intensity of it all', and about her deep sense of wellbeing. 'I don't know where this inner strength comes from and I don't ask', she said; 'I'm just grateful for it.' In the last weeks she spoke to us on several occasions about how extraordinary it was that she felt so alive.

Jackie's adult life had three quite distinct and fulfilling phases. After reading mathematics at Cambridge she travelled extensively, partly in connection with her role as Overseas Programmes Administrator for the charity War on Want. After we married she devoted ten years or so to bringing up our two young children. She then read for a PhD in the History of Mathematics at the Open University, and in 2000 made her first connection with Oxford where in due course she became Senior Research Fellow of The Queen's College and Lecturer in the Oxford Mathematical Institute. Among the nine books that she wrote, largely on developments in algebra during the sixteenth and seventeenth centuries, was her much acclaimed 'The History of Mathematics: A Very Short Introduction.' In Jackie's obituary in the *Guardian*, her friend and colleague at Oxford, Dr Peter Neumann, referred to 'her exceptional breadth of scholarship.'

At Jackie's funeral our daughter, Ellie, spoke of how her mother's deep sense of the past seemed to make her 'unusually comfortable with her own limited space in time and to give her a quiet confidence in the future.' This confidence and trust is beautifully conveyed in a message she wrote to young people – *'my beloved children, their wonderful friends, nieces, nephews, students'* – that she asked to be read out at her funeral: *'I want you to know how much I loved you; how much I enjoyed seeing you make your way into adult life, each with your own particular energy and expertise. I want to tell you that for a very long time I have been learning more from you than you could ever have learned from me; that wisdom and understanding are not the prerogative of the old or middle-aged, they are yours too. And I want you to know how profoundly I respected your values: your care and respect for me, for your own families, for each other, and for the world about you. I am confident of a future that is in your hands.'*

Jackie's own role in that future will, I believe, be more than just the influence that is inspired by memory; she was less sure of this. Life and death, time and space, the wisdom and beauty that surrounds us – we each had our own way of expressing our understanding and appreciation of these great mysteries. She was increasingly drawn to the silence of a Quaker meeting.

Some months before she died I told her that I wanted to write a book for her. 'You'd better hurry up' was her reply! Yet she knew what I meant and that I believed much could still be conveyed between the living and those who have died – albeit not in words as such, but through what lives in our hearts.

I hope, therefore, that what follows – the thoughts and feelings that prompted what I have written – will be a bridge of sorts, both to her and also to those who sense that there is indeed a bigger picture. Some of the poems are also intimations that in our efforts to extend boundaries of every sort there is, in fact, no shore too far.

Jonathan Stedall

Beauty

So often, as I stand in awe
of beauty in its many forms –
the flowers, a frost,
the kindness in a person's eyes,
our grandson three days old –
I long for you to see them too,
to share the joy,
to share the thrill
that life so often brings.

But then I think,
or rather hope,
that all this beauty isn't lost
because of where you are.
Perhaps, indeed, that joy is there,
and greater than for us;
for you can see
and you can hear
the essence of this world we love
in greater depth,
with brighter light
than those of us still here.

If this is so,
and not some ruse
to keep at bay my tears,
then when I kneel
to thank the world,
I know you're kneeling too.

A Bigger Picture

She said to me,
this brave and thoughtful soul
I so admire and love:
'Why all this talk of angels and the like –
there's so much beauty,
so much goodness here on earth.
Why should we look elsewhere?'

And she was right;
a world sublime
and wise beyond belief
indeed right here at every turn,
and in our daily lives.
And yet like so much else
we witness hour by hour:
the wind, our thoughts,
the life that calls forth flowers from tiny seeds,
we cannot always see
with eyes that have to close at night.

Miracles abound,
both seen and unseen,
day in, day out
and in the here and now.
So, too, the angels and the gods,
of whom I sometimes speak,
are not for me far out in space
or in another world,
but working in our daily lives
to help us out of bed,
and out into the rain;
to help us take the next step,
and the next.

And now she, too,
is nowhere to be seen –
my dear and precious friend,
my wife.
And yet she lives,
of that I feel so sure;
closer perhaps than when we still held hands
or disagreed about the meaning of it all.
Together still, united in our search
for what I sometimes call
a bigger picture:
a journey and a quest
that maybe never ends.

That Robin

That robin who became so tame
when you were ill
is back again,
but not so close.

Perhaps he knew –
not in his tiny brain,
but in his feathered being –
that you would welcome such a friend
when times were hard.
For what keeps animals at bay
comes tumbling down
when people drop their guard
and boundaries start to shrink.

The garden was your world.
You saw each flower and tree anew.
Perhaps you saw them as the robin does.
No wonder you became such friends.

In Touch

There is no number I can call,
and email doesn't work;
yet where you dwell,
just out of range,
is not that far away.
So I must make my own device,
and not with bits of wire,
but woven from the love I feel –
a love that flows through all our lives,
in sky at night,
in light of day,
and will do evermore.

Marmalade

When white, not orange,
cold, not heat,
reminded us our friend, the sun
was very far away,
you, carer of the four of us,
took down your cauldron from the shelf,
and chopped up fruit,
which boiled and boiled,
and filled the house with steam.

And so our treat for months to come
would slowly fill up jars;
and breakfasts were a daily feast
reminding us at start of day
of Spanish warmth,
and English frost,
and all those hours of toil.

Now all is quiet,
but nothing lost –
I live both now and then.
Your skills I miss,
but what remains
so links me still to winter days
when you brought warmth
to all our lives
in many different ways.

But now there's only one jar left,
and that I'll have to keep;
for stored up there
is treasure rare
which helps me not to weep.

Wings

'I'm not so far away,'
is what she sometimes seems to say.
Or is it my imagination,
my need to feel at peace,
to trust that all is well?

'There's nowhere else' –
unbidden come more words –
'I'm here, behind the scenes,
closer than touch,
in realms where time and space
exist no more.'

Then in the silence,
in the chill,
I listen for more help.
How forge those wings
to cross that gulf
and take me where she is?

'Stay where you are,'
her voice calls out.
'Your tasks are in the here and now,
and if you do them well
those wings will grow
and you will fly,
but not to somewhere else;
just closer still
to what is real,
to those you love so much.'

A Bad Day

Today was not so good
despite those lofty thoughts
on which I often dwell.
It all seemed far away,
so far away —
that paradise I glimpse
between the cracks
of daily life.

A tree whose beauty
I admire
in summer, winter,
fog and rain
today seemed dull,
just one of many
near my home
that grows without a care
for us —
or that is how it seemed.

Poor tree!
It's me that's dull,
that's only half awake.
I hope you understand.
And when tomorrow
I return
to gaze with wonder
and with thanks
at you, dear tree,
so silent,
so serene,
you will forgive
those sad, dark thoughts
that only humans feel.

A True Friend?

A few days before he was assassinated by a Hindu
nationalist, Mahatma Gandhi wrote: *'Death is a true friend. It is
only our ignorance that causes us grief.'*

You may be right,
you brave and honest man
who always tried to speak the truth;
and so, at evening prayers,
you died a martyr's death.

But bolder still,
you sometimes said
your truth today
tomorrow may well change.

I share your readiness
to let truth grow,
but have not yet
your total trust
to use that word for death.

Perhaps one's own death
when it comes
feels like a friend;
but not the death
of someone that you love.

A thief is what I see,
but maybe that is me,
forever thinking of myself –
and ignorant;
not always trusting
what I sense is true.

So still I'm sad
on lonely days,
too sad to trust
that all is well;
too selfish
to allow my lovely wife
that friend of whom you wrote.

Vision

Without my eyes
I wouldn't see the world;
but what I never see
are those two eyes themselves.

And as I search
for what it all might mean,
these wonders I behold,
I see not god as once we did –
a god we called the sun.

Perhaps that god has come to us
and lives in eyes
of quite a different kind,
through which we'll see much more.

And maybe such a power as that,
which needs our trust to grow,
is heaven's newest gift to us,
and like the eyes we've had awhile,
cannot itself be seen.

Immortal Life

In his book 'The Circling Year', the poet and novelist
Ronald Blythe writes: *'Our mistake has always been to have
believed that our immortal life begins when our mortal life ends, when in
fact these dual states of our being, the temporal and the eternal, run side
by side from our birth.'*

My mortal life is all too clear –
a baby once,
all new and loved,
but then one day I'll die.
I see that pattern in a flower –
a daisy grows,
a daisy dies,
though daisy species still exists
and reappears from year to year
in thousand small white flowers.

A human being is not a plant –
each one is quite unique.
Am I a species on my own
that grows and flowers,
then disappears,
but maybe comes again?

Yet while I'm here
in sun and rain
I live from day to day.
And what is real,
what matters most,
what gets me out of bed,
are not the thoughts about my death,
but what there is to do.

Yet somewhere lurks
a thought like this:
Immortal life,
if it exists –
what was and is
and will be evermore –
unlike my mortal frame,
was never born in time and space,
and therefore cannot die.
So side by side,
as Blythe suggests,
I live a double life.
And what I hear,
and what I see
without my eyes and ears
is all that lives,
has always lived,
behind what comes and goes.

And if I trust,
and if I pause
amid the daily rush,
so come the memories
faint but sure
of how to cope yet once again
with what I face from day to day
that mortal life demands.

And if I heed
what whispers thus
from lessons long ago,
so grows the strength
to take the helm
and steer my ship
through surging waves
and rocks that lie in wait.   >

Thus born anew
and head held high,
I throw a rope to those like me
who in our puzzled state
at times will doubt
that life persists
when winter slays the flowers.

Oh, welcome storm
and welcome rocks
that wake us from our sleep.
And thus a greater truth unfolds –
no more a double life.
For then we see a law at work
where what we do
while mortal beings
enriches that which never dies,
and also yearns to grow.

Lenses

The Elizabethan poet, Edmund Spenser, wrote in 'The Fairie
Queene' that once a man has missed the way, *'the further he doth
go, the further he doth stray.'*

We've learnt a lot
in recent years,
since Galileo ground his lens
and saw a mystery in the sky
that now we take as fact.

The danger that we face today
is that the lens through which we looked,
before these tools were made,
will wither, fade
through lack of use
and then we'll truly stray.

But I believe
that waking up
is what we're meant to do.
So as we meet along the way
what turns ideas upon their head,
we'll use our reason,
brains and skills
to polish up that other lens,
and so not miss the way.

Trust

How sad for you
if all we do
is weep and mourn,
and dwell upon the past.
And what is worse,
what must be worse,
is the belief that you have left,
that you exist no more.

For me, I know,
not in my head,
it really can't be so.
You feel so close,
so very close –
it matters not the hour.
You're in the air,
and in my thoughts,
and in the light by which we see,
but only see so far.
I also trust
our love, our bond
for you has never ceased.
And what we do
and what we feel
concerns you as before.

Yet some are deaf,
and some are blind,
with eyes that only see
what's on the surface,
comes and goes,
and leads us all astray.
And as they hurry
through their lives,
the danger is they miss that help
that souls like you can give.

For now a precious light is yours –
a light you kindled here;
and you can know,
and you can bring
what angels in their sheltered state
can only learn through us.
And what at times
caused hurt and tears
when side by side we lived,
you now can see
what made it worse:
the workings of those spirits flawed,
so troubled, in their fallen state,
by that great power of love.

And love's the word
that matters most –
it's what I'll always feel –
as I imagine how you are,
and how to help,
how not to cry,
in silence that is only there
when trust and hope are weak.

Insight

'The tree which moves some to tears of joy is in the Eyes of others only a Green thing that stands in the way … As a man is, So he Sees.' William Blake, in a letter to the Revd Dr Trusler, August 23rd 1799.

I see, dear William Blake,
exactly what you mean.
Your vision reached beyond
mere words and paint
and all those scenes sublime
you kindly left to us.
You saw what we
at times can also see –
not with our eyes,
but with that sight
that some will mock
when we see trees
not just as shapes,
as green things in the way;
instead imagine what they feel,
and what they ask of us.

But then I hear my inner voice,
the voice that's always there,
reminding me
that I must work,
and I must grow,
if what I see
that's out of sight
I wish to understand.

So on I go
from day to day,
with head and heart
both working hard,
though head at times
it skips ahead
and leaves my dreams behind.

But on that path
I sometimes pause –
my mind is out of breath.
And then I hope,
I always hope,
that this will be the day
when I will see
what's always there –
she hasn't disappeared.

Alive

'It's strange,' you said,
'how well I feel;'
and then you spoke
another word
that helped me cope,
that helped me see
a deeper truth at work.
'Alive,' you said,
'so much alive.'
And as your body slowly died,
that life in you
it grew and grew
and so outshone
what met our eyes
as words, too, fell away.

And that still lives,
I feel so sure,
the essence that is you.
But now the challenge
that we face
is build a bridge
of love and trust
so we can find
what oft is missed
as we rush round,
both on our feet
and in our heads,
to fill another day.

Our world for you
is not the same,
but not that far away.
And where you are
is closer still
if we slow down
from time to time
and try to share
in silent awe
what lives in us,
what lives in you
and never, never dies.

Letting Go

Letting go
of all the clutter in our lives,
I can imagine brings relief
and peace of mind –
a tranquil place to be.

And when I do the same at death,
and let my body go –
thus letting go of facts I know,
but not of who I am –
will those who weep
not start to see
that I who did the letting go
am still around
to take new steps,
with them not far behind?

News

I often want to tell you things –
not news I read
in big, bold print
that then tomorrow
lights the fire –
but little things
that make me cry,
that make me laugh,
that always give me hope.

Today I had to phone –
a bill that made no sense;
the tone was harsh,
the threat was real,
with sentences in red.
Press one for x
or two for y
and five for something else.
But then a voice,
a human voice,
at last came on the line;
a person who could laugh and joke
and made it all seem fine.

I thanked him then
for all his help,
and thanked him even more
for tearing up his soulless script
no human could have coined.
I thought of you,
you would have smiled –
indeed, perhaps you did.

Not Worth Repairing

'Not worth repairing,'
so they say –
my faithful toaster
and the mower in its shed.

But what of me?
One tooth is cracked;
I need a coat of paint;
I don't hear all that's said.

One day they'll say the same –
'Not worth repairing' –
forgetting that great workshop in the sky,
that's not that far away,
where I myself will one day toil
to make a brand new model,
an improvement on the last –
or so one hopes –
mistakes and faults observed,
some lessons learnt:
a kinder heart, perhaps,
and bigger ears
and smaller mouth,
to listen more
and say much less.

Let's try again
to never burn the toast
or cut the grass
when stones are on the lawn.
Let's have another bash
despite that one big snag –
I come without a guarantee!

Icy Winds

The poet John Betjeman wrote in his verse autobiography
'Summoned by Bells':

'For myself
I knew as soon as I could read and write
That I must be a poet. Even today,
When all the way from Cambridge comes a wind
To blow the lamps out every time they're lit,
I know that I must light mine up again.'

Those icy winds from Cambridge,
they blow through all our lives
if thoughts expressed
do not conform
to what *they* say
(whoever *they* may be).
'It's just imagination'
is a weapon often used –
'Let's stick to what are facts.'

'Hold on,' I hear her say,
for Jackie's still not far away,
and doesn't quite agree!
A Cambridge girl herself,
trained to spot flaws
in woolly folk like me.

Yet maybe what we think
and what we dream
will be tomorrow's world –
a whole new page of facts
which in their turn
will likewise be exposed
as merely signposts on the way.

Meanwhile it's clear to me, at least,
the truth I seek
right here and now
is not within my grasp.
But in my search for clues,
for signs,
of why we're here,
and who we are,
and what it all might mean,
I need the rigour in my work –
a rigour she displayed –
that clearly underpins the truth I seek,
the role that thought has played.

But maybe brains are not enough
in this our age-old quest.
We make machines with stunning skill
that take us to the moon;
but they are toys when you compare
those rockets sleek
to buttercups,
or pears upon a tree.

Far yet to go,
and not just journeys into space,
before we've grasped our own.
And so we light our lamps again
and try, as Betjeman did,
to say what stirs within our hearts,
despite being on our own.
And icy winds can sometimes help
to keep in check the dreams we have,
as poets all at sea.
For what we seek,
what fashioned us,
can feel *and* think,
and we must do the same.

One World

The confidence that you expressed
in those, your final words –
that what unfolds in hands still young,
will steer the world to kinder shores
despite the forces stark and strong
that rock our tender Earth –
this is a trust I also share
when I, too, look around.

For what I see are warriors bold
who fight without a sword;
and they are wise,
and just as strong
as what conspires to dull our hearts
and lead us all astray.
And this they do,
the young you loved,
despite the odds,
despite the spears,
and often thanks to you;
and thanks to all
who've striven thus
to listen to their inner truth
and keep what's false at bay.

And in return they think of you –
and so, of course, do I –
not only then,
when side by side,
as once we used to be,
but here and now
still trying to learn,
and full of praise
for light that does not cease to shine
when the body falls away.

And all those tasks you handed on
are not for us alone;
for you can help in other ways
to keep us strong,
to keep us wise,
on journeys we all share.
For we look up,
and you look down –
or so the saying goes;
but what I sense
is not like that,
for here and there,
and up and down
are just attempts to put in words
a sense we have that you exist
and have not disappeared.

The challenge then:
for us to trust
that our concerns
are your concerns –
our paths are intertwined;
and to affirm for all to hear:
'There only is one world.'

The Angel

There was an artist *
years ago
who deeply loved the world –
the beauty of a flower,
the clouds,
the faces of her dear close friends –
and wondered what it all might mean,
this miracle of life.

And as she worked,
and as she prayed,
there came the question
ever more:
how paint the angel,
pure, sublime –
the one she knew was there –
but unlike flower and tree and bird,
her eyes could never see?

Then slowly as she worked away
there came the thought,
there came a voice:
'I'm not out there,
alone, apart,
but live in you
when you create –
it's there that I exist.
So worry not,
your work is fine,
those paintings *are* of me.'

* *Margarita Voloschin*

The Night

Maybe that God of old,
when he expelled
the father and the mother of mankind
from Eden's peaceful bliss,
was not so full of wrath as told,
for they could keep one precious gift –
the gift He called the night.

And still we can rejoice,
when at the end of each new day
we fall asleep and find again
the place where we began.
And in the morning,
as we rise,
there lingers on a memory faint:
'That Garden still exists.'

Oh, happy Adam, happy Eve
and happy pardoned snake!
For all is well, and nothing lost,
despite our sinful ways;
for still we have the welcome night
in which to forge our plans.
And as we wake
from out our sleep
we bring into the day
what we've absorbed
in other realms
from wiser beings than us.
And thus inspired,
is that our task,
to build a garden here on Earth
where knowledge has a beauty fresh,
the beauty of a flower?

Time Heals

'Time heals,'
or so they say.
Why is this so?
It's true I've ceased to weep
at every mention of her name,
or when I find a note,
or object that she's made.

I hope she knows
it's not the case
that I keep going
and even laugh
because I care no more –
or less than once I did.

Perhaps the healing
comes from her,
for in my heart
I know full well
we're living side by side
through all that happens
hour by hour –
she in ways that I must trust,
and me, as best I can.
It's this that heals,
that helps me cope
and wipes away my tears.

And she in turn,
in different guise,
is closer still to all that helps
this precious world to be.
And being the person that she was
I'm sure she's working hard.
No meals to cook,
no clothes to wash,
but help in other ways.
Her wish to learn,
and on her walks
to marvel at the world –
this will not cease,
but grow and grow
in ways no words convey.

And if I pause
from time to time
and in the silence wait,
I, too, perhaps can sometimes share
a glimpse of what she sees and hears
that needs no eyes and ears.
To do this I must chatter less
and still my restless mind;
be open to what nowadays
might be dismissed
and thereby seen
as wasted, precious time.   >

Alongside this –
as bridge of sorts –
I give to her my love and thanks,
my sense that all is well.
Reminders, too –
if that's a help –
of that which only here is learnt:
above all courage,
and the trust
to flounder in the dark;
a courage she herself displayed
when faced with what to some
seems cruel beyond belief –
an end and letting go
without more land in sight.

Ideas

I often wonder
what you'd do,
or what you'd say,
as dawns for me another day.

Perhaps ideas
I think are mine
are yours as well –
they all combine.

Time and Space

Infinity's a word
we coined way back in time
for something that we sense exists
when distance peters out.
Yet day by day
and year by year,
on travels far and wide,
it's walls and boundaries that we meet
and there we have to stop.

Eternity is just the same
and not within our grasp;
for things begin
and things conclude,
and journeys start
and journeys end,
and in this box we live.
And yet we know it can't be so,
or why invent these words?

We live in time,
we live in space –
that's clear for us to see.
But still the thoughts
we sometimes have –
our reason, some would say –
suggest an insight,
maybe hunch,
that something else behind the scenes,
a something hard to grasp,
enfolds us now
and ever more
in realms without an end.

A Helping Hand

My need to share,
to share with you,
through poems that I write
on life and death
and love and hope,
grows stronger by the day.

When you were here
and we would talk,
especially at the end,
the words I spoke
were sometimes not
the ones that you would choose.
That matters not,
for now you know
(I hope you do)
not in your head,
and not in words
the truth of how things are.

What matters now,
for me still here,
is that I pray
and that I wait
for thoughts that help me
face my day,
so I in turn can give some help
to those who need it more.

With you in mind –
you're always there –
there is a chance,
I sometimes hope,
that what I've read
and what I've thought
about that realm
where you now dwell,
hold insights that contain some truth,
and even help you to adjust,
to see with clearer view.

And I meanwhile
feel very sure
that you in turn
help me to think
more wisely than before.
Perhaps we're even holding hands,
this hand with which I write;
and what I try to share with you,
it is perhaps your gift to me –
the poems are by us.

Morning

It's nearly light –
they're here,
the men who clear the rubbish
from the road.
Their flashing light
sends patterns on my wall.

I wish that someone else
would come and do the same
with all that rubbish
in my head.
What waste of space
those thoughts that often start the day.

I wash and dress,
and then I pause;
an effort is required
to put aside that list of chores
that clutter up my mind.
It all can wait,
I tell myself,
as I sit down beside my bed,
and try to think
with heart, not brain,
what matters most of all.

Give thanks, and pray
for those I know
who *can't* get out of bed,
or if they do,
have fear and dread
of all that lies ahead.
I also think of many friends
no longer here on Earth
who love us still,
as we love them,
our journeys intertwined.

And in the silence
that unfolds
another mood transpires,
in which I marvel,
as all creatures must,
that I am me,
and you are you,
yet none of us alone.

Then down I go,
descending to another day;
some rubbish cleared,
though more, I know,
will soon build up
as ideals slip away.
But with me still
the wish, the prayer
to honour and to share
what Dante glimpsed
so long ago –
'The love that moves the sun
and stars,'
and never, never dies.

Day to Day

Sometimes I try to live
from day to day,
as Jackie did;
to glimpse the everlasting
in the here and now.

Last week has been and gone
and cannot be undone.
Tomorrow, a surprise
and only planned in part.
Yet even thoughts like these
distract me from today.
Why do I question thus?
Why always look elsewhere?

In fact some days,
like most of us,
I see no further
than the nearby hills,
and headlines bleak,
in big bold print
that fill us with alarm.

But in my search for deeper truths
I am no wiser, nor as kind
as many other folk
who have no time
on bus or train
to think of other routes.

Some shop and cook
and stay at home,
to scrub the floor,
and mop up tears
of those they know and love.
Some need no church,
nor have the time
for piles of books
and heady thoughts
to keep them in the know.

Perhaps I need to be more still –
not just my arms and legs –
but in that head which sits on top,
and in my restless mind;
to look and listen
with more care
for that which whispers in the dark
from out the turmoil we call life
of wiser plans at work;
nor turn away from what seems dull
and often sad,
or hopeless in extreme.
Then let life speak in muffled words
of why we need to sweat and toil –
what muscles grow thereby.
So comes the strength
to smile, to hope,
and dream of better days.

Friends with Now

I chose when I was born,
so I believe.
It's why I'm friends with now:
this age that hovers on the brink
of so much good,
and so much bad.
We could go either way.

True, there has always been
a battle of some sort.
But now, I sense,
it's hotting up,
the choice is in our hands.
We have the tools to build anew
and not destroy
through thoughtless deeds –
destroy the Earth itself.

And far the greatest tool of all,
the one that really counts,
is my own choice of how to live,
how serve with head and hands
what in my heart
I know is right,
however steep the climb.

Some dream with longing
for the olden days,
when horses pulled our carts and ploughs
and life for *some*
was far less stressed
and went at gentler pace.
I have no wish to be back then,
when priests and kings,
they called the tune
on what to do
and what to think,
so they could stay in power.
Nor do I crave
some golden age
before it all went wrong,
for childhood is a blissful state,
but not a place to stay.

Perhaps I did,
like all of us,
tread on this Earth before.
I cannot tell,
nor do I know
what lessons and what scars
I bring from other times.
But what is clear,
to me at least,
in this, the age I live,
are stirrings of a basic shift
in how we think,
and how we feel,
and what we hold most dear.   >

But acts of kindness,
modest deeds,
are not what make the news;
still less the thoughts we sometimes have
that things perhaps could change.
For what we're told,
and what's proposed,
if experts are our guide,
are goals of quite another sort
to which we should aspire.

Thus many hurdles
block the path
for change to come about;
for what erupts from out the past,
from battles raging still,
are greed and pride
and surging rage
from wounded, blinkered minds.

And yet there's light,
and yet there's hope,
though sometimes hard to see.
It's why we try,
and try again,
and wipe away the tears.
The tunnel has an end in sight,
it may be far away;
but I rejoice that I am here
to help the world along.

Thy Will be Done

Perhaps that 'will',
the will of God,
it corresponds –
or one day could –
to how I act,
when the lives of others,
and our world's fate,
become for me of greater weight
than all those cares about my life –
success and wealth,
rewards, acclaim,
and aches that warn of death.

And such a thought
makes clear to me
that I exist,
am truly me,
to that extent
that you and I
stand not apart,
but hand in hand,
to better world create.

And so unfolds
what wiser beings
have hoped for from the start –
a harmony that's born of love,
but slowly has to grow.

The Gift of Forgetfulness

In Kenneth Grahame's story 'The Wind in the Willows', in a chapter called 'The Piper at the Gates of Dawn', he describes how Mole and Ratty – out early in their boat to help look for baby otter – have a brief and overwhelming experience of the god Pan. The author then introduces the phrase *'the gift of forgetfulness'*, suggesting that in order for the memory not to overshadow *'mirth and pleasure'*, and so that these two little creatures can get on with their lives as before, *'a capricious little breeze'* brings *'instant oblivion.'*

How little we remember
of what we read and hear and see;
and that can cause concern –
so much seems lost.
Or is it likewise,
as on that riverbank,
a blessing, not a curse
that we forget so much?

Maybe that 'little breeze'
is also there for us –
a gift from wiser realms,
behind the scenes,
where those who guard us still
are well aware that day by day,
and in our conscious minds,
we are not ready,
not prepared,
to be once more with Pan.

And yet he's close,
and so are they,
those spirits we once knew.
For none of them have turned away,
despite our doubts and proud belief
that gods of old were only there
until the age of reason dawned.
They understand, I trust,
that as the human race evolves
what matters most of all
are not the theories in our heads,
but how we help
and how we care –
like Mole and Ratty in their boat –
for others in distress.
Thus we can learn
a truth profound
through what we meet on Earth.

Nor is it quite oblivion
and nothing's really lost;
for as we wake all set to go
and face another day,
there lingers still from out the night
an intimation clear,
that baby otter matters more
than porridge getting cold.

Enlightenment

In forest dense
so long ago,
when night was night
and day still dark,
and all I had to find my way
was one small candle in my hand,
I saw but shadows,
shapes and forms,
and stumbled oft on rocks and thorns,
and nothing had a name.

But what I knew without a doubt
was here was home,
this place so strange,
whatever fear I felt.
And what was asked to stay alive
was trust in flame,
however weak,
to burn and glow despite the wind,
despite the rain –
a triumph over dark.

And now today I have a torch,
a powerful beam of light.
And so I see those shapes anew
and what they are
and how they work –
at least that's how it seems.

And at my bench,
and in my books
I learn more useful facts;
they help me build a safer world
with wood and bricks and steel.

The only problem with this torch,
and all the detail it reveals,
is if it stops us looking round,
and we forget,
or we ignore
the forest we once knew.

Perhaps one day we'll learn to make
a light that shines
not just on this,
not just on that,
but as the candle did.
Then it will show our home again,
a home in cosmos vast,
where rocks and thorns
and humankind
play different roles,
sing different tunes,
as part of one great whole.

And through the skills that we have forged,
as we emerged from out the woods
where once it all began,
so grows the power to see anew
the meaning of it all.
And could it be that torch we seek
is not a tool held in the hand,
but light of quite another sort
that flickers in our minds?

God

'Do you believe,
believe in God?'
is what I'm sometimes asked.
'What do you mean
by this word God?'
is what I then reply.

I have no problem,
as one fragile being
in a universe so vast,
to bend my knee
in awe and thanks
for all the miracles
that I perceive –
the sun and moon,
the air we breathe,
the body that is mine.
And looking round
I'm not convinced
that what exists –
these wonders I behold –
evolved by chance,
without a thought,
arose without a plan.

And faced with mysteries
so profound,
it's no surprise,
in days of old,
we said our prayers
and placed our God
far out in space,
among the stars,
and almost out of reach.
What else to do –
our challenge still –
but think in human terms?

But that's the past,
we now know more,
know what each star might weigh.
We've built machines,
and been in space –
no god appeared on screen.
And so for some those tales of old
are *only* myths that give no clue
to what it all might mean;
for stories are not really true,
if all we read are words.
What they believe must correspond
to what adds up,
to what makes sense,
to reason, as they say.

>

But what *my* reason tends to do,
when faced with questions about God,
is tell me that I need a further sense,
besides those precious five,
to help me grasp,
to help me see
what must indeed exist:
a wisdom,
and I hope a love,
of which we infants in this star-filled space
are largely in the dark.

Yet we exist,
as does our sun,
and little bugs that live and die,
too small for us to see.
Perhaps all this –
existence in its many forms,
including joy and pain –
is all there is,
and what could be,
another name for God.

Duration

It starts,
it ends,
the day, the year,
my life and yours,
and not just us –
perhaps the world itself.
Duration is the word I like
that helps me see how time unfolds,
but in this frame alone.

And so when something ends at last –
duration over and complete –
perhaps it doesn't cease to be
because it's out of sight;
but 'time' no longer is the word
that best describes what then transpires
through other laws at work.

And when I try to understand
what's always there,
that has no end –
a mystery for my earthly brain –
at least it has a name.

Eternity's the word we use,
despite our bond with time;
and there, perhaps,
is where we dwell
each welcome night,
or while we wait,
with other tasks,
for yet another life.

What I Do Is Me

In his poem 'As Kingfishers Catch Fire ...'
Gerard Manley Hopkins writes:
'Each mortal thing does one thing and the same ...
... 'myself ' it speaks and spells,
Crying 'What I do is me: for that I came.'

A flash of colour by the stream,
that bird the poet saw,
it had no choice except to be
its shy and radiant self.
And this it did
year in, year out,
while water, fish,
and plants and sky
its life and tasks sustained.

But what of me who cannot fly,
who learns so slowly how to walk,
and never builds a nest.
What task is mine?
Why am I here,
alone on riverbank?
And how can we,
despite our brains
and all the power we wield,
begin to make,
or even grasp
that miracle called bird?

And yet I sense that I am here
not just by chance and looking on,
but with a role to play.
And maybe, as we stand apart,
a deeper truth unfolds;
for bird is bird,
and fish is fish,
yet neither seems to give a thought
to what it all might mean.
But asking questions as we do,
as universe evolves,
perhaps is nature's way of moving on
and so create anew.

Meanwhile I am aware,
though member of the human race,
that every journey is unique,
that no one is the same.
And as our stories,
yours and mine,
unfold through many lives,
the cards we're dealt,
some red, some black,
not every one an ace,
can each be played
through what we've learnt
in games from long ago.

And such a stance,
if free from pride,
gives meaning to my lonely walk
along that riverbank.
For if I look
and listen hard,
I'll know for what I came.

Awakeners

What wakes me up –
not clock nor birds
to yet another day –
but something far more hard to hear:
to what that day's about?
And what it means,
and why I'm here,
and what I have to do.

Sometimes it's words
that ring a bell,
and call out from a book.
'Yes, that makes sense –
familiar, too,'
is often my response.
Yet years ago,
or just last week,
I might have skipped that page.

Perhaps I'll always find and see
what helps me take a different path,
but when the time is right.
Alongside this, I am aware
what speaks to you
may not to me;
but that is just today.

But words are not the only help
to stir us from our sleep:
the beauty of the natural world,
just like the music that we make,
is a window to the stars.

Awakeners come in many forms,
and come when they are called.
But if we're only half alert,
there is a danger that we miss
the message that they bring.
It's often people that we meet
who help us take fresh steps.
They tell us what we need to hear
in ways that sometimes hurt.

And all this help
from friends, from books,
from a world that's light and dark,
seem like reminders of a truth I knew,
and need to find again.
Perhaps this truth lives in my soul,
but not yet in my life.
To make it real,
to give it teeth,
is why I am alive.

Probes

We probe in space
for signs of life,
for life in forms we know;
for water, bugs and blades of grass,
and maybe beings like us.

Yet when we look at flowers or birds,
at friends across the street,
we only see their outer shapes –
the costumes that they wear.
But what's concealed,
at least from sight,
that mystery we call life,
has shaped, sustains,
and animates
the miracles we love.

If this is so,
and life exists
behind those solid forms,
then death itself,
as life withdraws,
is like the shedding of a shell,
but essence still remains.

To find *this* life,
this hidden thread –
a life that never dies –
will need another sort of probe:
among the stars,
or on the train,
that person by our side.

And as we start to sense,
to see
what truly is going on,
the stars, the moon,
the sun itself
will whisper in a gentle voice:
'We are alive like you.'

Promises

What are those promises
that I have made
that keep me on the move?
'Relax', I'm told,
'your job is done;
enjoy the rest that you deserve,
let others do the work.'

And yet I know
there's more to do,
and corners I have cut.
Those woods are lovely,
dark and deep;
I go there when I can.
But back at home are lists and tasks,
and friends to help,
and wounds to heal,
and poems still to write.

And if I pause
too oft, too long,
by fireside warm and safe,
there comes a knock upon my door –
another voice then speaks:
'Whence did you come,
and what to do?'
this stranger asks of me.
'What *were* those promises
that once you made
so many years ago?
And were they made
as you took stock
of all your deeds,
both good and bad,
through many lives
on other shores
in centuries long ago?'

And if it's true
it's true for all –
those promises we've made.
And what is clear,
it seems to me,
is on this journey often hard
it's not my task
to change the world,
or bend it to my will.
But what *can* change
is me, myself –
a harder task by far,
but one within my power.   >

Is that the promise that I made,
and did I write the plot –
a plot with open end?
A hero on a quest
who meets a dragon,
suffers pain,
is full of fear –
not sure what next to do.

But there the story need not end,
for then he listens in the gloom
not to the giants
who wield the power,
but humble folk
who have no gold –
a crone in rags
a child in tears,
or to a tree that talks.

And then he learns,
so slowly learns,
that once a spell was cast,
whereby the truth is out of reach
until he toils
and climbs and sweats
o'er rocks and mountains steep.

That's quite some promise
to have made;
no wonder I can't stop.
For night will come
and I'll be lost,
no castle yet in sight.
Then what comes next,
if courage fails,
those demons at my heels:
my journey stalls,
I quit the quest,
forgetting why I came at all –
no hero after all.

Bugs

If I am tired
or very stressed,
and days are wet
and nights are cold,
I'm almost sure
that bugs and germs
will hunt me out
and take up home
in body weak
that let's them in.

So, too, my soul
must be on guard
for what were called
in days of old
by scary names
like troll and imp,
and even bogey-man.
While on the windows
in the church,
amid the colour
and the saints,
were demons black
who crouched and schemed,
and lured us into sin.

But now today,
as time moves on,
we witness other scenes.
But if you look
and listen hard
they still are there
those imps of old,
but in another guise.

And if we're cold
in how we feel –
too cold to lend a hand –
those demons laugh
and jump for joy,
and spread the word around.
Then in they come
in twos and threes
to eat our souls away.

Message

'I've found another place to be,
and you can come there too;
and not just on the day you die,
or when you sleep at night,
but when you pause
and trust your sense
that what you see
and hear and touch
all silently proclaim
what ebbs and flows,
brings joy and pain,
but never, never dies.'

Crisis

The Swiss psychiatrist, Carl Jung, said in a lecture in 1929, entitled *The Aims of Psychotherapy* (published in 'Modern Man in Search of Soul'): *'About a third of my patients are suffering from no clinically definable neurosis, but from the senselessness and emptiness of their lives. It seems to me, however, that this can be well described as the general neurosis of our time.'*

When Nietzsche wrote that 'God is dead,'
he put in words what many felt
but hadn't dared to say.
It's not a thought that even then
had not been held before.
But now, it seems,
as Jung observed,
such lack of faith has left a hole,
a gaping hole,
for those who think there is no plan,
no meaning in their lives.

Yet in that hole
so bleak, so dark,
there lives a courage I admire
to keep on going,
to do one's best,
to lend a hand,
to help the weak,
without the promise of reward,
or future life of bliss.

'To give
and not to count the cost,'
are words that I recall
from prayers of long ago.
Perhaps that God I pictured then
would much prefer not love for Him
in heaven far away,
but love for those who share with us
a world that still is far from pure,
but slowly tries to change.

So on Jung's couch
let's start to hope,
and even start to trust,
that life makes sense,
that God is love
and does indeed exist.
And then we'll see,
between the tears,
that emptiness and void
for what it is –
a hole in us
that we ourselves,
with helping hand,
must slowly start to fill.

Devilish Clever

'Devilish clever'
was the phrase
that once we used
for new machines
that worked for us
in ever cunning ways –
machines on land,
then in the air,
that left the birds behind;
and now a gadget in my hand
that lets me speak to one and all,
and sends them photos of my car –
a car that parks itself.

Why use this word in such a way,
since devils don't exist?
– or that is what we think.
And marvels such as cars and phones
all help us cope with daily life –
they're blessings, not a curse.

Perhaps the danger that exists
is not what we create,
but rather that we start to think,
and even start to be
like those machines that chug away –
contraptions with no switch or dial
that tell them how to feel.
And if those devils *do* exist
they surely will rejoice
if we become, as time goes by,
not only slaves to our machines,
but slaves to those with other plans
for us who dwell on Earth.

So what's going on?
we well may ask;
these skills are here to stay.
So, too, the wheel,
the axe and plough,
and all that we have made
since first we asked,
as we looked round:
'What is there here to do?'

One help could be to stop and think:
where is the difference still
between the gadgets we create
and us who then look on?
They, too, obey the laws
that keep us on the ground,
but also do what they are told,
and faster than we can.
They ask no questions,
make no fuss –
nor scribble lines of verse!

So far, so good –
we're human still,
despite the words we tend to use,
as if our bodies were machines –
the heart a pump,
our brain wired up,
and then we're set to go.
So should we still
just jog along,
not always quite in step,
but grateful for the things we have,
that light the dark,
and warm the house
and help us get to work?   >

Or is there more to human life
and what we can create?
And is the clue
not in my brain,
nor just in nuts and bolts?
My heart it ticks quite on its own;
I breathe without a thought.
But no mechanic on this earth,
however good and kind,
knows really what there is to do
when things go badly wrong.
For what has kept me going so long,
besides my fuel of food and air,
is something no machine requires,
nor devil can create.
And so at death
what we call 'life' –
a mystery no one doubts –
is suddenly no longer there,
has seemed to disappear.

Perhaps the challenge that we face,
if human to remain:
to take good care of that in us
that maybe never dies.
And ask ourselves at every turn
where do my loyalties lie?
Then come those words
from long ago,
a balance to suggest,
when Jesus spoke
to those confused
of what to render,
what is owed
to Caesar and to God.

Descend we must
onto this earth
its laws to understand;
and learn what only here is learnt,
as Newton showed so well.
But there are other things to do,
and songs to sing,
and tales to tell
that free us from the ground;
thus in our minds
a ladder build
and step by step ascend.
For there awaits
what we ignore,
if all we worship,
all we see,
are things that rust
and things that rot
and then get thrown away.

And thus in time a home appears,
a heaven, some would say,
and friend from long ago,
where life itself
is forged, renewed,
where other laws prevail.
So nothing's lost,
and nothing dies,
for there dwells love
and there dwells hope
for all that lives and grows.

The River Wye

Sometimes in haste
and sometimes calm,
you flow towards the sea,
obeying law that apples know
when time to leave the tree.

Whilst on your banks
the trees and flowers
point upwards to the sky;
the reeds are straight,
those blades of grass
that bend awhile with dew,
they go not where the river goes –
to what do they aspire?
Perhaps my wish to play with words
is prompted by that same strong urge:
defy the gravity that holds me back,
but draws the river on.

Once, long ago,
we built slim spires,
expressions of our growing sense
of other laws at work.
Now they are dwarfed
by taller towers
that really have no point,
except to keep us looking down,
our noses to the ground.

So quietly and not quite alone
we try to build our inner spires
that point us to a higher truth,
to what we might become.
Thus stone by stone,
and trial by trial
there slowly will emerge
a triumph over Newton's law
and all that drags us down.

Glide on, obedient and seductive Wye,
and maybe we will meet again
at some place further on.
I hope by then I'll understand
the wisdom of both laws –
that things grow up
and things grow down,
and I am in-between.

The Stork

In olden times,
so it was told
to little girls and boys,
a huge white bird –
a stork in fact –
had brought the newborn child.

Why was this so
when what was clear
to old *and* young,
and all with eyes to see,
was mother's tummy getting large
and there this baby grew?
And children saw,
far more than now,
how cats and dogs,
and cows and pigs
had babies just like us.

It's hard for us
perhaps to see
how children understand
that stories about storks and gnomes,
and reindeers in the sky,
do not conflict with simple facts,
but tell another tale.

So was this bird
with great white wings
an image of a different birth,
where soul arrives upon the Earth
to take on shape,
a name and genes,
to live with us as welcome guest,
and learn what's still to learn?

Meanwhile that stork,
perhaps he stays,
but carefully out of sight;
and there he looks
and waits, and waits
like angels also do.
They want to help
but find this hard
if we believe,
like grown-ups do,
they really don't exist.

It's harder still for those who care,
but from this other realm,
if what they see
and what they hear
are cries of pain
and cries of woe,
and sorrow in our hearts.
For well we know how many lives,
as childhood falls away,
don't feel this welcome from the world –
it's not what they had hoped;
they notice, too, it's seldom asked
from whence they came
and what they bring,
or what they're here to do.   >

And yet we cope
and live in hope,
just like the Earth itself;
and some may moan,
and some are brave,
but all are here awhile.
Most do their best
to do no harm,
despite the fact
that what they find
at times feels far from home.

Then in the twilight of our lives
perhaps that bird is waiting still
to take us whence we came;
not to a heaven somewhere else,
but to the heart of life itself –
a source of hope that's always there,
which longs to see,
and longs to make
this Earth of ours divine.

A Double Life?

Despite my talk,
my hope and faith
in bridges to a timeless realm,
I often live that double life,
with a chasm in between.
What's out of sight
is out of mind,
as earthly tasks
and cares and trials
fill up my busy day.

But maybe this is not the case,
if what I think
and how I act
has as its source
that inner life
which never goes away.

Thus angels in another sphere,
and maybe Jackie, too,
don't need our thoughts
from dawn till dusk
but just from time to time.
For they are here,
and we are there,
and life and love are one.

Behind the Scenes

There is, I sense,
so much going on,
as in a play
behind the scenes,
not just the show on stage.
The faithful Sun,
the Earth itself
obey a wisdom
day and night
no telescope reveals.
So, too, those billion cells
that live and die inside the hand
that writes these simple words;
they keep some secrets
veiled, secure
from microscopes that probe.
My thoughts, my joy,
the sadness that I sometimes feel,
all this is hidden too.

So what of me on lonely quest
who longs to know,
who longs for clues
to what on earth's going on.
I take one step
and then the next,
dependent on a brain and legs
that do what they are told.
But I myself,
in what I do,
am less obedient,
less in tune
to what I sense is wiser far
than fragile human beings.

Perhaps in exile so extreme,
there stirs a challenge
for us creatures weak
to search within
and there to find
the wisdom that made you and me,
and all that we behold –
a wisdom that is still at work
and looks to us for helping hand
to move things on,
to have bold thoughts,
and so create what's new.

Imagination

What we imagine
has a power,
that as we wiser grow,
could echo what imagined us
in ages long ago.

But we are free
what route to take –
it could go many ways.
Creation that is fit to last
needs us to think *and* pray.

A New Heaven

'The stars once spoke to Man.
It is world destiny that they are silent now,
but in their silence there grows and ripens
what man speaks to the stars.'
From 'Verses and Meditations' (1906-1925) by Rudolf Steiner.

'I saw a new Heaven
and a new Earth ...' –
so wrote Saint John
for those of us
who puzzled then
and puzzle still
at what unfolds
both here on Earth
and in the skies above.

They touch us still –
a ring of truth –
those words from long ago;
but visions so profound, opaque,
are often hard to grasp;
for we've moved on,
the past's the past,
we live from day to day.

An Earth that's new is not so strange,
it's what we all desire;
a world where tears
and pain and strife
no longer haunt our lives.
But words like heaven can confuse
for those whose focus,
work and thoughts,
are in the here and now.

Yet there are some
who have a sense
that somewhere is a place serene
that's free of strife,
of ups and downs,
where only good prevails.
What is it then the prophet sees?
Why should that Heaven,
so sublime,
be also up for change?

Perhaps that picture
of the silent stars
is Steiner's sense
of evolution not on Earth alone,
but on a cosmic scale;
that Heaven, and the world we know,
are working hand in hand.
And so unfolds what's always been,
a dialogue of sorts,
in which the angels now must pause,
be silent for a while;
a rest maybe,
as God enjoyed
upon the seventh day.
Perhaps it's Sunday still,
and now it's up to us.   >

So what to do,
what is our task,
if Heaven's hope
and Heaven's trust
can one day be fulfilled?
And what on earth,
we well may ask,
can we create
that can compare
with what exists,
not least of all
what lives and grows –
the miracle that's life?
And harder still it is to know
how all our efforts,
what we do,
can be of help to those above
whose deeds and power,
exceed by far our own?

Some people say
that God is love;
and angels, too,
who care and guard,
have only us in mind.
But what of you
and what of me –
we creatures in His image made
who struggle still
to be like that,
to love as we are loved?

Perhaps our freedom is the clue,
and all the mess we make.
For if one day,
in years to come,
we do succeed,
just step by step,
to put the other first,
it will be out of choice alone,
not in obedience to some preacher's text,
or law that someone's made.

Thus grows an Earth that's truly new,
the one the prophet saw;
and what is more
there will exist
in the universe at large,
not just the harmony
of spheres and gods,
but knowledge honed
by us alone,
by us in pain,
of what it means
and why it's so:
the truth that all is one.

And then, and only then,
can we speak words
that have some worth
to waiting stars,
to silent stars,
and all that looks to Earth.
And so a Heaven
full of joy
will be enriched,
will be renewed,
and speak to us again.

Underway

If I observe not just the world
and all I see out there,
but turn instead,
from time to time,
and look at me who stands apart,
forever looking on,
it seems to me that what's revealed
are three quite different selves.

My body is not hard to see,
and mostly works just like a plant,
without much help from me.
It's fed and watered,
breathes and grows –
my heart beats on its own.

But like my cat,
or dog or horse,
I feel a bond –
it comes and goes –
for all that feels like me.
I can be sad,
I can rejoice,
and that's the me that's also here,
except when fast asleep.
Some call it soul,
it's out of sight,
but real as arms and legs.
It can be wise,
and sometimes not,
for passion there holds sway.

And then there's me
who thinks and plans,
who's meant to be in charge.
And when I am,
my soul obeys
and tells my body what to do,
which path to walk along.
One problem if the spirit's weak,
is soul and body partner up,
and what results is beast with brains –
no more a human being.
They can and should all intertwine,
these parts of me that make me whole,
that help me stand erect.
But if I sleep in daylight hours
then other beings invade.

And looking round at us, our world,
what doesn't help is simple fact
that human spirits are still young,
and not yet fully here;
while rocks and plants,
and flesh and blood
have been on Earth awhile.
It's therefore no surprise at all
that what we see,
and how we are
is still in such a flux.

The body's wise,
if on its own,
the soul goes either way.
So what must grow,
come more to Earth,
is spirit that is half with God,
and not yet here at home.

A Selfless Self

In 1931 Mahatma Gandhi was in London representing the Indian National Congress for talks with the British government on Indian independence. During his stay he was invited to tea at Buckingham Palace with King George V and Queen Mary. Dressed as always in his dhoti and sandals, Gandhi was asked by a journalist on leaving the palace whether he had felt properly dressed for the occasion. 'There was no problem,' he replied, 'the King was wearing quite enough for both of us.'

We smile at Gandhi's wit,
we even share that hunch
that all is not quite right
if people freeze,
and people starve,
while we consume so much.

I've read in books
and heard it said
by those who see ahead,
that as the human race evolves
the harder it becomes
to feel at peace,
to turn away
when someone whom we've never met
is in distress,
is not at peace
and calls to us for help.

To feel, to suffer
as the other does,
would be one mighty stride for Man –
like stepping on the moon.
To make that step,
let's not forget,
I need at first to have a sense
that I am me
and stand apart,
and so have thoughts like these.

Then all the hurt
we know so well,
when you and I
and life on Earth
compete from different sides,
will slowly start to ebb away,
as we emerge with thinner skins,
and kinder hearts,
and willingness to share.

And if we do achieve this shift
and put the other first –
not just my child,
or Mum and Dad,
or people just like us –
we've made a choice
quite on our own
to be a selfless self.
And love like that
perhaps is new –
a sign of what it really means
to be a human being.

Another Day

It's early still,
no birds awake;
and I am back,
but back from where,
in body once again?

Some fleeting dreams
now fill my mind,
but not for long,
and few of which
I really understand;
the chaos, I suppose,
of not being either here nor there,
between the night and day.
But where is 'there'?
I often ask;
no memory helps me out.

'Write down your dreams',
so I am told,
those messages I've sent,
and open now
as I wake up
to yet another day.

But what I really want to know
is where was I for all that time
from when I fell asleep
until a dream, a nearby sound,
or maybe just a wish
to have another go,
called out to me:
'Your time is up –
enjoy the here and now.'

Or is the answer
that I seek
quite simply out of reach?
If so, relax
and just rejoice –
I haven't passed away!
Perhaps the night is but a chance
to let the body rest.
No need to walk,
no need to talk,
and free from all those muddled thoughts
that permeate my day.

But while I *was* away,
asleep,
it wasn't total rest.
For like some great and complex plant,
my lungs and blood and all those cells –
that body I now move and dress –
continued to obey some law
far wiser than that lodger slack –
the lodger that is me –
who comes and goes,
and makes mistakes,
and leaves his room a mess.

Back Again

I've heard it said
that when you die
you live your life again,
but in reverse,
from death to birth,
before you start again.
And that's not all:
there is a twist
as time again unfolds.
For now you live
on the receiving end
of all you did
and all you said,
as well as what you felt.
A punch you gave,
it now hurts you,
and so, of course, does hate.

If this is so,
or partly true,
then talk of heaven
and that other place
has meaning once again;
though most of us,
who muddle on,
dwell somewhere in between.

So on return –
that's if we do –
we try, I hope,
to mend our ways;
punch less,
care more
for those we trampled under foot,
forgot to thank,
passed by,
all in our rush to come out top,
to favour number one.

Between the Lines

To read between the lines,
the lines of life,
is what I need to do.
So shut my books
and close my eyes,
but only for a while;
and there I'll see,
though not at first,
a story still being told
that gives me hope,
and gives me help
to open then my eyes.

As Above, So Below

That miracle out there at night
of stars in numbers that amaze
all those who raise their eyes,
is there again –
or so it seems –
when people speak of tiny cells
in numbers just as vast
that live and thrive,
and have their home
in universe that's me.

So what's the link
between what shines
far out in distant space,
and all that grows
and lives and breathes
on this our planet Earth?

In recent years,
as facts built up
and so replaced belief,
the universe to some
no longer has that much to say
on what concerns us here.

They see it now,
when viewed from Earth,
as some great clock
that ticks away
quite on its own
obeying laws
(well, more or less)
which mirror laws
that we have learnt
so we can build machines that probe
those lumps of rock above our heads
that twinkle in the night –
but speak to us no more.

Or is there still
some power at work
both in the stars
and here on earth,
in bodies such as ours –
in cell and limb,
and flowers that grow,
in hearts that beat
and minds that stir
with questions such as this?

Perhaps there is,
as once was said,
a cosmos that's divine.
And as above,
in heaven's realm,
so lives a force
in me below
that link us all –
some call it God –
to life that never ends.

Baggage

' ... trailing clouds of glory do we come
From God, who is our home ...'
From 'The Prelude' by William Wordsworth.

Some people speak about the afterlife –
that death is not an end;
but what is less discussed, I find,
and often not at all,
is life before we're born.

We talk of children growing up,
and that they surely do;
but what unfolds alongside this,
I'm prompted to suggest,
is something that is seldom grasped –
a journey growing down.

A lovely thought and lovely words,
the ones that Wordsworth wrote;
a vision that inspires me still
despite sporadic doubts.
Yet in the eyes of some, I sense,
a notion that is little help
in coping with their daily tasks –
the pace and stress of life;
and nowadays it's facts that count –
ideas that can be proved.

And yet we sense that all these facts –
the ones our experts list –
do not convince,
do not ring true,
if we are on a deeper search,
and meaning's what we seek.

Meanwhile I have my doubts
that every word that Wordsworth wrote
is absolutely true;
that what we trail on journeys here,
the baggage that we bring,
may not be quite as pure,
as white,
as poets like to dream.

I may be wrong,
and Wordsworth right;
for if indeed we come quite new,
still pure from home with God,
then yes, indeed –
at least to start –
it's glory that we bring.
But if we've lived,
as I believe,
and not just once,
but many times,
it's no surprise that what unfolds,
alongside heaven's gift,
has all the traces,
all the signs,
not just of lessons learnt,
but how we failed,
the hurt we caused,
and wish to put it right.   >

No wonder then we're back again,
not just with those
whose hands we've held
in battles long ago,
but those we've wronged,
ignored, despised,
in trying to stay afloat.

Thus growing down,
as we grow up –
it may take many lives –
we have the chance,
if courage holds,
to urge the world,
to urge ourselves,
a heaven *here* to make.

An Inner Voice

We needed them,
those priests of old,
when we were young
and they were wise
and listened to the gods.
But now it's often second-hand,
those words of wisdom
some still preach
in texts from far-off days.

It's true, the language
and the art,
created long ago,
still has the power
from time to time
to help and to inspire.
And yet for most
what is conveyed
seems far removed
from what we see
and what we face
as daily life unfolds.
Nor do those promises
of better things –
not here,
but in another world –
inspire the victims,
bruised and weak,
of wars we fight
not just with guns
but money in the bank.   >

Perhaps the challenge,
and the task:
to shape those words anew;
and one by one,
and on our own
to find the sage within.
And so, released
as from a spell,
an inner voice is born;
for evolution's on the move,
as it has always been.

And words of wisdom,
so one hopes,
will gradually emerge,
and so give strength,
and also faith
in what we'd like to build –
a world in which the human being
observes that one great truth:
that I need you
and you need me,
and all at heart are one.
So where we live
and how we live
no longer has to be
a race to win,
to come out top –
a jungle without heart.

And maybe all those gods of old
are not that far away,
but waiting now in silent prayer
for us to take the lead.
For that's their vision,
that's their hope –
it's never gone away –
that we create
the dream they had:
a paradise on Earth.

And now, as then,
amid the pain
and through the tears,
their message lingers still:
'Be brave, be strong,
and trust that voice,
however frail you feel.'
For what is right,
and what is wrong
is not enshrined in stone,
but carved in every human heart
for each of us to find.

Black Holes

I often think,
and with relief,
that I am not the only one
who faces gaps in what I know
that are so large from end to end,
I sometimes wonder if it's best
to simply start again.

And do such thoughts
occur to those
who gaze at stars,
then do their sums
and find huge gaps
in what they know
and what they thought was there?

They call them holes,
they call them black;
and one it seems,
I heard today,
is home to what they seem to think
are suns and suns,
and several billion more.

And then they pause,
these modern knights
in coats of shining white,
put down their tools,
wind up the blinds,
and off they go to tea.

And now's a chance
perhaps to glimpse,
if we are so inclined,
the holes in how we live and think
that aren't so far away.
Let's call them white,
these nearby holes,
for they have tidings full of joy,
where meaning's glimpsed
and hope restored
for those with eyes to see.

The Big Bang

Many years ago our ten-year-old son, Tom – nourished from
an early age on fairy stories, but also with a growing interest
in science – came up with this suggestion: *'Maybe one day God
became fed up with all those myths and dragons and things, so he decided to
blow himself up – and that was the Big Bang.'*

Our need to laugh,
so I believe,
not only keeps us sane,
but points to something quite profound
that seems to say –
'You're wise to laugh,
especially at yourselves,
at what you think you know.'

And yet we try
to find the truth,
it's what we long to do.
Alongside this,
our age-old task,
we need to pause
from time to time –
that's science at its best –
and see our theories as just that,
as steps along the way.

That Bang of which they speak
was big as big can be;
but trying to fix a starting point
to when it all began,
in some way seems
about the same
as pinning down what we call God
to seven days in which to make
the world, a snake and us –
with one day off to rest.
We scratch our heads
and stare at screens,
or words from long ago,
without much thought,
or so it seems,
for what went on
before that Bang,
before the day and night.

Another problem with the Bang
is that the brain through which we work
to have a thought like this
is trapped in time,
and has a life
that had a start,
but then one day will end.   >

A story, on the other hand,
has as its source a timeless realm –
the home from whence we came;
and sometimes in between the words
a deeper truth resides.
It may not give us precious facts,
but gifts of other sorts;
for what we crave is that which feeds
what lives in us and never dies,
but chokes when all that's on our plate
are chunks of logic,
dry and stale –
no herbs or fruit,
or songs to wash it down.

Yet brains are great
at what they do –
they help our minds to grow –
and that includes
a thought like this:
'We cannot give you
on our own
the answers that you seek;
for brains will die,
but you will not,
so you have work to do.'

Thus let's imagine,
also dream,
and think with head *and* heart.
And then let's laugh,
not in despair
at challenges we face,
but with much joy
and trust and love
for tasks that lie ahead.

Science

'Science, my lad, is made up of mistakes, but they are mistakes which it is useful to make, because they lead little by little to the truth.'
Jules Verne in 'A Journey to the Centre of the Earth.'

It might appear from what I write
that I dismiss what comes about
when all we trust,
all we believe,
is what our reason says.

This isn't so,
despite my sense,
that there exists
at every turn
far more than meets the eye.
For I perceive and I respect
that tools we use,
and how we think,
belong to here and now.
We look around,
we touch and hear,
and with our minds we do our best
to help it all make sense.
Thus once we moved from wood to bronze,
and then to iron and steel;
and now we see,
or think we do,
what made the stars and us.   >

And yet it's said,
as we progress,
the more we know
and more we see,
the less it all adds up.
Perhaps we need to listen more,
to pause from time to time
and hear what whispers in the dark,
for clues to what we seek.
And if we do,
and then have trust,
perhaps the birds,
and all those stars,
and plants we take to bits,
will speak to us as once they did
when first we walked the Earth.

'Keep looking,' they will gently say,
'and what you see,
and what you touch,
both near and far away,
will make it clear to all of you
what questions next to ask.
Be not afraid, if what you find
does not conform to what you think –
mistakes will help you on.'

To search, to question
is our task –
not always 'in the know'.
But if we're brave,
and if we work,
the world itself will find a way,
its secrets to reveal.

And if the truth *does* slowly dawn,
it won't be as before;
for then we knew as nature does –
our bodies know it still.
But we stood back,
and Eden left,
these questions then to ask;
no wonder that it takes a while
for answers to unfold.
But then one day,
when all is clear,
and we and world are one,
we can rejoice and call out loud:
'We did it on our own!'

Sleeping Beauty

I loved them then,
I love them still,
those tales of kings and queens,
and wicked witches in the wood,
and maidens waiting for their prince,
while sewing silken wings.

One slept a hundred years
in castle overgrown,
until a kiss dissolved the spell
and life moved on anew.
Briar Rose had found her prince at last,
as handsome as she'd hoped;
so they were married there and then
and, as such stories rightly end,
were happy evermore.

It makes no sense,
but no one cares –
we learn another truth.
For is the message we can heed,
through tales from long ago,
that wisdom is at times revealed
when logic falls away?
Or is it just escape, a treat
before we go to bed?

For now's the age
when reason rules,
and dragons don't exist.
Yet in *our* castles overgrown
we wait as ever for that kiss
to wake us from our long, long sleep –
the person of our dreams.
We fall in love
and see in her,
or see in him,
not how they are from day to day,
but what they might become.
And we in turn are blessed, inspired
by kiss and loving hand;
they come like gifts from God Himself,
and help us still to dream.

But maybe what we really seek
is closer than we think:
our other half,
not someone else
and not out there,
'across a crowded room',
but here already –
patient, still,
and waiting to be born –
if they can only hack their way
through all those hostile thorns.
And then a wedding of another kind,
where bride and groom,
they meet in me –
myself at last made whole.   >

If this is true,
or partly so,
let's thank the folk
who told those tales,
and those who wrote them down.
Let's also pray,
in years to come,
that someone writes some more:
how Sleeping Beauty,
while she slept,
and trapped by all those thorns,
learned what she had to learn,
as you and I must also do,
by sometimes being alone.

Thus we grow wise
in many ways,
and still enjoy such tales;
we also start to understand
that prince and wedding,
thorns and sleep,
are clues to what is yet to come:
that two are really one.

The Bat

The American philosopher, Thomas Nagel, wrote a celebrated paper, first published in 'The Philosophical Review' in 1974, called 'What is it like to be a bat?' Most people's first reaction to such a question is probably to think it must be rather boring, hanging upside down in the dark and eating flies. But the real challenge, so Nagel suggests, is to imagine what it's like for a bat to be a bat.

What miracle, the human being
with eyes and ears and fingertips
through which we meet and touch the world,
and brain that keeps it all in check,
that tells us when to cross the road
and helps us read these words.

But when it comes to Nagel's bat,
those skills, our minds
are at a loss
to step into the shoes –
if bats wore shoes –
of something hanging upside down
in darkness day and night.
What is it like
to not be me,
to live a life
so different from the one I know,
through which to meet the world?   >

Some talk these days
of trying to think
what's sometimes termed
'outside the box' –
perhaps with heart as well:
a different box –
no lid, no sides,
that we ourselves must make.
And so could grow
a window new
through which we sense,
or start to sense,
what life is like
not just for bats,
but those who've died –
for other states of being.
And life without an outer form
is not that strange for some,
who even now have dreams and thoughts
that hint of other realms.

But what's the point?
so some may ask –
I have enough to do.
No time, no need
to wonder thus,
to wonder what's going on.
That may be true,
and so life waits,
until the question bothers us
enough to think again.
But then we have to work and pray,
and slowly forge those latent powers
through which the answers that we seek
emerge from out the mist.

And curiosity is not enough,
nor must our motive be
to merely stock our precious store
of larder full of facts.
We want to know
and need to know
because we care –
a care for all
with whom we share this precious world
that waits on us to grow.

And so with insight,
and a glimpse
of what it's like to be
a bat, a flower,
a child in pain,
that person down the road,
then I myself can better serve
what longs to come about:
an evolution of the human being,
where what endures
is filled with love –
a love that knows no bounds;
and fit to hold
in times to come,
to hold the hand of God.

Freedom

'Go now,'
my angel gently said to me,
'a life that you and I have planned
awaits you now on Earth;
though while you're there,
and troubles mount,
it may not seem,
from where you stand,
the plan was always just.
And then at times,
when all seems quiet,
a blow will come that wasn't planned,
that happens just by chance.'

'But every night you will return
to home among the stars;
and there I'll be
to help you see
that what unfolds –
those choices tough
that you have made –
are what you need,
and what you willed,
so you can grow like me.'

'Nor will you be,
while living thus,
without the help of those you love,
who in their turn love you.
For by your side,
while storms may rage,
will be the friends
with whom you've shared,
through many lives,
this journey you're all on.'

'And if you're brave,
and if you're strong,
it's not the human race alone
that grows in wisdom, love and hope –
the universe evolves.
For you are free
to go astray,
and that you'll often do;
but in the end,
if you can love
without reserve,
the way we angels do,
you've done it out of choice alone,
so brought to life what's new.'

Herod

'Herod, who drove away the Child and wanted to kill Him, is an image of the world, which still wants to kill this Child in the pious man; wherefore one should and must flee it, if one wants to keep the Child alive within oneself; for the Child is the enlightened, believing soul of every man.'
Johannes Tauler, 14th-century German mystic.

Where is King Herod in the world today?
And should we flee,
or stand our ground?
And if we stay, are we prepared
to die upon a cross,
without a pension, fame and praise,
or clothes upon our back?
The challenge that we face is huge;
that Child I carry looks to me,
and only I can help it grow,
can help it stay alive.

But what of Herod
on his golden throne?
He knows a trick or two.
His suits are smart,
his shoes are clean,
he knows that two and two
add up, make four,
and keep the trains on time.
No need to murder babies in their beds;
seduction is a better ploy,
and force a clumsy tool.
The speed and glitter of our modern world –
it tempts us, one and all.

And yet the toys
we love to make
are not to be dismissed;
they have their place,
they help us cope,
can even make us smile.
But as we live,
what matters most,
to keep that Herod in his place,
is when we flag,
and lose all hope,
'Lift up our eyes unto the hills'
and whisper to our tender Child
our intimations and our faith
that some day dawns a better world –
a world where love is king;
and not a place just when we die,
among the stars and far away,
but here on Earth,
our precious home,
amid the rubble where once stood
proud Herod's glitzy den;
a palace far more frail,
unreal,
than this,
our growing Child.

Nirvana

There is for some
a strong belief
that if perfection is our goal
and Earth's delights a cunning trap,
we can move on to place of bliss,
and not return to all this woe
that human beings create.
No need to live another life
of pain and sorrow,
grief and strife,
for we've become serene, sublime,
whose noble path leads on and up,
away from dark to light.
But that's the trap –
let's call it pride –
for those who stand erect:
a thought, a hope
that their ascent
sets them apart from lesser folk
who scramble in the dust.

Yet some would feel –
or so I hope –
if such a day should dawn
when they were pure
and free from sin
in centuries still to come,
that they would shun
that tempting path
to land that's free of strife,
while others stay and struggle still
with all that's left behind.

For this they know –
tomorrow's saints –
that they have grown in stature fine,
not in a bubble,
sealed, secure,
but living side by side
and on the shoulders sometimes strong
not just of giants,
but those more frail,
whose pain and hurt,
or rage and fear
has been the block to moving on
from tears to hope,
from hate to love,
and sense that we are one.

Another reason to return
is wish to be with those who've dreamt
from very early days
not of a heaven somewhere else,
but how this Earth could be redeemed,
and so become divine.
And maybe, too, that tale of old
can help us on this path:
it tells of child –
a holy child –
who comes to Earth like us.
And as he grows and sorrow meets,
he speaks to us not of escape
to somewhere in the clouds,
but tries to show,
as others do,
that we are here to learn to love,
and that is all that counts.   >

A life so lived,
it opened up
a place for Christ to dwell.
It also shows what lies ahead
for you, for me,
when guard is dropped,
and hope is born
that I one day can see and know
my flawed and fragile self
for what in fact I've always been –
a son, a child of God.

And if we choose
to praise this man
in sounds and words sublime,
let's not forget when out of church
the reason why he came.
And so then try,
through deeds, not words,
to cause no hurt
to those who once
were little children too;
and came to Earth so full of hope
that here there could be change.

Is that the message
that he brought
despite his own deep pain:
that we are here,
and here to stay,
but through our work
create a place
that no one wants to leave?

Bluebells

I wonder whence the bluebells came,
with promise of more colour soon,
for spring is on its way.
One thing I know for sure:
those flowers were not beneath the ground
on winter walks
I made just months ago.
For if you open up a bulb
no baby bluebell can be found
curled up and waiting to be born
when warmer weather comes.

So then I start to think
about that human egg and sperm
that once upon a time was me;
though, like the bluebells in the wood,
I, too, was out of sight.
So was I, like these flowers in spring,
once helping from afar
to slowly bring to life and form
the bluebell that is me?

Becoming Human

We quarrel in the bedroom,
in the car,
at summits,
and with guns and bombs.

The root of all this friction,
I suspect,
is not the human being,
(they do not yet exist)
but rather a becoming
of something still so young
which somewhere down the line,
as bruises start to heal,
emerges as the Word made flesh –
a truly human being.
But for a while,
like every spotty youth,
we need to think that God is dead,
that father is a fool,
and slam the bedroom door.

Then truly on our own
we slowly start to see
how we, our world –
the worms and rocks,
the sea and stars,
a man across the street –
are not just this,
and not just that,
but part of one great whole,
in which unfolds,
from age to age,
a drama with no end.

Our task as human beings
is then to make this known
not just in words,
not just in song,
but in our gratitude to busy worms,
and kindness to that fragile man,
that man across the street.

Headlines

This morning's headlines
trouble us –
it's what they're meant to do.
But in the days and months gone by,
as millions went on that same train,
no one took out a knife or gun
to harm a person of a different race –
a human being like them.
But that's not news,
and yet it is,
that people under constant stress
will still say 'thanks'
and give, not take,
and often lend a hand.

Waiting

Created when the world was new
by God Himself,
so we began –
that's how the story goes.
And then it tells us even more:
He formed us from the humble dust
to look and be like Him.
Perhaps He wonders
what went wrong
in all that time between.
Or is it not so very bad
as might at first appear?

It's not that hard to see the hand,
the hand and will of God,
in all that grows,
that gives and takes
so we might live and stand erect
in bodies that are wise and strong,
that truly are divine.

My inner life,
what's called my soul,
is not at all the same.
I often feel regret, ashamed
of what I do,
and what I feel,
and even what I think.

But maybe that's the clue we seek:
who is it that's ashamed?
Is that the me
still on my way,
and not yet fully born,
who knows what's right
and what is wrong
but sometimes loses heart and map,
and courage on the way?

Meanwhile He waits
in silent trust,
like every parent in the world,
not just for our return,
but in the hope that we have learnt
through our mistakes
a little more
than gods who never stray.

Moving On

I sometimes wonder
if I dwell too much
on what to some
must often seem
not quite to do with life –
an intimation of a hidden truth
that draws my gaze
beyond the hills
to things we cannot see.

In my defence
I hope it's clear
I treasure what my wife so loved –
the beauty of the natural world,
the miracle of life,
and what we call,
when all goes well,
the joys of here and now.
But maybe that was always there,
my sense of something more;
and yet I've lived,
and had a job,
and know my left from right.

But as I age
and know for sure
that what I am,
and what I see
will not remain
forever as it is,
so then I think of little child –
and I was one of those –
who slowly wakes
to life on Earth,
but also sleeps a lot.

Am I like that,
but in reverse,
half here, half there,
already with one sturdy foot,
not in the grave,
but on the path
that surely lies ahead?

Water

It sometimes seems
when times get tough
that I, too, harden
like a block of ice –
sharp edges, cold
and on my own –
unlike the water whence I came,
so soft and mobile like a child
who runs through fields,
explores the woods,
and touches all he meets.

But ice can melt
and I can flow,
as once I did,
when I was young
and all was new
and called to me:
'Come nearer, please,
you restless thing,
and thus you'll learn
that I am tree
and this is rock
and you are you,
so full of life,
and long to tell me so.'

But then one day,
so I assume,
I'll want a rest,
the need to pause,
embrace a new surprise;
and as that water
nears the sea
another stage unfolds.
For if you stand
upon the shore
and look towards that vast expanse
that's ever on the move,
you will not see
what happens next,
for water disappears from sight,
as do the ones we love.

So, too, the water
that we heat
it meets a threshold new.
It turns to steam,
but then it's gone,
or so it seems,
until it rains
and we get wet,
and earth calls out,
all dry and parched:
'You're very welcome back.'

War in Heaven

A war in heaven,
out of sight,
and not with bombs and guns,
is not a subject much discussed
in our enlightened times.
Too many of our own, perhaps,
to bother with such thoughts.

Yet some still sense
our wars, our strife,
as well as blessings we receive,
are closely linked to other realms,
to what the angels do.
There, some are proud,
have other plans
of how we should evolve.

And so perhaps behind the scenes,
but not that far away,
are those who would in time rejoice
if all we worshipped,
held in awe,
were just the tools we make.
The arts, our songs
and dreams we have,
are not so welcome
to these spirits flawed,
who crawl with broken wings.

We owe to them our clever ways –
machines are what they love.
But there they'd like us to remain,
just in our heads,
and in that realm
where logic reigns supreme.

And they meanwhile
have their own dreams,
with aspirations out of place
to be themselves as gods.

And in another camp,
with countenance of light,
are rebels of another sort
who'd like me to believe
that I am right,
and others wrong,
and all that matters in the end
is my success and fame and wealth,
secure within my tower.
For them this world is not much fun –
it's better to escape,
to dream,
and live a life without the mess
that other people make.

Is this the war of which seers spoke
in centuries long ago?
And if it is,
and we're the prize,
what choices should we make?
One way to steer a middle path,
if that's what's best to do,
is use the *gifts* that each path brings
to beat the other at his game
and keep extremes at bay.   >

It's good and right
that we explore,
and make the world our home.
But if we also laugh and sing
it helps to keep machines in place –
not turn them into gods.
And that's the yeast –
our need to dream –
that takes us to the heart of things,
to life that's not machine.
So, too, our need to shine, succeed,
that leads to pride if too extreme,
can be toned down
and kept in check
if we observe our faulty selves
with that same rigour that we use
when building those machines.

But does it matter
whether we believe or not
in plots afoot,
that battles rage,
and all behind our backs?
Perhaps it does,
for then we see
what drives us all apart –
apart from God,
apart from Earth,
enslaved to narrow plans.

I stand alone,
and that is right,
yet arm in arm,
through ups and downs,
with each and everyone.
We're on the Earth
to learn its ways
and also leave our mark;
but we are also free to stray,
for that is how we learn.

And so, perhaps,
these traps we meet
are blessings in disguise.
For as we flounder,
make mistakes,
we slowly can discern
what path to take,
what voice to heed –
not in obedience to a wrathful God,
but out of choice
and from our hearts,
above all, out of love.

Here and There

It must be clear to those of you
who've read my lines so far,
that long and complicated words
don't always work
when writing as I do.
But 'here' and 'there'
are clear and short,
and crucial words
through which to share
my growing sense
that boundaries don't exist.
What's there is here,
though not in space,
but in the human mind.
And thus the stars
are close at hand;
so, too, are those we love.

Yet nothing that exists at all
feels so alone,
and so apart
as you and I
can sometimes do
as we look on
in fear and awe
and wonder what life means;
while tree is tree,
and is just that
without regard,
so I presume,
to why one day it dies.

But maybe that's a gift we have,
to be as tree
that lives and grows,
but also move about.
And as we do,
and as we think,
the world is not the same.
Perhaps it's why,
so long ago,
we left that Garden so serene
on quest to understand.
But we'll return
when what we've learnt –
have still to learn –
brings something new to life.

Meanwhile it dawns,
so slowly dawns,
in exile so extreme,
that we need flowers
who need the bees
who need the flowers
that give us air
so we can breathe
and thus enjoy
the sun above –
a sun that isn't just a rock on fire,
but home to life that's not like us,
and still belongs to one great world
that's huge in size
and yet exists
in bird and flower,
in star that's *there*
and me that's *here*,
and those now out of sight.

Microcosm of The Macrocosm

In his book 'A Guide for the Perplexed', the economist E.F. Schumacher wrote: *'What enables man to know anything at all about the world around him? "Knowing demands the organ fitted to the object," said Plotinus (d. A.D. 270). Nothing can be known without there being an appropriate 'instrument' in the make-up of the knower. This is the Great Truth of* adaequatio *(adequateness), which defines knowledge as* adaequatio rei et intellectus: *the understanding of the knower must be adequate to the thing to be known.'*

Time and again
as I pursue this task –
a testament to loss,
a longing to connect –
one word, one thought
still hovers there,
and often holds me back:
'Inadequate' is what I feel.

How write,
how dare to write
of what I call
'a bigger picture'
when what I see
and hear and touch,
and all that hems me in,
are mostly things that come,
then go,
and speak to me
and all of us
of death, decay and end?

Perhaps tomorrow,
as last week,
there'll stir in me
what corresponds
to that which never dies.
But I must trust it,
help it grow,
this 'instrument' still small and frail
of which the wise men speak.
It is not given,
like my eyes and ears;
but it is promised,
so I trust,
if I will do the work.

Though as I think,
and as I pray,
and inner world expands,
I'm ever watchful –
try to see –
that kindness is not left behind
in rush to learn still more;
without it I will never know
what matters most of all.

Words

"What must I do, to tame you?" asked the little prince.
"You must be very patient," replied the fox. "First you will sit down at a
little distance from me — like that — in the grass. I shall look at you out of
the corner of my eye, and you will say nothing. Words are the source of
misunderstandings …"
From 'The Little Prince' by Antoine de Saint-Exupéry.

That little fox
in desert home,
he knew a thing or two.
And yet,
despite his warning about words,
I write,
forever searching for the ones
that best express the glimpse I have
of what it all might mean —
your death, our lives,
and now the silence that remains.

I'm also well aware
the words I write,
the words I speak,
you neither read nor hear.
But maybe what we feel and think
need neither eyes nor ears.
And foxes know what we forget,
that in the silence —
if we trust —
a truth appears
of which our words
are still but symbols pale.

And on that path,
the bumpy road,
that all of us are on,
the words we use,
the words we've coined,
describe this world,
or how it seems,
while only here awhile.

It's not so easy
words to find
for what I sense
behind the scenes
but cannot touch,
and cannot see,
that makes no sound at all.

Perhaps one day
new words will come
when angels and *their* world
become as real to us on Earth
as trees and rocks and sea.
Meanwhile I fumble in the dark
and in that silence wait
for senses of another sort,
while only half awake.

The Little Death

If sleep is what I sense it is,
then when we die,
I like to think
there's no surprise
at what we meet,
at what unfolds
as blinkers fall away.
For every night,
while body rests,
we likewise reconnect
with what it is,
so wise, so pure
that underpins our world.

And in this state I cease to be
inside my shell and looking on
at bird or fish,
at flower or tree,
at all that isn't me.
Instead I pause
and enter in
to what it is to be like them:
to sway in wind,
to be that wind,
in sun and rain rejoice.

And then I turn to those I love,
to some no longer here.
And they, like me,
have now let go,
our masks are laid aside.

And in that realm
where time and space
no longer hems us in,
we can reflect on what we've learnt
and sense the tasks ahead.

And then it's time to wake again,
to put our armour on.
And in the battles that we face,
one hopes there lingers still
a memory faint,
albeit real,
of why we're here
and why we need
at times to feel alone.

And if I'm right,
or partly so,
then this explains
what oft was said
by sages long ago:
the sleep we need,
the sleep we crave,
is like a little death.

To Be

To be,
or not to be?
He had no choice
and nor have we;
it matters not
if prince or serf,
or tree upon a hill.
What is exists,
it comes and goes,
in ever-changing form.

And yet we humans
stand apart –
or that is how it seems;
for what we know,
unlike that tree,
is I am me,
and you are you,
that cat is cat,
and cloud is cloud,
and busy being just that.
And thinking thus
we stand aloof,
so often proud
and knowing best,
yet cannot swim
as fishes swim
or fly just like the birds.

So is this progress
to look on,
and name and weigh
and draw and paint
what others simply are?
Perhaps it is,
like Hamlet's quest,
a phase along the way;
a path that leads
to finding bird
and fish and flower
not just out there
in field and stream,
but in each human being.

And if that time
should one day come,
the world itself will change,
and know itself
for what it is,
no more in bits,
but as a whole,
in the seeker that is me.

Outside of Time

'How long till lunch?'
we sometimes ask;
or 'Has the post arrived?'
But rarely do we ask ourselves:
'How long until I die?'
Some things we know,
or maybe guess,
but others not all.

Have faith, some say,
explore within
and read what's in the stars.
Or should we just relax,
live life,
and simply wait our turn?

Some feel that death,
that final step,
is like the end of day;
however good,
however rich,
however full it's been,
enough's enough,
you're tired, replete
and ready to let go.

Then all's revealed,
so they believe,
and in that realm
that's out of sight
old friendships are renewed.
And there, perhaps,
my wife and I
can pick up treasured threads.

For me it doesn't quite make sense
that bonds so strong
are put on hold
for years and years to come.
And so I sense –
perhaps it's hope –
that every night,
like death itself
when so much falls away,
a space appears
outside of time
that both of us can share.
Then she helps me,
and I help her,
for there what matters,
what endures,
is the love we forged on Earth.

Horizons

There is a limit,
some would say,
to what we can
and cannot know;
horizon is the word
that often comes to mind.
Yet if you climb,
but just a hill,
you see beyond the trees
to yet another wood;
and higher still,
if not too puffed,
the distant sea appears.

So what of knowledge –
is it much the same;
no limits if we climb?
I know for me
what holds me back,
besides my feeble brain,
are lazy days
in valley safe
and sheltered from the storm;
content, as well,
with what I know –
no frontiers still to probe.

Too often,
maybe every day,
we settle for this easy life,
afraid to rock the boat.
And if we do,
our cargo frail
might quickly come to harm;
for in our hold
are crates of facts
that tell us how the world goes round,
though not what it might mean.

The hills are there,
the paths are steep,
but questions drive me on.
And what I find
will feed my soul,
the higher that I climb.

No Shore Too Far

'Why is there something rather than nothing?' wrote the German philosopher G.W.Leibniz in 1697, in his essay 'On the Ultimate Origin of Things.'

This is a question so profound –
it stops me in my tracks.
For I'm aware,
and I believe
that if we think the way we do,
and fail to shift,
and fail to heed
what stares us in the face,
we'll never cope with such a thought
and all that it implies.
Nor will we ask,
nor think to ask,
and far less understand,
what Leibniz wrote
and Leibniz asked
with more than just his brain.

So I have hope
that what I feel,
and what I try to say,
is not a flight from common sense,
but intimation frail yet clear
that if we grow,
as grow we could,
and if we think
and learn to act
with head and heart entwined,
they will reveal,
and will confirm
quite other laws at work.

And so I trust
what's sometimes said,
that in a cosmos
vast, sublime,
despite our size,
our faults and crimes,
there is for us
no shore too far.

Exploration

We feel so small,
just tiny specks,
the more we're told,
the more we learn
about another billion stars
that someone's found
while peering into space.

And yet in other ways
we're huge,
as huge as each new thought
that takes us to those billion stars,
and to a truth
beneath our feet
and in our hearts –
a truth that knows no size.

Farewell

Farewell feels better
as two words:
'Fare well' is what I pray.
And so on journeys,
long or short,
we wish each other well.
And for a while,
and in the quiet,
we may seem out of touch;
though in my heart,
where trust resides,
I know it isn't so.

And then one day
when I, too, shed
the costume that I wear,
we'll truly meet
without our masks
in preparation for another life,
for yet another play.

And there off stage,
outside of time,
outside of space,
and thought by some as dead,
we'll gather in the crowded bar
to reassess our roles;
the words we spoke,
forgotten lines,
the laughter and the tears.

We'll write the script,
but just a draft –
there must be space for change.
And let's be bold,
let's not forget –
we creatures on the move –
that we ourselves,
not just the gods,
are destined to create.
So on we go
to play our parts
in dramas still to come;
and add some lines,
as well as jokes –
the universe evolves.

Acknowledgements

My thanks to the following for their help and encouragement at various stages of the writing: my son and daughter, Tom and Ellie Stedall, and my sister, Dede Bark; Alex Barakan; Eva Marie and Simon Chadwick; Charlotte and Saied Dai; Jon Earnshaw; Allmut ffrench; Colin Glascoe; Christopher Goode; Pip Heywood; Ronald Higgins; Liz Hingley; Vilna Kembery; Jeremy Naydler; Vivien della Negra; Moses Papo; Raphael Papo; Susie Radford; Tatjana and Rodney Peppe; Richard Ramsbotham; Louanne Richards; Chris and Signe Schaefer; Ann and Mischa Scorer; Sue Smee; Lucinda Sowerbutts; Mary-Anne Sutherland; Richard Tarnas; Ruth Thomas; Alex Verbeek; Norman Voake; Katrina Zaat; and above to all to my brother, David Bryer, for the thoughtful and sensitive way he wielded his red pencil!

I am also most grateful for the support and trust of my publisher, Martin Large, and his wife Judy; so, too, for the skill and creativity of my book designer, Lucy Guenot, Miriam Macgregor for her wood engraving of *Two Hands*, and Saied Dai for his painting on the cover, *Moonlit Cove*.

The author is grateful for permission to quote from the following books:

Summoned by Bells by John Betjeman © The Estate of John Betjeman 1955,1958, 1960, 1962, 1964, 1966, 1968, 1970, 1979, 1981, 1982, 2001. Reproduced by permission of John Murray Press, an imprint of Hodder and Stoughton Limited.

Poetry of Robert Frost by Robert Frost, published by Jonathan Cape. Reprinted by permission of The Random House Group Ltd.

The Little Prince by Antoine de Saint-Exupéry © 1943 Editions Gallimard. Katherine Woods English translation © 1945 Editions Gallimard. Published by Egmont UK Ltd and used with permission.

Bibliography

Ashe, Geoffrey, *Gandhi – a study in revolution*,
William Heinemann, 1968.

Blythe, Ronald, *The Circling Year*,
The Canterbury Press Norwich, 2006.

Grahame, Kenneth, *The Wind in the Willows*,
Charles Scribner's Sons, 1908.

Hopkins, Gerard Manley, *Poems of Gerard Manley Hopkins*, H.Milford, 1918.

Jung C.G., *Modern Man in Search of a Soul*,
Routledge and Kegan Paul, 1933.

— —, *Memories, Dreams, Reflections*,
Random House, 1961.

Leibniz, G.W., *Leibniz: Philosophical Essays*,
Hackett Publishing Company, 1989.

Nagel, Thomas, *Mortal Questions*,
Cambridge University Press, 1974.

Schumacher E.F., *A Guide for the Perplexed*,
Jonathan Cape, 1977.

Spenser, Edmund, *The Fairie Queene*,
Penguin Classics, 2003.

Steiner, Rudolf, *Meditations and Verses*,
Rudolf Steiner Press, 1961.

— —, *Staying Connected* – lectures edited and
introduced by Christopher Bamford,
SteinerBooks, 2000.

Verne, Jules, *A Journey to the Centre of the Earth*,
Penguin Books, 1970.

Voloschin, Margarita, *The Green Snake: an
autobiography*, Floris Books, 2010.

By the same author, an autobiography
also published by Hawthorn Press in 2009.
ISBN 978-1-903458-90-7   Hardback 592 pages

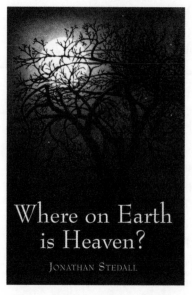

'A deeply thoughtful book, the result of a lifetime of thinking, reading, and conversations with an amazing cast of people' – Mark Tully.

'Jonathan Stedall brings the same sensitivity and spiritual insight to the printed page that he brought to his many television documentaries' – Theodore Roszak.

'A wonderfully written book, with much insight, tenderness, and candour' – Arthur Zajonc.

'A real quest, with outward work perfectly integrated with an inner search' – Karen Armstrong.

'A thoughtful book by a thoughtful man' – Ben Okri.

Hawthorn Press

DISTRIBUTORS: UK: BookSource, orders@booksource.net
USA: Steinerbooks, service@steinerbooks.org
AUS: Footprint Books, info@footprint.com.au

www.hawthornpress.com